TANGENT
DREAMS

A High School Football Novel

Joe Torosian

ISBN: 0692588175
ISBN 13: 9780692588178

NOTE FROM THE AUTHOR

About eight years ago then South Hills HC Steve Bogan said I should write a book about high school football. "I'd read it," he said.

The thought stayed with me, but there was always something going on to keep me from banging it out. Also in a subject as rich as prep football, what would I write about?

I didn't know. Until I took the time to watch not just a football season but a football career end. I wondered how close the player's dreams came to the reality achieved. How did they cope with walking off the field for the final time?

Everything that follows is true. It happened. Only the names, faces, teams, schools, times, dates, races, genders, faiths, and outcomes have been changed to keep my car from blowing up when I start it in the morning.

I want to thank my wife for allowing me to build the RamCave. I want to thank my entire family for allowing me to live in the RamCave while seeing this project through.

I want to thank Pat Cherry of www.blackheartart.com who provided the cover art and for putting up with me. A big thank you to the services of MGT-Editing.

I've always said because you write football, it does not mean you really know football. So, thanks to Temple City alum Riley Saxon for correction and enlightenment with the Xs & Os.

Thanks to the Omelette, Josh Ouellette, for providing the foreword while in the middle of a life change. Thanks to those who read early drafts and gave me a thumbs up. I'd also like to apologize to the advance readers I, unfortunately, sent unedited drafts to. I apologize for that torture.

Finally, you're going to notice over the next several hundred pages a battle between words and story. I came to roughly 180 crossroads where I had to choose which way to go. I chose story

FOREWORD

Tangent Dreams, a lofty title about football in the San Gabriel Valley, captures exactly what it is to be caught in the whirlwind of the life of every player who takes the field above, below, east, and west of the 10 and 210 freeways.

Torosian shows what it's truly like to take the gridiron in one of the most diverse areas in the country, and yet still brings up almost every possible scenario that can happen to a coach, a team, a school, and a community during the craziness of a prep football season.

This isn't Friday Night Lights and "Texas forever," nor is it the story of some of the new elite football schools in California like Corona Centennial or Oaks Christian. It is the everyman story of former greats like Temple City, Arcadia, and Arroyo with beckoning calls to past glories at stadiums in need of a facelift and the proud traditions of off and on powerhouses like Monrovia, Rosemead, West Covina and so many others.

A veteran sportswriter, Torosian has been the fly on the wall in the SGV for the past 20 years. As one of the most trusted informants and historians of the worshiped pigskin in the area, he brings a little bit of every story that has ever crossed his desk into the pages of a book that anyone, football fan or not, will have a hard time putting down.

Every face on your own high school football team flashes through your mind as you flip through the pages of the world Torosian has created at the fictional West El Monte Poly on the not-so-fictional Flair Drive.

The coming story brings you more than football, it brings you life in its most raw emotions. Faith in standard and non-standard form, the love of being in the moment, and the awkward teenage years with the haunting future that real life is only a few blinks away.

Speaking as a former member of the San Gabriel Valley football fraternity and as one of the fat guys already starting to bald covering prep football… Anyone who has played in the area, or even thrown on the pads at all, will be able to immerse themselves into the story and ride all of the ups and downs coming for Dale Andrade as he searches for his own tangent dreams in the pages you're about to read.

—Josh "The Omelette" Ouellette

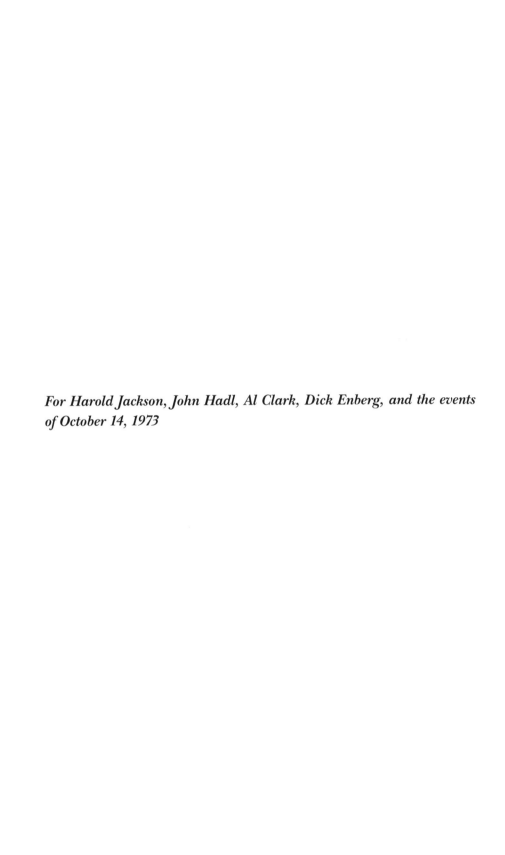

For Harold Jackson, John Hadl, Al Clark, Dick Enberg, and the events of October 14, 1973

"What is this moon? This grifter of time? The joy of the under current, masked days, the fortune of solitude…And the tangent dreams of buffalo long for the land and times that are so far gone."
    ---Ann Longshire

TANGENT
DREAMS

PART I

1

My father once told me, "When someone wants you, Dale, appreciate it." His feet were on the coffee table, head resting in clasped hands behind his neck. We were half-heartedly watching a Lakers game. "Because they're not always going to want you."

His tone was advice, but faint lament was traceable. It fit his situation: divorced, single father, with three different jobs in five years. Thank God it wasn't my situation. It was his. My situation, as a sophomore in high school, like everything in my life, was hassle enough. I didn't need to pick up Dad and put him on my shoulders.

He turned slightly and gave a knowing wink. "It's a simple fact of the world." I nodded like I understood. "It's something I know far too well. Time and circumstances make us all fall out of demand." His eyes went back to the flat-screen. "Trust me on this."

Dad was a computer guy, Mom was a unit secretary at a hospital, and our financial fortunes were always on the edge of break down. He went from one job to another, getting outsourced each time. Hard to be a tough guy, full of the vinegar required to tackle the world, when every eighteen months you were tossed to the street.

He got depressed, Mom got tired, and then she split for a hospital administrator offering a better deal. Dad was only a drag to be around when it came to Mom. When she came to pick me up, drop me off, met us to celebrate a birthday, or they had a phone conversation, that was when I hated being with him. Always passive, always weak, as if some soft gentle display on his part was going to win her back.

Dad's problem, not mine. He was out of demand, and I was in. Desi Bradley, a junior, asked me to escort her to the school spirit dance. It wasn't exactly Christmas, but more like getting everything you ordered at a drive-thru. A nice win. Her interest in me was a stamp of approval for my classmates to see. Dale Andrade was regarded highly enough to get a date from a girl of physical note and a grade level above.

Truth is, I was in the hallway of the administration building, Desi was in the hallway, we passed each other everyday. The chances of us connecting were very good. She wanted me because she needed a date and was between boyfriends. I was available, my acne was in control, and looked like a safe choice.

Desi had the stuff any guy my age desired, but she never made me nervous. Never made me gush, never made me think tomorrow could be better than today, or about anything beyond getting my hands all over her body. Later I'd learn being underwhelmed was a great place to be in a relationship.

It should have been the highlight of the last semester of my sophomore year, but it wasn't. It didn't compare at all to the day Fred-X said he wanted me. I can't say he made me gush, but he did make me dream about tomorrow.

I'd never been a football guy, watched it some with Dad when he was home, didn't have any brothers to knock me around, and gravitated towards volleyball because I played it during a quarter rotation as a freshman. On this day, though, the puzzle pieces of fate aligned. I took P.E. to be lazy. Fred Ritter and his friends took it because they had an open spot for an elective.

At five-eleven, I was above average at West El Monte Poly. I had big hands, which made volleyball easy, but it wasn't a volleyball Fred picked up during P.E. on the day my life changed.

For Fred, when he smiled or tilted his head back in acknowledgment, you felt you had found favor with prep football aristocracy. His royal credentials read twenty-seven touchdown passes and twelve more rushing as a junior on a team finishing one game short of making the playoffs.

For other schools making the playoffs was a sign of achievement. For West El Monte Poly almost making the playoffs (since it never had before) was cause for a hallelujah jubilee, and it made him the five-foot-nine-inch tall prince of the campus.

If Fred was a jerk, the story would be different, but he wasn't. Instead, he was electric. If you were tired when he came into a room, you were wired as if double espresso from Starbucks had been mainlined into you by the time he left. He made a lousy day good, the good day great, and the mediocre football team a contender.

So on this particular spring day I was stretching because Coach Von Huson, directing things from his golf cart, was going to make us run before we started our thirty-five minute session of coed touch football.

"Go deep," Fred said, but nobody moved. "Somebody go deep. I got to see if I still got it." He pumped the football with his right arm. Two girls standing near, neither his girlfriend, giggled. "I'm serious. We're getting ready to start again. I've got to loosen things up."

"I got it," Pineapple said, getting off the grass and rubbing his hands together. Why Pineapple was called Pineapple, I didn't know. He was Samoan with frizzy wild hair, and I assumed it took three spins of the scale to measure his weight. His last name was Bartholomew and he was one of a half dozen Bartholomews in the school district.

"You're too slow," Fred said. "Pineapple, by the time you go twenty yards the class will be over." He looked around. "Yo! Gavach!"

He was calling to me and pumping the football in his hand. The girls continued to giggle not because he picked me, but because he was talking, and they were close enough to smell his deodorant. Fred-X could advocate for dolphin extermination, and they'd continue to swoon over him.

"Me?" I pointed to myself. He had said *gavach* which was short for *gavacho*, which meant white guy. My last name was Andrade, which made me Hispanic, which is technically white, unless you are on a campus, working a job, or getting arrested. He was darker than me, but his last name was Ritter. So goes life in the San Gabriel Valley.

"Yeah," he said pointing at me and then to the other end of the field. "Go deep."

If Pineapple had asked, I would have shrugged him off, but this was Fred-X: The Man, King Cool, at West El Monte Poly. I had nothing to lose by going deep for him. I nodded and took off running. That was the kind of power he had.

In shape, stretched, I felt fast on the grass field. He cocked his arm back and waved me deeper with his left. A thought came he might only be messing with me to give the girls another laugh. If so, he'd pulled it off.

None of that mattered because this was Fred-X, the guy the sports blogs described a touchdown pass from as a 'Fred-X Delivery.' I kept running. He let go of the ball, to great relief, in my direction.

The spiral was perfect, but as it approached it drifted over my left shoulder off target. I wasn't going to catch it, but knowing everyone was watching because of who was throwing, I bent back as far as I could, reached with my left-hand and cupped the nose of the ball before spinning down to the grass. From the ground, I held it up.

If nothing else happened for the rest of the day, at least I had created a memory by making a really great catch. When he was in the NFL I could say I caught a pass from Fred-X in high school.

"Paydirt!" He yelled raising his hands to signal touchdown. Even better, he came jogging towards me with his loyalists in tow. Getting up, slapping cut grass off me, I casually flipped the ball back to him. "You a sophomore?"

"Yeah," I said.

"You playing football?"

"Never have," I said.

He dropped an f-bomb (You know what an *f-bomb* is. The rest of this story is filled with them) and said what I could do with *that*. Then he told me I was playing football and spring practice began in three weeks.

How special did I feel? It was like being one item on a giant aisle loaded with items in a giant store filled with long aisles of merchandise and getting picked out. Fredrick Xavier Ritter wanted me, and there was nothing that matched the feeling of being wanted.

2

Read The Blitz
By Grip Teague

Charles Irons has resigned as HC at Walnut stating he wants to spend more time with his family. Irons led the Mustang program for two years and leaves with a 7-13 record...Multiple sources have confirmed Arcadia running back Jefferson Pham has transferred to Bishop Amat. Pham rushed for 776 yards and twelve touchdowns as a sophomore...West El Monte gains one but loses two: Fighting Scots left guard, Josiah Chavez, has transferred to Cathedral, and linebacker, Anthony Ciccone, is leaving for Rosemead. But Coach Skip Piccou has confirmed that Ayala quarterback, Billy Hudson, has enrolled for second semester classes on Flair Drive. Hudson, a freshman, started the final two games of this past season for the Bulldogs. "West is great academically which is important to my wife and I," said Billy's father, Nick Hudson. "Plus the football program is well coached and the system we feel fits our son's strengths."...Schurr confirmed its Zero Week date with Glendora...Things are not looking

*good at Monrovia this year...Pomona's Tank Davis has
been offered by Nebraska...Los Altos HC, Tom Holstead
said Jeremy Chandos will be his starting quarterback until he does something to lose it...*

My pending football family prepared me on how to argue
with my parents if they said I couldn't play. Since I was
living with Dad, all I really needed was his permission.
Mom would give some protest because she'd feel the need to demonstrate a concern, which was not overpowering at this point. I received a list of promises and assurances about being responsible,
grades not suffering, etcetera, etcetera.

"Parents are only worried about three things when it comes to
football," Fred said. He made it plain I didn't have to keep calling
him Fred-X.

We were sitting across from each other in the Jack In The Box
on Flair Drive, down the street from the school. Pineapple, next to
Fred demolishing a dump truck's worth of tacos, contributed only
the sounds of his lips smacking between bites.

"Grades, money, and getting hurt," he said. "They want to know
how much it is going to cost. I showed you right here," he pointed
to a notepad. "That's what it's going to cost. Then they're going to
want to know about your grades. You tell them Coach Von Huson,
our offensive line coach, the old guy who has been around for f-
bombing ever, does grade checks and homework checks every week
for everybody on the team."

"That shouldn't be a problem," I said.

"It shouldn't be unless you're a f-bomb up like Chavez. Then as far as getting hurt you'll be new so you won't be returning kicks. You'll be a receiver, if we run a thousand plays this year, maybe you'll catch fifty passes. So the chances of you getting hurt are really small. Do your parents know anything about football?"

I shook my head.

"Did your dad play?"

I shook my head again.

He smirked. "Dude, you ain't going to have any problems. Country looking white boy like you with no tats, your parents probably wouldn't even yell at you if you stayed out all night."

"They would," I disagreed. 'Country looking white boy' made me sound soft. I didn't like it, but it was only the beginning.

"They might, but they're sure not going to keep you from playing football. Just tell them you'll follow through on all your responsibilities. They won't even notice when you start to slack off late in the season."

"Do you slack off?"

"No, but a lot of guys do," he said. "Guys who ain't going anywhere."

"Which guys?"

"F-bombers like Chavez and Ciccone," Pineapple said before unsheathing another taco.

"Where are you going?" I said.

Fred smiled at me then half punched Pineapple in the shoulder. "We're going all the way."

৯

Turned out I didn't need any of it. Mom said over the phone to check with Dad. Dad was good and asked how much to make the check out for, or if online payment was available.

"Really?" I said to him going out the door the next morning. "You're not worried?"

"If you end up with a scholarship, I'm keeping your college money," he said.

"I got college money?"

"No, I spent it on pizza last week."

Now all I had to do was go see Coach Piccou.

৯

"Oh hell no," Coach said from his office desk. He dropped an f-bomb as a punctuation. Then got up, put some files into a cabinet, and looked back at me. "Did you lose a bet or something?"

I didn't have a list of promises for him.

"You're looking up the wrong skirt here, Andrade," he said sounding like he was protecting me. "I can't stop you from coming to tryouts, but save yourself the sweat and humiliation. Stick to volleyball. These guys will break you in two."

"I want to try," I said. Fred inspired me to push. All Piccou could do was say no, and if he said yes, I was in Fred-X's world.

His tone moved into discouragement. "We've been lifting weights since January. You've never played football before, and you've never been hit." The sound of baseball players spikes on the concrete click-clacked as they left the locker room behind us. I loved the sound of it, as if they were marching off to something important, something distinct to be a part of. "I don't have time to teach remedial football at the varsity level. Do you get me? Maybe if you were going to be a sophomore, but not a junior. It's too late kid."

"But Fred-X told me to come see you."

His eyebrows lifted.

After two weeks in the weight room, my body came back to life. Everything still hurt, but not as bad as it did after the first few days. Every time I was in there, so were Fred and his boys: Pineapple, shirtless, sweaty, with his gut protruding; 'Fast Eddie' Edwards, thin with zero body fat, wearing a Property of Arizona State shirt; Bustamonte, who always looked like his hair was blow dried; and the leader of the defense Gelbaugh. The middle linebacker truly frightened me with his thin stringy blonde hair and thick face. It was like a square block with flaring nostrils. Not long after high school was over, when the rest of his hair was gone, I was sure he'd be part of a biker gang.

None of them thought much of me and tolerated my presence only because of who wanted me there. I hated the way they looked at me. I hated lifting weights. I hated having Coach Gugliotta, the defensive coordinator, tell me what a joke I was every time I touched the free weights or sat down at a machine.

"Look at Andrade over there," Gugliotta said to Coach Jackson, the offensive coordinator. "The little stiff. Who does he think he's fooling? He's going to get all busted up."

"Boy, you are softer than your mama's love," Coach Jackson said to me. He was African-American and retired from a twenty-five year stint in the U.S. Army. No one asked him about it, but word was he'd seen serious action. "Yeah, that's a lot heavier than a volleyball isn't it? You're going to have to pick it up if you want to stay at this son." They walked off laughing as I continued bench-pressing reps a fourth grader could have done with one arm. I had no upper body strength, but I did have the most powerful man on campus in my corner.

And it wasn't Principal Mathers.

"Handsdrade! Getting it done in the weight room!" Fred-X said, walking from one machine to the next. When we left the locker room, those words were the pinpricks of energy helping me lift just a little bit more each time, to push through the burn in my developing muscles.

I also loved how he called me *Handsdrade*.

"Handsdrade, I'm going to make you All Mid-Valley this fall. Grip Teague is going to put you on his show."

"Teague has a show?"

"You've never seen Teague and the Bald Guy?" He said.

"The writers, they do the Friday night football show," Edwards said.

"Forget those guys," Pineapple said. "What you want is to get Trudy Shields to interview you."

"Is she hot?" I asked.

"She's hot for me," Pineapple said, and groans rolled over the sounds of players lifting in the weight room. "That's why she's on my list."

"List?"

"Yeah," Pineapple said to me with a short laugh, and the leer I'd soon become very familiar with.

"I don't get it," I said.

"Wait till you see her," Fred said.

"What list?"

In the hallways and around the campus, Fred included me in whatever was going on.

'Handsdrade come over here.' 'Handsdrade we're getting pizza.' 'Handsdrade we're going to the mall.' Suddenly, I was having lunch and spending all of my free time with him and his friends. Pineapple and Edwards softened. Bustamonte, too busy with his hair, never spoke to me.

The closer we got to actual football, Gelbaugh started to hang out more with Dan Feliz, Dinh Lee and the rest of the defensive players. This was fine by me because Gelbaugh, emotionally, was a stick of sweaty dynamite. He always seemed like he was ready to blow.

On Saturdays, I'd meet with the offense on the practice field to run routes. After I'd go to Fred's house for lunch and play Madden. He'd go through the diagrams of the plays on the video game to teach me the team's spread offense.

I was 'Handsdrade,' and I was to be his slot receiver. Coach Piccou wouldn't buy it at first, Fred said, but it was going to happen. I needed to keep lifting, keep working, and I had no intention of doing anything else.

3

READ THE BLITZ
By Grip Teague

Do you round up or down from 66%? I'm no fan of math, but there are rules to it we cannot get around no matter how enlightened we try to make ourselves feel. Which means if Johnny has two apples and Danny takes one apple, then Johnny only has one apple left. Meaning no matter how good or bad we feel about ourselves or what injustices we may have suffered, two plus two will always equal four.

And if you are going to round 66%, you round up and not down. The next stop is 70%, but for right now 66% is the number of varsity head football coaches in our coverage zone who are walk-ons. This means they don't teach at the school. Some are on campus working security, three that we know of are heads of maintenance, but this number is ticking higher and higher all the time. It was 64% a year ago.

Walnut High School replaced Charles Irons with Mark Hauser, a walk-on who works for the United States

Postal Service. Now Hauser, who coordinated the defense for Diamond Ranch a year ago and got blown out along with everyone else on Kent Miller's staff, has a big job in front of him.

Just like life, and everything else, we're all given obstacles. A coach is given ten obstacles over the course of eleven weeks in the fall and just to get to those weeks they have to:

Find a staff (largely off campus), manage the boosters (loud parents), oversee fundraisers (because it will be his butt if he doesn't), deal with player issues (that goes more into the 'father figure' realm), deal with parents (who want more playing time for their sons), grade checks, transfers, potential transfers, message boards, injuries, and must constantly hope the activities director didn't cross up the athletic director and give the band the football field during practice time. Then they can go and take care of their own family.

Did I mention he has to find a couple of hours of sleep in there too? In addition, he could probably make more money flipping burgers at In-N-Out...Which I did in college, paid pretty well, and had zero stress after I clocked out. A varsity football coach never clocks out.

Spring practice began the first week of May. On the first day, there were ninety-seven of us. Coach Piccou opened by giving us an expletive inspired speech about how far the program had come, and how we were laying the foundation for those coming after us. If no one was prepared to commit fully to the team they needed to leave now.

I'd heard the same spiel at the start of the last volleyball season and began to figure it was a union requirement of the brotherhood of coaches.

"I usually like to be only about football, but before we start we need to touch on this. Mr. Yanto is no longer the president of the booster club. Mr. Garamonde has taken over, and we're gonna need help at the firework stand. So have your parents call either me or Mr. Garamonde. We're covering many of your initial costs with money from the fireworks stand, so I don't want the coaches and me spending the Fourth of July working for you. So f-bombing get on it and get your parents signed up. I'm reminding you about this now because when this workout is over you're going to have trouble remembering your own name. There will be flyers stuck in your lockers."

Then he got back to football.

"F-bombing Rosemead, f-bombing Arroyo, f-bombing-El Monte, f-bombing-South, think they f-bombing own this f-bombing league." Although capable, he wasn't frothing or raving. The words rolled off his tongue as if they were coming down an assembly line in the City of Industry. He manufactured obscenities so perfectly, he should have been working grocery retail. "I'm tired of all their f-bombing talk on the f-bombing message boards. It is our f-bombing time right now!"

Then, for the next two hours, we didn't touch a football. We ran. Forwards, backwards, high steps, side steps through ropes and tires. Then we crawled and tumbled over cushions, which I later learned were called step overs. I was in shape, decent shape at least, but my lungs were begging for air. Going from one station to an-other, I could feel my breakfast and lunch starting to argue over who was going to break out first. For a few moments, as my stomach voiced a small growl, I wasn't sure if the direction of things would be up or down.

"What are you breathing like that for? You want to quit?" John Robles said. "Go ahead and quit." Robles was thick-legged and nicknamed Fat John because he was fat pig. He was picking on me because he was a veteran, and I wasn't. "You want to be on this team you gotta run!"

I clenched my mouth before starting another set of sprints.

"You want to win a championship you gotta run, rookie!" Fat John spit. "What the f-bomb? You're so f-bombing weak!"

"F-bomb you Robles," Edwards said. "All you do is trot that big butt of yours. You never run."

"Don't be soft on him Fast Eddie," Fat John said huffing away. "He's gotta learn what it takes."

"I won't be," Fast Eddie said. "I don't want him to turn out like you." Then he looked at me. "You got to run harder Handsdrade. I'll yell at you, Fred will yell at you, and I'm not going to stop Gelbaugh from yelling at you, but Fat John is a lazy dog. We won't let him yell at anybody."

Going easy on the water with small sips, the feeling of throwing up came, but I ran until it passed. This happened several times. Moments came when I thought I couldn't do anymore, but then found sanctuary with a few more steps or a few more reps. Luckily, I avoided the dreaded side cramp.

Somewhere, during the conditioning, a whistle blew, and Coach Piccou said we were going to have to do our quarters again. This was a drill that had us start on the goal line, run to the ten, touch, then go back to the goal line, and run out to the twenty, and so on. In the confusion, I got lost and touched the twenty-five instead of the thirty.

"When you f-bomb up we all have to run!" Gelbaugh screamed two inches from my nose. His hair hung in wet strands down the side of his face. No one told him to shut up because he was the madman in residence.

Only seventy-two of us were on the field for the fourth day, in shorts and blue tee shirts with 'Alba Gu Bràth' printed on the back, when the footballs came out. I found out later 'Alba Gu Bràth' meant 'Scotland Forever!'. Since we were the Fighting Scots we were also required to watch the movie *Braveheart* by the end of the first week. A written test would be given on the film by Coach Von Huson.

The practice broke up by position, the assistant coaches were yelling, everyone was dispersing, and I was lost again. Every time I seemed to get a grip of what was happening, the routine would change.

"Andrade, if you want to waste time go do it somewhere else!" Piccou screamed at me. "You're looking like an f-bombing moron! Get your head out of your…"

"F-bombing, Andrade!" Receivers Coach Paleo screamed at me. "What the f-bomb are you doing? Get with the f-bombing receivers!"

"Handsdrade!" Fred called and waved me over. "You're here!" He pointed to where Bustamonte and several others were in two lines on either side of him. "We're running the passing tree. Remember the passing tree?"

"Yeah," I said.

"You're going to go from my line to Hudson's line and then back again. Got it?"

"Got it."

"Then let's do it!" He punched me in the shoulder. "My man!"

Getting in line, I was laughed at. Bustamonte, an all league receiver with sixty-three catches and twelve touchdowns the year before, talked trash to the others about how soft I was. "The white boy can't play," he said.

Jesse Maez was okay with me. Jesus Ponce, who was going to be a sophomore, wasn't. The punk looked right through me, never acknowledging my presence. Charlie Califf, who was heading into his senior season, was on the low end when it came to talent. He wasn't exactly welcoming because, if everything worked out, it meant he wouldn't be getting much playing time.

The verbal abuse was brutal. I despised it less when they told me I sucked to my face and really came to hate it when I'd hear them talk under their breath about me. Hated it so much I flirted with quitting, but the ace up my sleeve was the quarterback wanted me.

I was to be his 'Y,' his slot receiver, so I ran 'slants,' 'ins,' 'flats,' 'go's,' 'skinnys,' 'corners,' 'comebacks,' 'curls,' and 'posts.' When they told me to go stand over there, I went and stood over there. When they told me to run, I ran. When I was told to fetch water, I fetched. I even got water for Ponce who had as much varsity experience as me. I didn't have any standing to argue back so I kept quiet and reminisced about how easy volleyball was.

The running, when not winded during conditioning, was easy. Route running, and then observing from standing in line before the next one, was easy as well. The passes were perfect, like gloves, the ball perfectly fit into my hands. Fred said never to use my body, to always use my hands and to watch the ball all the way into them.

"Some guys take forever to figure this out Handsman," he said during a seven on seven session when Billy Hudson was running the offense. (*Handsman* was another nickname he gave me.) He said Bustamonte used his body too much and rounded his patterns. "Boosty cost me two picks last year because he didn't get his hands out in front and the ball bounced off his chest," he said. "Then I got a third when he fat dogged it on an out pattern."

"Fat dogged?"

"Lazy," Fred said. "Don't get me wrong he works hard, but some-times he gets sloppy on his routes and rounds them out. Those cuts have to be sharp. That's how you get separation and give me a tar-get to throw to."

"What does he say?"

"All he ever says is that he's f-bombing open and for no one to touch his hair," Fred said. "You run those routes sharp, and Coach Paleo and Coach Jackson will notice."

By the seventh day, the under the breath mocking from my fel-low receivers had stopped for the most part. Bustamonte wasn't tak-ing me out for pizza, but his comments about me were now going undetected.

Ponce was still acting like a jackwagon. "You got to run that route tighter rookie," he said to me after I ran an out-route. "Keep watching me and maybe you'll learn something. Why don't you go get me some f-bombing water?"

"Get it yourself f-bomb face," I said, too tired to care.

"About time you said something," Maez said and patted me on the butt. "Some of the guys you have to take stuff from, but this little piece hasn't done anything yet."

"I played last year!" Ponce said.

"Who did you play for?" Maez said. Ponce didn't want to say freshman football. "I thought so."

On the tenth day I noticed something else; the coaches had stopped cussing at me. When we lined up in seven on sevens, I was inserted into the slot halfway through the offensive sets. I was out there with Bustamonte, Edwards, Maez, a sophomore named Mike Miranda, and Fred-X.

This also meant I'd moved ahead of Ponce.

"F-bomb," I heard him sigh when my name was called ahead of his.

The more we got into the offense the more I got into everything. I never had so much fun. Running my routes, the passes just kept coming to me, and if they were anywhere within reach I caught them. On the fourteenth day of spring practice, Coach Jackson was calling out the starting lineup and he said, "Handsdrade, slot!"

Hearing him say 'Handsdrade' was even better than hearing him say 'slot.'

The weight room work I came to understand better because the only place a defender had a chance with me was at the line of scrimmage. They'd try to jam me and force me out of my route, but if I got by them, I was going to catch the ball.

Especially loving the slant routes, I thought of pass patterns when walking around the campus or my house. I always planted my foot, simulating a cut, and pushed off with it to get an extra boost. I started counting my steps going from class to class, at the mall, and shopping at Sam's Club with Dad.

On the seventeenth day of practice, I heard something marvelous. Catching a slant pass, I broke away from my immediate defender and took it to the end zone. Gelbaugh never failed to curse me as I went by him. He always threatened me with death.

Maybe I was drunk with building confidence, maybe my insult filter was clogged, but I responded, "Can't kill what you can't catch, Jack," then wished I hadn't. No one called Jack Gelbaugh by his first name. It was too soon to be popping off, but I was tired of being treated as a less than.

He eyed me and nodded. If Pineapple, Edwards, or Bustamonte wanted to tear me apart, I knew Fred would step in. If Gelbaugh came at me, he'd have a more difficult time stopping him.

"Handsdrade!" Fred yelled with raised hands to signal touchdown as I crossed the goal line.

"Andrade!" Gelbaugh said as I came back across the field. "Soon." He smiled. I didn't like that, but what I heard next was great.

Now my hands were big, but my ears were normal. Nothing extraordinary about my ears except when powered by egomania;

then they could pick up good stuff from West El Monte to San Luis Obispo. Returning to the offense, I ran behind Coach Piccou and Coach Jackson.

"You notice how he runs those routes?" Piccou said. "He's embarrassing Bustamonte out there."

When it's good, you hear it all.

"Everyone thinks he's fast," Jackson said, "but you're right. It's the way he runs the routes, very crisp for a newby. He gets more reps under his belt, we might have something by midseason."

I was feeling six-five.

Why would anyone play volleyball when they could play football? It just didn't make sense. I wasn't the best player, I knew that, and, except for a little teasing of Gelbaugh, my ego was in check. No one was worried about me crashing to earth. The best player in the San Gabriel Valley was the guy who picked me to be his slot receiver, his insurance guy. Volleyball was for chumps.

The job was easy: just run the f-bombing routes. Because of Fred, I knew those routes before the coaches taught them to me. I learned the patterns while playing Madden and on napkins while we ate burgers at The Habit. Those patterns were sketched out in straight lines, so I did everything I could to make those moves, those cuts, as straight as something out of geometry.

He forced me to spend time with Pineapple, Fast Eddie, Bustamonte, and even Gelbaugh when we went to his house to watch *Braveheart*. The linebacker's family was kind to me, and Gelbaugh himself was polite enough not to stare.

When prom time came, I was Desi's date, more like escort, but Fred made a pointed effort to invite us to the after party the football team was having. He was there with Angela Barbero, who wasn't his girlfriend, but very attractive.

The invite to be with the team made me feel important, and it sure didn't hurt walking in with a girl, Desi, of equal caliber with Fred's date. They wanted me, and I belonged.

4

Read The Blitz
By Grip Teague

The best part for any sportswriter's season is to go back when it's over and check to see how he did on the predictions he made. I did well last year. I picked West Covina's title run, picked South Pasadena's playoff bid. I even wrote that West El Monte would be improved but would not make the playoffs.

All of that was easy. Those were good teams, and I wasn't the only one. No, the harder choice is picking out the dogs. I'm not talking about teams that lose their quarterback a month into the season, but the teams you know right now, in June, are going to suck before the first kickoff.

There are three things to look for: One, who are they returning? Two, stability in the coaching staff. Three, did the HC give his team the kiss of death with these words: "We're gonna be young this year…"

Amigos, take it from Grip (and the Bald Guy I work with), if you hear your coach, the coach of your favorite team, say, "We're gonna be young this year" head for the hills because what he is really saying is: "We're gonna suck this year."

I don't want to be a negative dude, like my former colleague Landestoy Luke (scumbag), but when a coach starts trying to explain things, before the Fourth of July, your team is in trouble.

Notes: Jefferson Pham has been cleared by CIF. He will be suiting up for Bishop Amat Week One…Arcadia HC, Tab Figueroa reiterated that he wishes Pham well…Look for relocated Pasadena Bulldog Montel Gaines to be at quarterback for the Apaches when the season starts at El Rancho. Figueroa said the senior is now number one on the depth chart…Frank Khoury, a walk-on, has resigned at Gabrielino and taken an assistant coaching job at Golden West College. Khoury led the Eagles for three seasons and to a playoff birth last fall. No word on a replacement, yet… Mark Ramos has returned to Covina to coach Freshman football. Ramos played (center) for one season at Mt. SAC before blowing out his knee three years ago…Word leaking out of West El Monte Poly has newly arrived Billy Hudson pushing Fred Ritter for playing time…Dominguez quarterback, Alec Jammon, has been offered by Utah…

The setting sun always turned the sky the obligatory fiery pink when looking west towards Los Angeles. Seeing it was like lifting my head above water for the first time in weeks

(*Wow there's a sun?*). I got the schoolwork done to finish my sophomore year, but everything from English to math, to world history-
geography felt like another part of the football journey I was now
committed to.

Football had become everything, devouring all aspects of my
life. Everything was done in the name of football, motivated by
football, controlled by football. Fresh air wasn't green grass, a cool
breeze, or a day at the beach, but the heated dampness of the locker
room. What it smelled like, what it tasted like on the inside as it
passed through my system after practice.

Taking in the sun as it went down was odd and out of context.
We knew the sun rose and went down every day, but to watch it go
down was doing something new. We should have been showered,
dressed and gone an hour before, but Fred decided to hang out, so
I stayed with him. Our bodies ached a bit, but it was the good kind
of ache, coming from a solid workout. At least for me, it was a good
kind of ache. I didn't have to do what Pineapple and the rest of the
beasts were doing with weights, sleds, throwing tires, and running
while harnessed to a bungee cord.

"Handsdrade!" Fred said like an announcer. "Let's talk."

It was graduation day. We sat on beach chairs in front of the
double doors of the locker room. Coach Paleo wedged a trashcan
in front of one of the doors, so it wouldn't lock us out. Everyone
else bolted before they got stuck. Campus security was directing
overflow cars to the outfield of the baseball diamond because everything was congested on Flair Drive.

We chilled and listened over the loudspeaker.

"Your folks sign up to work the firework stand?"

"I was going to ask about that," I said. "My dad tried but never heard back from Garamonde."

"You're not going to--he quit--have your dad call Piccou."

"Is he running it?"

"Until someone else wants to take over the booster club."

"Sounds like a hassle," I said.

"Believe me, it is. My dad took it over for a while last year, just to fill in. He lasted a month. No one is ever happy."

I'd been on the campus late before, but usually it was coming out of a building and going straight to a waiting car. Just sitting as the day faded was surreal, as if ghosts from years past were going to emerge and reconnect with one another. The place felt haunted.

"Your grades good?" Fred said.

"I've always been a good student," I answered. It was true. I mean, I had very few distractions until football, so things always got done.

"Cool, I thought so," he said. "That's how you get a couple of letters like these."

He tossed me two envelopes. At first, I didn't know what they were. I saw his name "Fred Ritter," and then I saw where they came from: Illinois Wesleyan and Luther College in Iowa.

"Hey!" I was excited. "You're being recruited!"

"Yeah," he said. "D-three. They saw my highlights online."

"That's awesome." What everyone was talking about since the end of last season was starting to happen. Fred-X was ready to go big time. I wanted to throw a party for him. "This is great."

"They don't give full scholarships, but because my grades are good, they can work out financial packages. It's just the beginning though."

"The beginning of what?"

He kept staring towards the stadium. Its lights had already started to take effect, and most of the seats were filled. The event didn't interest him as much as it seemed to concern him.

"What do you want to do, Handsdrade? Because I want to have a great season," he said. "I want to play Division-one next year, not for some school no one's ever heard of. If I do well at the quarterbacks camp at the end of July, if we have a great year, more people are going to see us play. I know the offers will get better."

His junior year was his first year as a starter, the team didn't even make the playoffs, and now schools from the middle of the country were after him. If we had a great year and made it to the finals, he could go anywhere, I thought.

"Dude, I think you're on your way," I said.

"Coach Piccou says, unless you're a lineman, Mexicans don't get seriously recruited from this area," he said. "Scouts don't think we're athletic enough to play at a high level."

In the distance, the band started playing the marching music, and cheering came from the football field. The graduates were coming into the arena. Next year, Fred would take the walk. A year later, I would.

"You proved coach wrong," I said. "Offers are already coming in."

"Look at me," he said, raising his right arm off the beach chair. "I'm twice as dark as you, and my last name is Ritter because my old man is white a guy. Your last name is Andrade, but you look like you're from Sweden or something."

"Birth lottery," I said. "My dad's quarter Mexican, and my mom's from Glendora. She was named Debbie Schmidt when they got married. Let them think you're a white guy. They won't be able to argue with your numbers. It works for you."

"It does, but I just don't want scouts to write me off at a camp because I'm Mexican. You don't wear a helmet at those things," he said, taking the envelopes back from me.

"I don't think everyone thinks like that as much as they say they do. If you can play, you can play, right? And you can play."

He kept his eyes on the stadium. "I want to play on Saturdays. I'm gonna be that guy standing on a ladder in front of the student section at USC waving the sword. I'm gonna do whatever it takes to get there. I'm gonna do it on the field. I'm gonna do it in the classroom. I'm going to hear that music, and I'm going to play in the Rose Bowl. I'll do anything I have to do."

My dream was just to play: to be on the field in the awesome silver and blue uniform and catch the touchdown pass to beat

Arroyo. I wanted people in the hallway of the administration building to look at me just a little bit like they looked at Fred. It was a respectful look but also the kind of look you got when you were headed somewhere. Happening. I wanted to be happening. I dreamed of it.

Garbled sounds of speeches wafted our way. We both had people we knew who were graduating. Their parts were over. It was almost like they were dead, and the ceremony was their funeral. They weren't going to get to play football this fall, and when Fred-X quarterbacked USC to the Rose Bowl, they wouldn't be there unless they bought a ticket.

"Jimmy's graduating," he said. "Do you know Jimmy?"

"Jimmy Machado? Yeah, I mean, I know of him. Is he playing somewhere next year?"

"They talked him into going to a school in Arizona to learn about air conditioners. Dumb butt didn't do his work in class, so now he's going to spend the rest of his life working on f-bombing air conditioners."

"That sucks," I said. "Didn't he get any letters?"

"Idiot didn't even take his SAT."

Cheering came from the stadium. The night was becoming dominant, and Fred's mood moved from mellow to motivated.

"That's not going to happen to me," he said. "Because we're going to go all the way this year. Then we're going to get offers and go to the colleges we want to go to." He looked at me with his big smile. "So you're coming, right?"

"Coming? You mean inside?"

He grinned at me like I was a little brother. "No man, are you coming with me to the finals? We're only guaranteed ten games, fourteen if we go the distance, so I have to know that you're not going to f-bombing quit when we start hitting. We have great things in front of us, things that are going to make people wish they were us. So, are you coming?"

I'd been dragged to church two out of every four Sundays for the first twelve years of my life, but I'd never been preached to like Fred-X preached to me from his beach chair. The Pastor was always telling us to go and experience this, and to go and experience that, and how it would change our lives. Until then, nothing ever changed me the way Fred-X changed me with his sermon from the beach chair and how there was something golden waiting for us. I'd practice all night with this guy. I'd get straight A's for this guy. No one was going to work harder than me to make it happen.

"I'm coming," I said.

"Órale," he said.

"Do you speak Spanish?"

"Nah, my uncles just say, 'órale' a lot."

We laughed. Then laughed again when he learned I didn't speak Spanish. I told him Gelbaugh scared me. He admitted Gelbaugh scared him too but masked it by scaring Gelbaugh back.

"I just get in Gelbaugh's grill. I'm the quarterback, and I'm good," Fred said. "Not to sound like a jerk, but everyone should be afraid of me. I mean, what's the option, Billy Hudson?"

"I read online he's pushing you for playing time."

"Yeah," he said, and we both laughed again. Hudson was no-where near taking his job.

The sun was halfway below the horizon, and the sky was covered by shadow. A district administrator was giving his speech about how the graduating class could go out and conquer the world. This was followed by the salutatorian's speech about how the departing se-niors could go out and be anything they dreamed of being and that they would change the world.

Fred got up.

"I've got to get my gear and pull the door closed," he said. "You need anything inside? If not, it'll stay there till Monday."

I shook my head. My gear was on the ground next to my chair. He went inside the locker room, and I pulled out my phone. No texts or Facebook messages, but my news feed was brimming with shots and comments from the graduation. I slid the phone back into my pocket as the valedictorian gave her speech about how the graduating class would shape our future world and…

"Hi," a girl's voice said.

I looked, and I gushed. It was an involuntary chemical reaction inside my body. Must have been, because it hit my system and took control. The hair was black, the eyes were green, and the smile was bookended by subtle dimples. If my head didn't know it, heart and physiology did. I was face to face for the first time with the love of my life.

"Hi," I said, getting out of my chair. She was familiar and unfamiliar at the same time.

"I'm Lena. I'm supposed to meet Fred," she said peering around me. Then she looked at me a little closer. "I know you, don't I? Didn't you come to my church?"

I stammered and tried to shake my head cooly. It had been a while since I'd attended church, and if I had met this creature called Lena, I never would have stopped going.

"I know I've seen you there before," she said.

I wondered if she was capable of not smiling.

"Lena!" Fred called from behind me and then came to hug and peck her on cheek. "Do you know Dale?"

"I was just telling him, I think we've met before at church."

I still didn't have anything to say.

"Handsdrade goes to church?" Fred gave a phony shocked look. "Dale Andrade, this is Lena Durkin, my girlfriend. Lena, this is Dale who will be all league next year."

She made her mouth small, tilted her head, and gave a look of being impressed. "That's awesome."

She was parked on the far side of the campus away from the traffic. We walked around the building and through a small faculty lot. One car was parked there, a yellow Challenger with a window slightly cracked. It was easy to see the couple in the front seat making out.

"Coach Paleo is getting his," Fred said.

"That's not nice," Lena said as we kept walking. Coach Paleo and his girlfriend didn't notice. I didn't care about Paleo because the girl I was walking next to was a supernova.

"I'm just happy for the guy," Fred said. "He was a senior when I was a sophomore, and he couldn't buy any lip."

Too polite to laugh out loud, we smiled.

"You want a ride home, Handsman?"

I refused saying my dad was meeting me at Jack In The Box, which was true, but what I really wanted was to get away from Lena so I could start to breathe again. Her looks combined with whatever perfume she was wearing devoured me. Right then I knew she was going to be trouble.

5

Fred-X Says: "I'm Not Transferring!"
By Trudy Shields

(West El Monte)--- West El Monte Poly quarterback Fred Ritter, also known as 'Fred-X,' stated on Wednesday he is not transferring to Cathedral High School and has no intention of leaving the Fighting Scots program.

Message boards commenter "MaxAtax" wrote a long post on Grip Teague's site, and the story lit up over the weekend about Ritter joining former Los Altos running back Julius Morales in heading to the Phantoms. During yesterday's four-way throw at South Pasadena, Ritter made it very clear.

"I'm friends with Julius online, I met him at the Arroyo Shootout last summer, and I haven't seen him since we talked last January at a basketball game. I'm not transferring and would be a fool to leave. On top of that I grew up in El Monte, I'm playing for an El Monte school, and no matter what anyone says or writes I will be the starting quarterback."

Ritter said there was no friction between him and newly arrived Billy Hudson, who transferred in from Ayala. Hudson has already been cleared to play by CIF...

S even-on-seven passing leagues ran through May and July. Instead of humbling Gelbaugh, and the rest of the defense at practice, I was now running by defenders from other schools.

We rotated around the San Gabriel Valley with throws against Baldwin Park, West Covina, South Hills, and La Puente. These were the regular schools, but we lined up against a lot more. All the attention was on Fred, at quarterback, Bustamonte at receiver, and Edwards out of the backfield, as it should have been. All three were legitimate standouts. No one was concerned about me.

A safety, not as fast as a cornerback or a second stringer usually had me. If I was lucky it was a linebacker. After a few rounds, they'd tighten up on me, which freed Bustamonte to make big plays.

Coach Piccou, now calling me Handsdrade, never let up with his instructions. I was always the first to show for practice and didn't fat dog it in the weight room. Running sprints after practice, I dug in all the harder. When no one was left on the field to throw to me, I practiced my routes.

I told Hudson I'd run routes for him if he wanted to get in some work after practice, but the shake of his head indicated it wouldn't be necessary. So I counted my steps, made my cuts, and imagined I was catching strikes from Fred-X. Coach Paleo often stuck around after practice to help me.

Edwards, smooth doing things out of the backfield, was fast and reminded everybody he was going to play at Arizona State. He was the only African-American on our team and came from Pasadena after a freshman stop at Alhambra. Fred liked him but said he didn't like to run between the tackles and had a limit on the hits he would take before giving in.

"Fast Eddie's great," Fred said, "but he's Mission Valley League fast."

"I don't understand."

"It means he's fast for this area, but not fast enough for major college. Plus, after a while he don't want no more."

"Want what?" I said, and Fred lifted his shoulder to simulate getting hit.

"Great guy but if he goes to ASU it'll be to study, not to play."

Bustamonte, after making sure his hair flowed properly from his headband, was more physical and much stronger than those trying to defend him. The guy thrived on lifting weights and carried himself like he'd already received a dozen offers to play Division-one football. If you asked him about it, he'd say it was only a matter of time.

Pineapple, the entertainer at left tackle, was the offensive player with the most upside, according to the media. He constantly cracked to the coaches they were hard on the team because their wives were mad at them. He spit all the time, sweated profusely, and operated like he had a perpetual case of jock itch, with his hands always down the front of his shorts. His favorite past time, besides walking around naked, was trying to catch someone off guard by offering a polluted hand to shake or for a high five. When he got a victim, he released his slow laugh and long leer.

He was down to his butt-huggers after a late June practice when Fred came running into the locker room after him.

"What are you doing?" Fred said.

"I'm getting ready to take a f-bombing shower. What does it look like?" Pineapple said. "Your woman might like you all smelly, but mine don't."

"You ain't got a woman Pineapple," Bustamonte said, walking by with only a towel draped over his shoulder. It surprised me so few of the guys showered. Pineapple, Fred, Bustamonte, and myself were the only ones who regularly did.

Fred, at five-nine, 165 pounds, grabbed the six-two, 325 pound Pineapple by the elbow and dragged him from his locker. Coach Jackson, in a conversation with Hudson, didn't even bother to comment as they went by. First, I was shocked, everyone else was laughing, and then I remembered Fred saying everyone was afraid of him.

Following behind I saw Pineapple shoved out to the cement where Fred and I watched graduation a month before. The big man didn't fight back but looked at his quarterback with loss.

"What's crawling up your rear?"

"What's crawling up my rear? You're a f-bombing team captain! You skipped out on the push-ups at the end of practice! You lied there on the grass while everyone else worked! And the reason something is crawling up my f-bombing rear right now is because

I got a bad feeling Ruiz and Estrada from Arroyo, after they get by you, are going to be crushing my rear when we play them!"

I saw it, the coaches heard it, and there was Pineapple standing in the summer sun with his hairy belly hanging out over his Fruit of the Looms. He shook his frizzy brown head and started to walk back to the locker room.

"Screw it, I'll make it up tomorrow," he said.

Fred-X, not Fred, stepped in front of him, his winning presidential smile replaced by something colder. "No, you're going to make it up now. Because I'm not going to get a concussion in October and miss half the season because you're too lazy to do push-ups in June." Then the quarterback's voice boomed from West El Monte to the Inland Empire. "Do them or I'll fry your hairy butt!"

What exactly 'frying Pineapple's hairy butt' meant, I didn't know and assumed it was something connected to football I'd learn later.

Hands touched my back as I leaned out of the locker room's double doors. Edwards and several others were looking over my shoulder as Pineapple, cursing, went down to the ground and began doing push-ups. Fred counted them off.

"Faaa," Edwards said, which was his abbreviated form of F-bomb. "Better not mess with Fred-X."

"No jack," I said.

I passed my *Braveheart* test with an eight out of ten. The two I missed were from his speech before one of the big battles. In the Fighting Scots program, this is serious business.

"You need to brush up on your Scottish, Andrade," Coach Von Huson said as I sat at my locker before practice. He was the only coach not calling me Handsdrade or Handsman. Von Huson, in his sixties, didn't seem to care about anything except a National Geographic magazine he kept rolled up in his back pocket.

"I don't own the movie, Coach," I said.

"It's fifty cents to rent on the computer," he said walking away. "Califf! You didn't turn in your math homework." He turned the corner and was gone. "It's f-bombing summer and it's the only f-bombing class you have!"

"You're supposed to be a son of Scotland, Handsdrade," Fred said parking himself next to me. "You can't write down 'son of England' on your test."

"I got confused."

"Well, get unconfused," he said. "I'm vouching for you. You're making me look bad."

We dressed and were ready to hit the field when a black guy, about my height, came in the locker room wearing earbuds. Sculpted, with fine tuned muscles, he gave me a nod, headed to the next row of lockers and began to dress out.

He looked like a receiver and fear came to me. Of course, it had been easy to beat out a low life like Ponce but that didn't mean I was really good. Insecurity told me they were probably bringing this guy in to take my spot.

"Who is that guy?" I said to Fred as we walked across the concrete to the field. My concern took away the pleasure I always got from hearing our cleats clack on the hard surface.

"Patterson," Fred said. "He transferred in from Pasadena."

"Is he a receiver?"

"I don't know," he smiled at me. "You worried?"

We stretched, we ran, did our quarters, and instant relief came when we broke into our groups. Patterson went with the defensive backs. Unless you were in a private school, it made sense to want out of Pasadena, but my new teammate had found his way to West El Monte Poly. A heck of an address change to a part of the valley not known for having a large population of brothers...or sisters, as Fast Eddie often complained.

Patterson spent his time connecting with Lee, our free safety, and Gelbaugh. Coach Gugliotta plugged him right in. First, he locked up with Maez, then drove Bustamonte crazy for a half hour, before settling over me. I tried to get into my routes, but he roughed me out of them. I wasn't going to beat him with speed, and I couldn't keep him from manhandling me even with the punch and swipe techniques Coach Paleo taught me.

"I can't shake this guy," I said to Fred between reps.

"So do something about it." Fred's look wasn't a look that said I should quit, but more about how I should get it done--meaning there wasn't any choice but to get it done.

I lined in the slot again. Patterson came and pressed right over me. *Press*, I had come to learn, often meant man-to-man coverage. The last half hour of practice I got chewed out for not being fast enough, strong enough, and mentally tough enough to do anything against the Pasadena import.

"Handsman, you look about as tough as a French soldier," Coach Jackson said. "You're surrendering before the ball is even snapped."

"I thought you said the French soldiers weren't as bad as everyone says?" Coach Piccou said.

"You're right," Jackson said. "What an insult to the French soldiers. Handsman, you got to pick it up. This isn't Pasadena Marshall."

The less than feeling I had early in the spring returned. It surprised me to find out I wasn't as good as I thought. Even worse was the feeling Fred might be done with me. The other guys struggled. Neither Maez nor Bustamonte did anything against Patterson, but they were the same as they were before.

Afraid to ask them about it, I began putting on my clothes when Patterson came by our row of lockers. He high-fived Fred, gave me a head nod, and went out the doors. At least he wasn't a jerk, but, then again, the jerk-position was already filled.

"You got schooled out there today, Andrade," Ponce said, tying his shoes. "Not that easy, is it, boy?"

"Did you even catch a ball today, Ponce?" Maez said.

"Did you?"

"When you're ready for a little chingasos, let me know," Maez said

"'Chingasos?'" Ponce let out a laugh. "What are you? Some seventies vato with a filero in your back pocket, esé? You still cruising in your low rider, holmes?"

"You want to find out, debilucho?" Maez efforted a pair of cold eyes at the sophomore. Ponce didn't want to find out and turned back to knotting his kicks. "Don't worry about it, Handsman. Patterson made us all look bad today."

We kept dressing. Maez, having my back, helped with my being humbled. I left out the double doors with Fred. We walked through the school to the student parking lot. Even for summer, the place hardly looked abandoned. Cheerleaders were practicing, the band was practicing, janitors were working and leaning against the hood of Fred's Frontier truck was Lena, wearing white shorts, flip flops, and a plaid pink blouse with sleeves rolled.

"You want a ride?" Fred said.

"Sure," I said, without much energy. The memory of Patterson faded, and I could feel myself weakening the closer we got to Lena.

"Two things you have to know about today," Fred said, naturally assuming my disposition was stuck on the former and not the latter. "Patterson is a really good athlete, probably better than most of the guys you're going to see this year. Especially in league, but it will help you. You see, so far you've been bigger or faster than the guys you've played against, but you have to learn how to use your brain."

Lena hugged Fred and gave me a great smile. "Hey, Handsman."

I smelled her. Five feet away, I could smell her, and after she got into the front seat of the truck, I could smell it even more. In the mall the previous weekend, I went by a women's store and smelled the same scent. I found out it was Royal Jasmine. That was what I smelled when I was near Lena. No whiskey, I was sure, could make me feel as drunk as that scent did.

"You have to learn how to outsmart guys faster than you. I know if we lined up on the goal line to see who could throw the ball the farthest, Hudson might beat me…"

"…Hudson's a…"

"…Yeah, I know, he's a jerk. He might have a little bit better of an arm, but I'm a better quarterback. I think faster, and I know I make better decisions."

"So what do I do about it?" I said, trying not to stare at Lena through the side mirror.

"Get the job done," Fred said. He revved the Frontier's engine and rolled out of the parking lot.

"How?"

"By doing whatever it takes."

"Bad day at the office Handsman?" Lena said, smiling back at me.

"Nah, he wasn't as bad as he thought," Fred said. "You just have to sell your moves with your eyes and shoulders. You did exactly the same thing on every snap today, and that makes it too easy for someone to defend you. Paleo has told you about this; you got to change it up sometimes Handsman."

The conversation segued away from me. Lena and Fred talked about their plans for the next few days. It seemed as if I was invited to everything but their next make out session. In the last few months, I'd fallen for my quarterback. I'd have done anything for him, but, as we drove, I kept hoping for him to say or do something wrong in front of Lena. I wanted him to be rude to her in some way, so somehow I could find a wedge to just ethically dream about her. For now, he was proving to be an even better boyfriend than quarterback.

We pulled in front of my house, and I got out.

"We're doing that swim party with the church this week," Lena said, leaning across Fred, who was holding the steering wheel. "You need to come. Fred's coming."

He shrugged like he didn't have a choice.

I nodded, feeling like I'd taken a double hit. Not only was Fred driving off with Lena, but I was probably going to lose my job to Patterson. Coach Jackson had to be excited about getting a guy like that involved with the offense.

"Handsdrade!" Fred called out from the truck as I reached my lawn. "I didn't tell you the second thing."

"What's that?"

"Patterson," he said holding up his hands, "manos de piedra!"

"What's that?"

"He's got hands of stone," Fred said smiling. "He's not playing offense."

I went to the swim party. Fred didn't show. Familiar faces from grammar school days went by me. People were polite, especially Lena. She wore a very modest one-piece bathing suit, but I couldn't corner her, couldn't find a way to keep her next to me. Every time I thought I'd turned the trick, someone else needed her for something or someone else horned in on our conversation. She was like the Fred-X of the church teen group.

The Youth Pastor's devotional was about how I needed Jesus, but I couldn't take my eyes, or thoughts, away from Lena. She listened from the edge of the pool with her feet in the water. Too many positive vibes were countering my negative ones. I hung for about forty minutes and then carefully went out the front door.

"Passing League tournaments and throws are never supposed to be about one team proving they're better than another. It's never about winning a trophy or a title in the summer," Piccou soberly declared while we were on one knee before the first match of the SGV Shootout at Arroyo High School. "What everyone really wants, what we want, is the hardware they give out in December. That's the victory we want. The purpose today is strictly about getting better individually and as a team."

Sure, and there's no cactus in Arizona.

I began to notice the opponents we threw against frequently in midweek four-ways were teams our coaches were good friends with. We were taught fundamentals, technique, and playbook. Some laughing kept it all in control, but if something got out of hand they, immediately policed it. The coaches always preached sportsmanship except when we played schools with coaches they didn't get along with. Then it would get quiet and turn into something else. We were given the pep talk about doing what we were supposed to do, but, between the lines, it was made clear we were going to react if someone tried to dump on us.

We opened the tournament against El Monte on a hastily laid out field near the tennis courts with cones and chalk. Everything was cool, except they beat us when their quarterback, Anthony Ledesma, hooked up with Carter Ochoa twice. On the same field, we won against Los Altos, and I caught a touchdown from Billy Hudson, who did have a good arm. Then, before lunch, we moved closer to the stadium and beat Crescenta Valley.

We ate sandwiches, orange slices, and pounded Gatorade under the easy-ups by the baseball field's backstop. Some guys rested on their backs with towels over their faces to steal naps while others made the circuit. I watched the carnival atmosphere around me. All the event was missing was jugglers, fire blowers, and clowns.

Up to this point, I had no idea a world like this existed. There were food trucks, vendors selling football equipment, the smell of hamburgers and hot dogs burning on grills. The easy-ups for all the teams ringed the grounds. The players were in shirts with team colors and themes printed on the back. A few were in Latin, most were in English, and all were some form of rah-rah; *'Hate to lose, love to hit, hit to win,' 'Seize the day!'* in English and Latin, *'Semper Fidelis'* and *'Hard work beats talent.'* Chino High School's theme was a more progressive: *'Suck on this!'*

"Why did we choose alba gu bràth?" I said aloud under the shade of our tent.

"Because we're the Fighting Scots," Dan Feliz, a linebacker, said. "It means Scotland Forever. We've only seen the movie like a hundred times this summer. Get with it, Handsman."

"I haven't seen it a hundred times," I said.

"Well, you should," Feliz said. "It's better than porn."

"I doubt that," Bustamonte said, lying back on the grass with a towel over his face. "I've seen it, and I've seen porn. I kind of like porn better."

I knew guys who loved porn, and they all seemed to have a bad odor to them. I wasn't a saint, but I stayed away from it because it didn't seem right to me. First person shooter games, in my old life, were more my speed. Now, I was hooked on Madden and wouldn't have time for porn even if I wanted it.

"You're sick, Boosty," Feliz said.

I had other questions but let it ride. Everything out of my mouth continued to make me look like the novice I was. So when I saw Fred talking to some guys from Arroyo, I let it go because I knew the answer would be, "Because he's Fred-X."

After lunch, we threw with Alhambra on the big field inside the stadium. It was as if a shooting war had begun, and we were

Marines parachuting into North Korea. Even in the warm-ups, Piccou looked like he wanted a fight to break out.

The seven-on-seven with the Moors began with me getting swung at on the first play by a runt of a cornerback. *'Triay'* was printed on the back of his shirt, and *'No One Gets Out Of Here Alive'* on the front. I quickly established a Ponce-like hatred for him.

On the second play, I got a hard palm across my neck from my new friend. The series went on, the day got hotter, the grass started sticking to my skin, my arms itched, my legs itched, and I thought maybe this was why everyone doesn't play football. I mean, I could be resting up for a round of parking lot volleyball with the church tonight.

When the defense took the field, Coach Paleo found me. "Handsdrade, what did you expect? You waiting for a kiss and him to ask you out?"

"The f-bomber took a swing at me. You want me to swing back?" I was new to football, but I knew I wasn't supposed to get into a fight. What was the point of getting thrown out?

"No! I want you to kick the little f-bomber's butt when he tries to jam you at the line of scrimmage. That's not Patterson out there, that's a bug, and that bug is allowed to do anything he wants to you until the ball is in the air. You ain't been lifting those weights since spring to look pretty in the mirror. Come on, we showed you the technique, slap his hands away, sell him some shoulder. He's laughing at you right now because he thinks you're soft. Hell, I'm beginning to think you're soft. So is Coach Jackson. Now, go out there and give him the kind of hell I know you can."

Patterson was now in a shouting match with an Alhambra receiver, and Lee pulled him back. Coach Gugliotta hollered at Gelbaugh to get his unit focused. Coach Piccou was jawing at the official for a flag.

"Handsdrade, listen to me," Coach Jackson said, joining my counseling session. "Son, you see the short little fat dude with the whistle in his mouth talking to Coach Piccou?" I nodded. "Don't wait for him to throw a flag. He wouldn't throw a flag if Pineapple walked past him on the field naked. All he's doing is checking his watch and waiting for it to be five o'clock so he can get some pizza. You, on the other hand, have to make it happen out there. You get your job done. Get to where you need to be for your quarterback. No one is going to give you anything out there, so go take it. This is football. You can't be soft."

"If we didn't believe in you, Handsman, you wouldn't be out there," Paleo added.

On our second series, Bustamonte caught a perfect pass from Fred on a go-route for a score. Instead of giving the ball to the ref, he spiked it, raised his hands in the air, and told the Moors they could go f-bomb themselves. This started five minutes of shoving that fell short of escalating into a full brawl.

The scrawny corner, who had been swinging at me, jumped on Fast Eddie from behind, but Gelbaugh grabbed him and launched his carcass across the turf. This prompted a drunk, shirtless, uncle, with a protruding stomach to come onto the field, his arms wide apart begging for Gelbaugh to challenge him.

"Throw me white boy," he said. "Throw me! Come on, I'm a man!" He was a disgustingly gross looking man: round, balding, and stupid--the guy we all prayed we wouldn't become ten years down the road. "I'm a man! Come get some of this!"

"You want me fat f-bomb?" Gelbaugh said pointing to himself. Accepting the challenge, Gugliotta and Jackson kept him back.

Coach Piccou, with his freshly shaved scalp sunburning, screamed at the official after they were separated. "The mother-f-bomber under the goal post has been sounding off all day." The drunk uncle was back in his beach chair and reaching into an ice chest for added fortification. "Get him out of here or I'm going to turn my guy loose on him!"

When the official went to the Alhambra coaches, Piccou screamed at us for getting tossed around. A few hours before, he told us championships were won in the autumn and summer was for preparation. Now he wanted us to jackhammer our opponents into the ground.

The uncle was removed. We huddled while Fred was getting the play from Coach Jackson.

"What did we ever do to Alhambra?" I asked.

Bustamonte pulled his mouthpiece out. "They ran the score up on us four years ago, and Coach took it personal. I was a ball boy that night. Piccou and Chalmers got into it after the game when they lined up to shake hands."

"Who's Chalmers?"

"The Alhambra HC, dumb butt," Fast Eddie said.

I was unaware learning the name of the other head coach was part of my job. It was difficult enough for me to remember technique, how many steps to take on a route, and seek ways to get by Triay.

"Did Alhambra run it up?"

"We finished 2-8 that year. The grandmas at the rest home could have run the score up on that team," Maez said. "They sucked."

Piccou was still frothing. The official gave him a warning, then blew his whistle for us to resume play.

"Coach!" Fred-X said. "I got it!" He gave a thumb's up when Piccou looked at him. "Don't worry, I got it."

In the huddle, he called the play. I dipped my shoulder to the center of the field and then finished off a corner-route. The pass was gold, and I scored a touchdown. Mindful of events, I handed the ball to the official and ran back to our side of the field, trying my best to make it look like I'd done it a thousand times before.

"Handsdrade!" Pineapple clapped his hands from the sideline with the rest of the team. "I knew that mother-f-bomber could play! I knew it!" He said to the rest of team and reached a hand out for me to high five. Suspicious of its previous location, I decided to ignore it and not take the risk.

Except for the center, Kiel Basler, who snapped the ball, linemen didn't participate in seven on sevens. Some of the tournaments we went to had competitions where they lifted weights, played with truck tires, pushed SUV's, did tug-o-wars, and ran laughable relay races. The SGV Shootout didn't, but because the team was there, they were there.

I accepted Edwards's high-five, and Maez gave me a respectful nod. While Ponce ignored me, Bustamonte gave me a pat on the butt. "F-bomb them," he said. "Great catch."

Triay took a swing on the next snap, and I ducked out of the way. The pass was incomplete. Piccou had to be held back by Gugliotta. "What the f-bomb! What are you guys watching out there?"

"Next one coach," the official said. "One more. Next one and you're gone."

"Coach!" Fred-X said. "Don't worry about it!"

Next snap came and I got by the shorter defender, but he tripped me. Fred completed a pass to Maez to advance us forward, and Piccou dialed the frothing down to seething.

"Let's go, Handsdrade," Patterson called from the sideline. Getting acknowledgment from Patterson was inspiring. It confirmed he really was my teammate and not a candidate for my position. "Toast those mofos!" (That's not abbreviated. He really did say *mofos*, and I'll let you figure out what it means.)

"Andrade, I can be pissed at you, or they can be pissed at you. It's your choice," said Gelbaugh offering his own form of motivation.

I lined up in the left slot, and the little defender came across from me. "Handsdrade," Triay said slowly, with disgust, loud enough for only me to hear. "Who the f-bomb do you think you are? You..."

The ball was hiked, and I beat him straight up field on a post-route. When the f-bomber stuck out a leg to trip me, Fred-X put the point of the ball in his ear. He went down hard. Even with his headgear, it had to hurt.

"Handsdrade, that was my bad!" Fred-X said touching his chest. "I'll get you next time. That was my bad, Coach Jackson. I'll get the next one."

Everyone on our side of the field laughed because they knew.

The official came to our huddle. His face bubbling with sweat, knowing everyone hated him. I felt some compassion because all he was working for at the end of the day, according to Coach Jackson, was pizza.

"Did you throw that football at his head deliberately?" He said to Fred.

"I don't know," he answered. "Did he try to trip my receiver deliberately? Tell him to cut the 'Bad Dude' act or it might happen again, maybe in the money-spot."

The official went to Chalmers.

Fred pulled us into a huddle. "Should I do it again?"

When all of us agreed with Fred, I noticed it really was us against everybody else. I hated Ponce, but Ponce was for me to hate, not another team. Gelbaugh might not have liked me, but he liked our opponents even less. I was his teammate. These were my teammates, and I began to think they might be something even more. In our circle, I was the weak rookie, but against other teams I was learning they had my proverbial six.

"These guys aren't going to the playoffs," Fred-X said plainly. "So let's finish it straight up. Boosty, don't start anything."

"Bull..." Bustamonte started.

"Don't," Fred-X said. "They're not worth it. They're not worth any of us getting hurt or suspended. This is gonna be your year, jefe."

What coaches and officials couldn't do, Fred-X did by just giving an order and ear-holing Triay with the football. The cornerback didn't return and the drama ended. We beat Alhambra but lost to Charter Oak in the next round. CO's quarterback, the left-handed Del Chance, was awesome to watch even when he was beating us.

Coach Jackson told us we had a good day. Coach Gugliotta told us we needed to get better but got it done when we had to. That was it because Coach Piccou had already left to work the team's firework stand.

I'd never reminded my dad about taking a shift.

6

Read The Blitz
By Grip Teague

Some might say it's too early to pick winners, top tens, league champs and champions, but I think we all know who the winning teams are going to be. I don't think we have to talk about CIF champions or go into much detail on this July day to talk about the individual leagues themselves (that's what a preview is for).

Here's our top ten for you to enjoy, tear apart, or just salivate over. Word of warning: the comment boards are monitored, if you're vulgar it won't go through. If you wish to curse at Bald Guy, or myself, our emails are below for you to do so privately.

1. *Cathedral: Best team around. We know, we know, we know about history, but we're not talking about history. We're talking about right now. They've had a great free agency period. Julius Morales is no joke.*

2. *Glendora: Tartans bring back a bunch of talent. Did you know, at one time, this was a basketball school?*

3. *San Dimas: You heard it here first, beware of the Bone-Spread and a quarterback named Shane Delfman.*

4. *West Covina: Graduation took its toll, but the Bulldogs and Courtney Graye can still make life tough for opponents.*

5. *Pomona: In three previous seasons, has anybody blocked Tank Davis? Oregon, USC and Nebraska are among those who have already offered this Red Devil.*

6. *Bishop Amat: They won the Jefferson Pham Sweepstakes, but time will tell if they are the best in the Catholic League.*

7. *West El Monte Poly: Fred-X brings back his magic for another season. Is it good enough for a title? We'll see, but it seems to be good enough for everyone to want to be a Fighting Scott (see Billy Hudson).*

8. *La Serna: They've been acquiring Whittier's best for a generation now. No reason to think this coming season will be anything less than stellar. Again.*

9. *Dominguez: Alec Jammon is hands down the best quarterback we cover. Better than Del Chance at Charter Oak, better than Ritter at West El Monte, and he's reason enough for us to put the Dons in our top ten.*

10. *Charter Oak: Leave it to Chance. Chargers quarterback, Del Chance, like Jammon at Dominguez, is the only hope CO has.*

If something happens to him, then it's lights out this season for the tradition rich program.

Notes: El Monte HC, Dan Valencia confirmed we will see Carter Ochoa at receiver, running back, quarterback, defensive back, and returning kicks this season. Bald Guy asked Valencia if there was any chance of Ochoa playing left tackle, and he said it was still a possibility. I asked Valencia if Ochoa was better than Lions legend Justin Ta'amu, who ran for two-thousand yards nearly a decade ago. "I'll tell you after Week 14," Valencia said. "Ta'amu took us to Week 12, so we'll see." ...Former Ayala/current West El Monte quarterback, Billy Hudson, says he's not content with waiting until his junior season to take over the reigns for the Fighting Scots: "I respect Fred-X, but if I have a better summer, and camp in August, then I should be starting." ...Downey linebacker Gilliam Gilliam (yes, that's his name) has been offered by Colorado State...

Dead period for us started the third week of July and went through the first week of August, which meant we couldn't play at the school or to get instructions from our coaches. All the schools had to observe this three week break, but we had Fred-X and that meant we were different.

We took one week off and spent the next two weeks meeting every day on our own, including Sundays, for ninety minutes in the park.

During the week off, I spent three torturous days at my mom's in Glendora. She wanted me to be happy, but she was the one who moved out and went to live with her boyfriend. I couldn't buy into the unstated assumption we were all happy and everything was just fine.

I filled my time with running and studying my play sheets. I also exchanged Facebook messages with Lena. She posted pictures of her family vacation in Colorado. I commented, she commented back, I messaged her, she messaged me. It was great, but while I was in love, she was only falling into friendship with me. In the moment, it was great. In the eternal, it sucked.

When I got back home, I went for my physical and found out I was an inch taller than I was the year before. Six-foot was a great number, and no matter what happened in my future, I could never be accused of being the short guy. Dad was only five-ten, so I took it with gratitude.

Fred-X went to a quarterback camp in Orange County where all the high-end signal callers in the state were on display. This was the camp he'd been aiming for and why he never stopped working out when the previous season ended. He told me many of the guys who made good showings at camps like Steve Clarkson's or Orange County Elite got offers no matter how well their senior year went. It didn't hurt to have stats in high school, but it was a bigger deal to have a great camp playing with the best passers, receivers, and everything relating to you measured.

When he returned, he invited the team to his place to play Madden and eat burgers. With parents around, I didn't have to worry about Gelbaugh mad dogging me, so I got to relax. Ponce and Hudson were bad enough, but they were kept in place by the seniors.

Mr. Ritter was grilling. Mrs. Ritter was making sure all the chips, dips, and sodas were stocked and within reach. It felt like a birthday party without the cake, candles and sappy singing. It was an average house, made better by Fred's dad who knew his way around a toolbox. Nice without looking like it was so soaked with money you feared spilling something on the carpet.

"No, no, no," Mrs. Ritter said when I offered to help get some more ice. She was tiny, barely five-foot, and her genes were probably the reason her son was only five-nine. "You're our guest. We're happy Freddy has such good friends."

Freddy? I wouldn't have called him Freddy with a gun to my back. Neither would anybody else. She leaned across the breakfast bar and whispered. "Don't tell him I called him Freddy. He hates it."

I waved a hand to let her know I wouldn't say anything and moved on.

Everyone was moving around from the living room to the dining room to the patio. A Jacuzzi was churning away, but no one was in it. Bustamonte was loading up at the buffet table with Hudson chattering away next to him.

"I swear, I never said those things to Teague," he said, trying to convince Bustamonte. "He just wrote it wrong."

A new slew of threads on the message boards appeared, arguing West El Monte would be better off with Hudson at quarterback and Fred in a split backfield with Fast Eddie. It didn't take long for the guys to figure out one of the most frequent commenters on Grip Teague's blog was Hudson's uncle, Clint. Clint Hudson was the new president of the boosters, the third since the spring if you were keeping track. His postings as "MaxAtax" revealed things that outed him as a moron and Billy's uncle.

"You should tell your uncle to stop talking so much," Bustamonte said. "It's going to get you in trouble."

"It wasn't me," Hudson said. "That's all I can say."

"That's not how the guys see it," Boosty said. "For starters, I wouldn't talk to Teague. Him and Bald Guy are just looking for trash to spread. It makes you look like a rookie."

"I'm not a rookie," Hudson said.

"You're a rookie," Fat John said, passing by, with a stacked plate on his way to the patio.

I moved to the living room where Fred's little brothers were playing a video game. It was a first person fantasy game I knew too much about. I hadn't played anything but Madden since March, but the nerd inside me knew exactly what he was seeing. What the Ritter brothers should have been doing to get to the next level was clear to my trained eyes. If the team really knew what I was into before, I don't think they would have wanted me around.

Behind the couch, where the brothers were sitting, was a Ritter family portrait from a few years back. We didn't have a picture like this at my house. I studied it and wondered if they were all as happy as the image indicated. Fred, a little chubby, looked like he was in junior high but already beginning to master his award winning smile.

Shelves holding books, nicknacks, and photos lined the off white walls of the family room. An unframed color picture of him and Lena by the Jacuzzi was on a shelf. Even on cruddy copy paper, she stood out. I could almost smell Royal Jasmine coming through the ink. Then my eyes saw a small stack of envelopes to the right of the picture. Fred's name was on them. Whittier, La Verne, and Southern Oregon were some of the colleges reaching out. I was happy for him, and if he could just find a way to tell Lena she'd be better off with me, the world would be perfect.

"Burgers and brats!" Mr. Ritter yelled, entering through the glass doors. "Get'em before Pineapple does!"

"Brats?" Kiel Basler said. "That hits me where I live."

More of the guys poured in from the patio. There were more envelopes, but I didn't want to touch them so I backed away. Took another look at Lena...

"Better get something now Handsman," Mr. Ritter said. His white skin was sun drenched and wrinkled from years of construction work. "Or the offensive line will take it all."

"I'm coming." I got in line.

"Watch your hands," Fred said, sliding in behind me. "Pineapple might mistake them for a hamburger."

"You want me fat or thin, Ritter?" Pineapple said. "Make up your mind."

We all moved in a circle around the buffet table.

"Was the camp good?" I asked as we loaded up.

"Where's the beer at?" Pineapple said. "If you serve brats you gotta have beer."

"You mean root beer," said Mr. Ritter. "It's out on the patio." Then he looked at Fred. "Where did you get these friends of yours?" He walked back to the grill. "The Home Depot parking lot?"

"They're all mojados," Fred said.

"They'll give you a vacation if you say that at school," Basler said.

"You maybe," Fred said. "Look at my skin. You think they're going to say anything to me? I am a mojado."

The guys shook their heads and laughed. It was so different from being at school. When we were at school someone or some group was always hacked about something. It was refreshing to have all insults available and free to use.

We worked down to the condiments.

"So how was the camp?"

"It was tough," he said. "Those guys were good, a little lazy, but good. I got some decent throws in."

"Who was there?"

"Jammon from Dominguez, Parker from Servite, and Meisner from Capo Valley looked good. Homeboy is big."

"Chance?"

"Yeah, Chance was there, but he was one of those guys who fat dogged it some."

"He dogged it at camp with all of those scouts?"

"A little bit," Fred said. "I think he thinks he's right up there with those other guys. He's not even close."

"What were the receivers like?" I checked to see if Bustamonte was nearby. He was a good receiver, for our area, but no invites to any camps had come his way. It was a tough pill for Boosty when the subject came up.

"I'll tell you," he said capping his burger, and scooping French fries, while maintaining a smile powered by Edison. "They weren't as good as the ones I have back home."

For the next two weeks in the park, he threw to us like we were the number one receiving class in America.

When dead period ended, we came back to three days of conditioning before being issued helmets and pads. All the lifting, all the work I had done from spring through summer, all the passes, and studying made me part of the team. I even made it into Bustamonte's graces, perhaps not his good graces, but he at least high-fived me now.

The feeling of belonging went away, however, when we dressed out for the first time. I had no clue, none, on which way my pads went or what to put on first. I was a volleyball player all over again.

When it wasn't on the list of things for me to buy, I assumed I would be issued a cup. I could have gotten away without being embarrassed, but I foolishly asked out loud. Asking would be better than staring right?

"Is your junk special, Handsman?" Coach Paleo said.

"They don't call him Handsman for nothing," Pineapple chipped in.

The team laughed hard at me, but there was nothing I could do. The coaches straightened me out on the cup issue, but it was Fred who ordered Edwards to teach me some visible cool to take into battle. He showed me how to tape up, how to use eye black, how to tie my laces, and how to let a thin hand rag hang from my hip so it could wave as I ran.

When finally assembled for the first time, I studied myself in the full length locker room mirror. I looked like a mechanized future warrior. Powerful, with all the latest technology, I wasn't close to being a star, but I looked impressive in the silver and blue colors. The last volleyball jersey I wore had a white collar and long preppy sleeves. Why didn't everybody play football?

We did our jumping jacks, our ups and downs, and knees to chest. The breathing was easy, the eighty degree heat a little after 7:00 a.m. was cruel. Before we broke off into stations, the coaches had us gather and take a knee. Coach Jackson went over housekeeping about our gear and what the schedule for the day would be. Coach Gugliotta gave us a lecture about drinking our water, staying hydrated and letting them know if we were feeling sick or light headed.

"Someone talked to their mommy because they were butt hurt about something and now I got a headache." Coach Piccou held up a letter. "I don't have enough headaches coaching you guys, running the firework stand, keeping Bustamonte from carrying a blow dryer in his back pocket and Pineapple from scratching himself? Now, I got to deal with this?"

We looked at each other, then back to coach.

"Someone went crying to his mommy, who went crying to the PTA, who went crying to the administration about me and the staff cussing too much. I told them it's football. We're supposed to cuss."

"F-bomb yeah," Pineapple said.

"So I have been warned not to cuss anymore, or I'll be written up. I'm also supposed to tell you the following, so listen." Coach Piccou brought the letter up to read. "Over the course of the last several months if I, or a member of my coaching staff, has offended you with coarse talk or obscene language, I do apologize. While I am human and my passions sometimes get the better of me, I and my coaching staff are representatives of West El Monte Poly. We are expected to act and speak with all appropriateness. In the future, myself, as well as the coaching staff, will think very carefully about the words we choose to use as we communicate with each other and the players in the program. Again, I extend sincere apologies."

It was quiet before Pineapple raised his hand. Piccou pointed at him.

"What the f-bomb does that mean?" He said, and the team burst into laughter. "I just don't f-bombing get it. Can we f-bombing cuss?"

"We can f-bombing cuss," Basler said, "but the coaches can't f-bombing cuss."

"That's not f-bombing fair," Gelbaugh said.

"So since Coach can't cuss should we cuss for him?" Pineapple asked the team.

We answered in unison: "F-bomb yeah!"

7

Local Coach Arrested at Practice
By Trudy Shields

(El Monte)--- El Monte Police Tuesday arrested a West El Monte Poly High School assistant football coach on suspicion of engaging in sexual acts with a student at the school.

Rick Paleo, 20, was arrested at the start of practice after police received a tip Monday evening regarding "unlawful sexual activities" involving the coach and a student. After a prompt investigation, police arrested Paleo the following afternoon.

Detectives handling the investigation believe Paleo's sexual contact with the victim took place on school grounds the Friday before. Paleo was booked in the Los Angeles County Pre-trial Detention Facility and then released on $100,000 bond.

Paleo's relationship with the minor, whose name has not been released, began when he was in high school. The arrest occurred as the West El Monte team was on the field for Tuesday afternoon's practice.

"I've known Rick Paleo since he was a freshman here," said West El Monte Head Football Coach Skip Piccou. "This is a miss-understanding. He just turned 20. She's 18 in October. They started dating two years ago when he was a senior. I've spoken to the girl's family, and they were as surprised as the rest of us that this arrest was made."

The school's administration has not issued a statement. The school district is expected to release one very soon.

On Wednesday, we were still in shock at seeing Coach Paleo taken away. The day before, the cops walked onto the field as he was explaining a play called 'Thirty-two Trips Richie.' They read him his rights and slapped the cuffs on him. Paleo, who always talked tough around us, began to shake and looked like he was about ready to cry.

Coach Piccou came across the field and followed the cops out. He yelled at them for doing it on the field. "You couldn't talk to me first? You couldn't wait until after practice? This is bull..." His voice faded away. When he was behind the bleachers and near the locker room, we heard him again, "Son of...," and a trashcan went tumbling.

We didn't know whether to laugh or cry for Paleo so we just stared in the direction of the locker room. Jackson and Gugliotta cursed us to get our minds back on practice and to remember we had Downey in Week One.

The next day, strapping up for practice in the locker room, we heard the news Paleo had been released. We were laughing and happy. Pineapple did the circuit naked as we heard the band practicing somewhere nearby.

"The lesson to be learned, Handsman," Fred said, "is make sure, if you hook up with a younger chick, not to make out with her in the school parking lot."

The team laughed all the harder. It was going to be murder when Paleo came through the double doors.

"So who played rata and made the call?" Maez said. "That's a cold thing to do to somebody."

"He's a coach and he was making out with Candida Rodriguez in his car on campus," Fred said. "He's stupid and I'm going to tell him he's stupid when he comes back."

The coaches came out of their office. Piccou marched right by us and out the double doors. The noise of the band came through even louder.

"Bring it in," Gugliotta called. "Bring it in now!"

We gathered, most of us half dressed, when Jackson spoke. "You know the good news. All charges against Coach Paleo have been dropped."

The guys cheered and couldn't wait to ride him when he came back.

"The bad news is, we had to fire him. I'm now the receivers coach until we find someone better. Now get dressed and get to the field."

"Why did he get fired?" Pineapple asked.

"Because he f-bombed up," said Jackson. "The world is like that. It's always waiting for an opportunity to f-bomb you over the minute you f-bomb up. Remember that. Hopefully, you won't have to remember it when people are shooting at you."

"I thought you guys weren't supposed to cuss anymore," Pineapple said.

"I'm a walk-on," Jackson said. "I don't get a paycheck. I say what I want. Now get your big butt to the field."

I didn't particularly like Coach Paleo in the sense that he was never somebody I would get super close to, but I hated to see him go. He'd given me his time, and I'd learned a lot from him. Coach Jackson knew something about everything when it came to football, but he wasn't going to have the time for us Paleo did.

Dressed, we came out in full gear, ready to scrimmage. Outside of the double doors, our cleats tapped in near unison over the pavement toward the stadium. The clacking of cleats again inspired me, reminding with each lift and touch I was part of something great.

The music grew louder. I stopped hearing our footfalls, looked around, but didn't see the band on any of the fields around us.

"What the f-bomb is this?" Bustamonte said.

Coach Gugliotta then came with his hands raised towards us. "Back inside! Back inside!"

Storming behind him was Piccou. No cap, no whistle, no clipboard, arteries in his neck bulging at stroke level. "Back inside! All of you get back inside!"

We sat on our benches inside the locker room. It was tight, a preview of what the season would be like. Through the double doors, we could hear the band playing, and I was completely lost.

"So what time do you want us back tonight, Coach?" Fred said.

"The band has the field till six. I'll see you guys back here at seven if my wife doesn't divorce me first."

The next day, late in the afternoon, we were scrimmaging. The temperature had cooled to the high eighties, which wasn't bad. Things were going well. I caught a couple of slants, a post, and a corner off a Smash play. I especially liked the Smash because when Boosty ran a hitch I took off on a corner. Fred would lead me with the pass, and the safety was always chasing me.

The defense made adjustments. Dinh Lee settled in across from me in the right slot. The signal was for me to run a slant. The ball was hiked and Lee pushed with both hands into my shoulders. I lowered myself and brought an arm up to swim by him on the inside. Making the cut, my head turned, my hands rose, the ball was high, I caught it, and then something emerged in my excellent peripheral vision.

Feeling nothing, except the sensation of flying backward in the air, I cradled the football. When I landed on my back, the light around my eyes pulsed and darkened. My lungs locked. It was the worst thing I'd ever felt. I was dying.

Some voices were talking, but I couldn't understand them. Helmets started hovering over me, but I only recognized one.

"I got you," I read off Gelbaugh's lips as he looked at me transitioning into death on the ground. "I told you I'd get you." He mouthed a profanity and disappeared on the other side of my blinking eyelids.

Coach Jackson kneeled next to me. My lungs started to move with a guttural screech. Fred with his helmet off, his black hair wet with sweat, gave me a smile. "Nice catch," he said.

"Handsdrade," Jackson said. "You okay?" He smiled at me and then at everyone else. "Looks like Handsman got a little taste of the boom, boom, bash."

What was he smiling about? I was dying.

"I'm dying."

"No, you're not dying," he said. "You got the wind knocked out of you, boy. Relax."

As air seeped back into my body, I rolled over and dug my hands into the grass. "F-bomb...that hurt."

"It's supposed to hurt. That's why it's called football," Jackson said. "Come on kid, you ain't soft."

At last, I finally understood why people played volleyball.

They deposited my carcass on the sideline. I sat on the single wood bench as the team trainer, Sondra, asked me a series of questions. I answered them. She looked at my eyes, felt my torso and asked if anything hurt. Satisfied, she walked away to give Coach Piccou the update.

They ran two more plays and then broke for two minutes.

"I played slot last year," Bustamonte said, grabbing a water bottle and sitting next to me. "With Machado graduating and me moving to the outside, we knew we needed somebody tough to take that spot. There was no way any of us wanted it to be Ponce, and Califf's too slow."

"Did you ever get hit like this?" I said, seeing Gelbaugh across the field. His helmet off, he was laughing with the rest of the defense. It looked like he was showing them how he lowered his shoulder and wrecked me.

"Gelbaugh cracked you good," he said adjusting his hair and headband, "but you're going to get hit like that a bunch this season."

"Why didn't you guys tell me?" I felt betrayed. How could they not tell me I'd be getting hit like this? They couldn't mention it over burgers at The Habit?

"Did you really think you could keep going across the middle and not have somebody clock you? Come on gavach, you're smarter than that."

All of Gelbaugh's threats over the summer during the passing drills came to mind. He couldn't hit me when we were in tees and shorts, but now, with gear on, he settled business.

"Fred likes you," Bustamonte said, standing back up and fastening on his helmet. "We're all starting to like you, but we have to find out if you can take a hit. I mean," he shook his head and grinned, "you were a volleyball player."

No session with the weights or mockery over trying out for the football team were as much of a challenge as putting on my helmet and getting back on the field. My first instinct was to never be hit like that again. I sat there and they started to run the offense without me. Bustamonte explained things, but Fred didn't say a word. He didn't even look my way.

The crossroads had come.

No one cared if I played football. My volleyball friends didn't care if I played football. My parents, while I knew they cared about me (even my mom), didn't care if I played football or not. The guys I'd spent the last five months with did care and their leader, Fred-X, was the one that wanted me.

The hard part was standing. Putting the helmet on and going back out onto the field was easy.

When I got home from practice, there was a pizza on the table with a two-liter bottle of Pepsi. Dad was parked in front of the television, watching the news. This was his routine: work, pick up some food, plant himself on the couch, and then go to bed if he didn't pass out. Some mornings I'd wake to find him curled up and sleeping.

"How was practice?" He said, without looking my way.

"It was practice," I answered, wondering if other sons came home to their fathers and told them about surviving their first run in with an army tank. I had no energy to offer up the conversation. Dad had no energy for a conversation. He didn't have energy for anything.

Practices continued. Our varsity roster was at thirty-eight, and Coach Piccou's plan was for no one to play both offense and defense. Only Patterson would play both. He excelled at corner, but his hands were so bad he was locked into a three-way rotation with Ponce and Califf at the fourth receiver spot. Coach Jackson wanted him out there for his speed to run go-routes.

Gelbaugh, my good friend at middle linebacker, would line up at fullback when we needed one, but in the spread offense Jackson was running we seldom needed one. We didn't have a punter either because Piccou and Jackson had no intentions of ever punting the ball. When we did need one, it was going to be Fred to keep the pressure on the defense. Bustamonte would handle kickoffs, but there was no practice time spent on field goals or point afters.

Limiting our huddles, going for it on fourth down ninety percent of the time, and exclusively using the two-point conversion after touchdowns weren't new ideas to prep football in the San Gabriel Valley. El Monte, Pomona, and a few others had done it with differing amounts of success over the years.

Plays from the sideline would be signaled to us, but Fred could override them at anytime based on what he saw at the line of scrimmage. During the summer, Fred had us practice this when we threw at the park. The plan was for us to use the signals and huddle occasionally. We were ready.

Boiled down, the lead receivers were going to be Bustamonte, Maez, and myself. Ponce, Patterson, and Califf would rotate. Fast Eddie was our featured runner and sophomore, Mike Miranda, backed him up. Pineapple was the left tackle, Matt Grieb the left guard, Kiel Basler at center, Ben Montoya at right guard, and Fat John Robles at right tackle.

Sportswriters, Grip Teague and Trudy Shields (whom I had never seen), liked Gelbaugh but said the defense lacked depth and would likely be our undoing. They praised four names: Gelbaugh, Lee, Patterson, and defensive end, Edgar Escandon. They didn't talk about anyone else but did drop in the names of Dan Feliz, Bobby Lucia at cornerback, and strong safety, Tom Preece.

When my name was finally mentioned, I was slotted as someone to keep an eye on. A project with potential. I cannot adequately express how good it made me feel. Just a dab of the fame drug was potent.

Pressing on with the weights, I'd become strong enough to shred defenders at the line of scrimmage and get into my routes. I had daily fantasies about planting Triay from Alhambra into the ground. I looked the same, but the extra inch, cresting me at six foot, increased my confidence.

I'd been tackled around the legs, taken down in Oklahoma drills, and drilled by Gelbaugh, but my struggle was blocking. The technique was hard for me to master but on this I received surprising understanding from the staff. They worked me, told me to do my best, but I wouldn't really get good at it until the end of the season because it was something that developed over time.

"We'll keep teaching," Coach Piccou said, "but what it really comes down to, Handsdrade, is getting a nose for it. To be willing to do what the team needs."

That was the convincer, *to do what the team needs.* The idea of letting the team that had accepted the volleyball player down was sickening. I'd surrender my body before letting it happen.

For now, my job was to get separation and catch the ball. My hands felt stronger, I'd adjusted to the equipment, and I was flying around the field. The biggest regret was I'd wasted two years of high school playing volleyball. I loved it so much, I never stopped asking myself why anyone would choose volleyball when football was available.

PART II

ZERO WEEK

Read The Blitz
By Grip Teague

Cathedral is playing Garfield tonight in a long awaited intersectional matchup. However, due to all the ongoing brush fires, they will be playing the game at Torrance High School. The Phantoms will also be playing without transfer running back (Los Altos) Julius Morales, who sprained a knee yesterday in practice. Word leaking out is Morales will be sidelined for three weeks...When we start talking numbers tomorrow morning, expect us to be talking quite a bit about El Rancho quarterback, D.K. Germany (great name)...The Dons are hosting Arcadia and former Pasadena passer, Montel Gaines, will lead the Apaches offense...Name a worse place to be than between Arroyo defensive ends Chao Estrada and Miguel Ruiz. You can't, can you?...Los Altos and Pomona will meet this evening at old Excelsior High School where Norwalk plays. The Conquerors, Jeremy Chandos, will make his first varsity start. I can think of easier ways to start a prep career. I have a feeling he's going to get run over by a Tank tonight...Former West El Monte receivers coach, Rick Paleo, says he's been approached by two schools to join their staffs but has decided to sit the year out. All charges against Paleo, who was recently arrested, have been dropped. "I'm playing with the idea of filing some charges myself," he said. We'll keep you posted.

The afternoon of our scrimmage, I got to the school and noticed equipment being put away. Three forest fires were burning: one in Santa Clarita, one in the San Gabriel Mountains just above Glendora, and another in Orange County. Every scrimmage in our area was canceled, and every Zero Week game was relocated to unaffected areas, mainly towards the beach cities.

When word came Maranatha wasn't coming, I got a sense of relief I didn't admit to my teammates. I slumped back in my locker and carefully let out a nervous breath. The desire to play was there. I did want to play, but it was like the feeling you get before jumping into a cold pool. Hesitancy, procrastination, and too much thinking about how to get through the process got the better of me.

"Cool," Fred said, clapping his hands. "More time to look at Downey film."

Gelbaugh destroyed the trashcan outside the double doors. When he finished with it, shredded pieces of plastic were in the locker room, the shower, and the parking lot. No one stopped him; no one appeared to even consider it.

Questions were dangerous to ask, especially since I was trying to transition far away from the novice everyone perceived me as. Still, I did notice Gelbaugh wasn't the only one upset by the canceled scrimmage. It was a scrimmage, and I didn't get it at first, but then I picked up from the veterans, they didn't just want to play, they wanted the contact.

Gelbaugh's leveling of me wasn't just to settle a score for talking a little bit of trash, but also because he wanted the impact of body and equipment. Almost prayed for it. Before the fire and ash took it away, the beginning of the week was like a countdown to Christmas or New Year's for all of them.

WEEK ONE

Read The Blitz
By Grip Teague

Say the name: Courtney Graye. Then add: West Covina Bulldogs and defense. Now you're talking trouble for anyone and everyone the WC comes in contact with this season...I encourage you to read Bald Guy's story on Rosemead's Anthony Ciccone. It will give you some insight on the emotional struggles the young man has had and what he's doing about it...Nice job BG (Bald Guy, not Bell Gardens--although I hear they are sup- posed to be improved this year.)...With its 16-7 win over South El Monte, Duarte is 1-0 to start a season for the first time in a long time. Don't order the CIF rings just yet, but you might want to buy a ticket or two to see Falcons running back, Kelvin Smith. He's a good little back...Everyone is going to trash me for this, but I'm telling you it's Monsoon season down the 605. Mayfair is for real...Cal High isn't looking too shabby either...

W e weren't allowed back outside to practice until Wednesday, and through Thursday, it was great. I was at home in practice. I got hit more often, but nothing was like the punisher Gelbaugh laid me out with. The playbook was printed inside my head. My body felt strong, and I felt like I could run all day when we boarded the bus on Friday to take the 605 to Downey.

I left Dad on the couch. He said he was thinking about coming. I didn't think he would. Once on the couch, he was generally rooted there until a one in the morning infomercial woke him up. It didn't matter to me. Maybe it was fear he'd drive all the way through traffic to see me do nothing. Maybe it was because football was my thing, and I didn't need to share it with him or anybody else in the family.

We bounced on the bus for nearly an hour. There was some talking, there was some joking, but for the most part, we were all getting lost in our own playlists. Some guys slept, some guys simulated dance moves, others, like me, stared into the traffic. When I decided to play football, I thought of practice, and, of course, the game, but I never thought of these in between moments. I didn't know if I should be nervous or excited, so, I kept quiet and followed the herd.

Chalk it up to not understanding the game enough, but while I was hit with some nervousness in the locker room at Downey, the veterans were at another level. Some were puking; some were suffering stomach cramps and growlers. Others paced around the concrete gray floors and light blue painted lockers, repeating stretching exercises over and over again.

Gelbaugh didn't do any of that. With blue streaks of paint running vertical on his face, he sat in front of his locker with eyes wide, staring at nothing. Beads of sweat emerged on his forehead as his body ticked down to kickoff with small vibrations and slow ratchet cranks of the muscles in his neck.

Pineapple had a growler. We could hear him screaming all the way from the toilet and making promises to God about never eating again. Bustamonte played with his hair, put on his helmet, took it off, played with his hair some more, put his helmet on again, and took it off again to check how it looked when he took it off. Kiel Basler and Fat John Robles pounded shoulder pads and encouraged one another about what they were going to do to the Vikings' defensive line. Fast Eddie was napping with butt on the floor, back against the locker, and legs up on the bench listening to music through earbuds. Jesse Maez stood in the corner with headphones on, massaging a Crucifix, and producing enough sweat to lather him.

Fred-X? He checked his wristband, looked at himself once in the mirror, made sure his cleats were tied, then walked the locker room, hitting pads, and telling everyone to have a good game. The only inward action he took was a pause at the back of the lockers where he carefully touched his pinky fingers to his thumbs, then his ring fingers, middle fingers, and index fingers. He repeated it several times, rocked his head side to side, and came back to his locker, calmly, ready to go.

As for me, I got dressed and began to feel nervous about not feeling nervous enough. I wasn't sweating, puking or putting my shoulder pads into the side of a row of lockers like Dan Feliz was. I didn't even have to pee, let alone suffer a growler, but I did wonder how it was going to be. The sound of the Downey band could be heard through our doors.

The knock came, and we turned our attention to Piccou.

"Our season started last winter when we came back into the weight room. It's not about what we've done the last couple of weeks but about what we've done the last nine months. This team is ready to play football," he said. "Have each others' back, play hard, ignore the scoreboard, kick some butt, break it down!"

We came outside in pairs, the sound of cleats hitting the cement and then the track. Our side of the stadium was half full; theirs was about three quarters to capacity. For an August 31st, it was a pleasant evening with a cool breeze and no sign of darkness yet. We got into our passing lines, alternately catching passes from Fred and Hudson. Right away, I noticed Coach Jackson's demeanor was different. He was patting us on the butt, telling us we were ready to take care of business.

"Handsdrade, be the man!" he said as I ran by him and got my slap. "You have a nice game tonight, make some memories kid, and make them remember you. This is why we play, this is why we play, Friday night lights. Yes, sir!" He said this to everybody. "This is why we play! We've been blessed by the best to play this game! Blessed by the best!"

I felt like I'd wandered into a new place, a place where they should have checked my credentials at the gate because I wasn't sure I belonged. My helmet, which felt heavy the first time I put it on, was now a comforting canopy allowing me blend in with everyone else.

Under our goal post we stared at the banner the cheerleaders made. It was ready for us to run through. This was really happening. I was really in the uniform, I was really wearing a helmet and pads, I wasn't at home watching the game on TV, and I wasn't dreaming about being a special person in a special moment. I was here and it was now.

Fred-X took his turn to encourage. "Sons of Scotland, what will you do with your freedom? Will you fight?"

"Yes!" We answered.

"Will you fight?"

"Yes!"

Then he paused, looked at all of us, and shrieked with a raised fist, "Alba gu bràth!"

When we ran through the banner, I might as well have floated to our sideline. Jackson called the offense over by the benches. He said something about the first series, the first hit, maybe something about a spaceship from another planet. I had no idea because my hearing was offline. The moment was jumbling all the words. I knew I was going onto the field and that was all. I could hear my heart thumping.

"You alright?" Fred said. "Handsman!" He whacked me upside of my helmet. "Are you alright?"

"Yeah," I said. "I'm cool."

Bustamonte took the kickoff to our forty-six. I ran to my slot position on the line of scrimmage, listened hard for Fred's signals, and when the play called for me to run a slant, I kept one eye on the defense. The Vikings were big and every one of them seemed to eye me the way Gelbaugh did.

"Don't f-bomb up rookie!" I couldn't see him, I don't know how I heard him, but it was Ponce.

Basler snapped, Fred fired, and the ball went through my hands, incomplete. I got hammered into a near death experience by Gilliam Gilliam, the middle linebacker. I kept my wind, but everything attached to a nerve throbbed. He laid on me and pressed his facemask against mine. No abbreviations or code words can express what he said he was going to do to me, which was sexual in nature and probably illegal even in New Orleans.

Through the crowd noise and the screaming coaches, I heard Ponce: "Soft mother-f-bomber!"

Hate to admit they were too tough for me, but they were. It was like being trapped fifty miles behind enemy lines, and I wasn't sure, after dropping the first pass of the season, if I still had a spot on the bus home. Fear was getting the better of me, and I fought to keep it under control. I breathed, breathed again and headed off a split second of nausea.

The Vikings were motivated. They blew past Pineapple and Fat John to get to Fred-X twice in the first quarter, then scored a quick touchdown after we failed to convert a fourth and four at our own thirty-three.

Building a 13-0 lead midway through the second quarter, the Downey players were starting to talk trash about our manhood when Fred-X broke away from a tackler and delivered a fifty-six-yard strike to Bustamonte. Edwards added the two-point conversion.

Conversation at the line of scrimmage ceased after this play.

The two connected again just before the half on a deep post-route. Bustamonte ran through the free safety, coming across the field and made another defender pay with his shoulder pads before going seventy-nine-yards for a touchdown. Fred-X's pass attempt on the extra-point was incomplete.

In the locker room at halftime with a 14-13 lead, Piccou didn't act like he was happy, but he sure didn't sound displeased. Questions were being asked and returned rapidly. Coach Von Huson was talking to the offensive line about protecting Fred and getting something, I didn't understand, called leverage. I didn't get yelled at, but the only encouragement I got was from Jackson on the way back out.

"Don't be afraid," he said with a hard slap to the top of my helmet. "It's just football."

In the background, I could hear Ponce complaining about me and how he needed to get on the field more. A bit of an edge returned to my thoughts. I wasn't going to let Ponce talk me out of this game, and I wasn't going to let anyone see what was running through my ears.

The third quarter opened with Bustamonte catching his third touchdown pass and then making a one handed grab for the deuce. Several times in the second half, we turned the ball over on downs, but the defense held the Vikings to just a field goal.

The defense was good. Defensive end, Edgar Escandon, had two sacks, but it was Gelbaugh who delivered. By my count, he had three hits on ball carriers equal or more punishing than what he did to me: two of them left the field, one didn't come back. As I watched him do his thing, I vowed inwardly I would never again say anything, anything at all, to offend him.

We won 22-16. I didn't make a catch, and, again, felt like a volleyball player in a football aquarium. The team was happy, the coaches were pleased, and I realized just having the uniform on wouldn't be enough. So I got on and off the bus decidedly unhappy.

Due to poor communication within the booster club, there was no team party and I decided to walk home.

"You sure you don't want to go, Handsman?" Fred said. "We're getting tacos at Adelbertos." I shook my head. "Okay, see you in the morning...And stop worrying."

I came through the front door and saw Dad sitting in the same spot. The glow of the TV was the only thing lighting the room.

"Did you win?"

"Yeah, we won."

"I'm sorry I didn't come," he said. "I don't know...I just..."

"No worries," I said. "You didn't miss anything."

The next day we did some light running, and Fred passed out donuts while we looked at film.

"You guys sucked!" Piccou said and then stared me down like he was from Downey, ready to get a piece.

"What the heck happened to my slot receiver?" He said.

"You f-bombed up, Handsdrade," Ponce sniped in low voice. "You're too soft."

"Handsdrade will be okay, Coach," Fred said. "He'd never even scrimmaged before and Ponce is too small to play the position."

Later in the locker room, as Pineapple passed by us completely naked and scratching himself, Fred encouraged me some more. "What happened after you dropped the ball?"

"It was incomplete," I said.

"Nah man," Fred said. "You still got lit up. You're going to get hit no matter what, so you might as well hold on to the ball. You might have to give them your body, but you don't have to give them both. And that second thing you give them is the catch, and that's like letting them take food right out of the mouth of your friends. That's the kind of thing that will keep me from getting to USC. I mean you do want me to go to USC, don't you? You want my life to be successful, don't you, Handsman?" He laughed and slapped my cheek like he was an uncle making a point to a nephew.

Pineapple came back, still naked, and looked at me. "You're going to be alright man. We all get nervous first time out," he said lifting up his hand. "High-five."

I slapped palms with Pineapple and a smile erupted on his face.

"Alright," Pineapple said. "Handsdrade knows where to get some love. Fred?" He offered the same to our quarterback.

"I don't think so, nature boy," Fred said.

I hadn't been to a church service since starting high school. I'd gone to a couple of events over the summer at Lena's urging but nothing else. When this Sunday came, a strong need to be there hit me.

Dad was asleep when I left. So it was good not having to answer the "where are you going?" question and its inevitable follow up: "Why?"

I needed to give thanks for getting to play football, which contained some truth. But I also hoped my presence would inspire God to keep Jesus Ponce from taking my job. No one told me I was on thin ice, but it felt like it. I had to do something to reclaim the satisfied feeling of catching the ball. All the confidence I felt through the spring and summer was now splatted like road kill on the 605.

At the end of worship Pastor David, the music minister, invited anyone who wanted to pray to come down to the altar. The moment had come to get right with God, to throw my request at his feet. I watched people crying as they went to the front of the church and gathered around one another. Hesitating, I let the moment pass. What if someone really asked me what I was praying for? Would saying I hated Jesus Ponce be well received? Would I have to give up my fervent wish he'd wreck his knee and be gone for the season?

The pastor prayed, the offering was taken and the kids were dismissed to children's church. Lena Durkin led them out by way of the center aisle. She smiled at me as she passed by. Any time you were in the direction of a Lena smile, you felt blessed. I took it as a good sign.

"I know you understand that everything in this life is temporary," Pastor Domres preached. "And that includes your temptations. The things that lead you astray, that promise you the world. They are the most temporary. The scripture in First John tells us everything in the world---the cravings of sinful man, the lust of his eyes, and the boasting of what he has and does---comes not from the Father but from the world. The world and its desires pass away, but the man who does the will of God lives forever."

I sat through the whole message. An old guy with thick, black and white hair and glasses made it a point to shake my hand. It was all good, but it was Lena's smile that helped me forget the Downey game, at least until bedtime when I dreamed Gilliam Gilliam was knocking at my door, asking to be let in.

WEEK TWO

Read The Blitz
By Grip Teague

The good news for Arcadia? Montel Gaines has locked up the quarterback spot and as long as he's healthy, you have nothing to worry about offensively. The bad news for Arcadia? HC Tab Figueroa needs to fill in another eleven or so pieces on defense. No shame in losing, but to lose to El Rancho, 55-28 in Zero Week, and then 61-21 to St. Francis last Friday means you have defensive problems... Speaking of The Ranch: Yes, I am a D.K. Germany fan. I know people are complaining, but the Dons are going to need something more than Germany to get into my top ten. In fact, West Covina should work out a deal to acquire Germany for its ailing offense. If today they can get Germany, tomorrow, they can get the world! (Think about it)...Los Altos quarterback, Jeremy Chandos's sprained shoulder is now being called a separated shoulder after running into Pomona's Tank Davis at the end of August...Anthony

Ciccone had a solid debut for Rosemead against Workman. Word is the volatile bruiser might get some carries at fullback for the Panthers...And since we're speaking of West El Monte Poly, did the Fred-X deliveries against Downey at Allen Lane Stadium really surprise you?

For as hard as the hitting was at Downey, there were only bruises. No sprains, strains, tears, or broken bones. At least, none anybody would admit to. Kiel Basler put athletic tape around his wrist, and Edgar Escandon used the same roll to wrap the pinky finger on his left-hand.

Monday we got the game plan, Tuesday the offense worked it, and Wednesday the focus was our defense. In a heartbeat, Friday arrived. Our Week Two opponents didn't generate the same emotions Downey had. The Arcadia Apaches came to Flair Drive with a decent football team and hardly any fans. There had been better days for Apache football, but it was flat now, according to Coach Piccou.

"I'm telling you," he said in the locker room. We were dressed and ready to hit the field. Dan Feliz and Dinh Lee joined Gelbaugh with the blue face paint. "Respect Arcadia. They're a good football team, they can put points on the board, but their fans don't care. I don't believe it's enough to just play for yourself. There has to be someone else in your heart or mind you want to play for. Win, lose, nobody except for the coaches are going to get on their butts about it. There's no energy there. It hasn't been a football town for years."

Anticipation was on our side as our fans came out in force. Alumni showed up, some wearing old varsity jackets, bad reminders of some really bad teams, but Alonson Stadium was currently the place to be on a Friday night. We were good, and people came because they expected to see a show.

The band played an ancient rock and roll song as we hit the field. Going through warm-ups, I saw Mike Patterson and Arcadia's Montel Gaines in the distance shaking hands and bumping shoulders. It was then I remembered both played for Pasadena the year before.

Nerves were building in me as the national anthem played. Fred knocked his shoulder into mine. "You're going to get on track tonight," he said. "This thing is going to be over before the popcorn is popped. You eat popcorn, Handsman?"

"Yeah," I said.

"Then you know you just have to be patient," he said.

I nodded and prayed deep down he was right. It would be nice to go back to church on Sunday and not have to beg God to give me my starting job back. I wasn't ready to join the growler brigade and didn't feel like throwing up, but I had anxiety. It was the team and the coaches watching me. The fear of letting them down was almost too much to take.

Arcadia's cardinal and gold uniforms looked good, but they couldn't lay a hand on Fred-X, who threw five first half touchdown passes, two going to Bustamonte, as we blasted off. No one talked on the Apaches defense, no one taunted or cursed us. They tackled, but they didn't hit.

"Tackling is fundamental," Gugliotta told us in an August meeting. "But hitting is essential if you're going to be a great football team. You have to make it so they don't want anymore."

Gelbaugh and his boys gave it to them. So much so, it became apparent, even to my first year football eyes, Arcadia reached a point where they just didn't want to get hit anymore. I understood. I don't think I would have wanted a blue faced Gelbaugh chasing and screaming after me for forty-eight minutes.

My first catch came at the start of the second quarter in the flat, and I was tackled around the legs. Eight minutes later I caught another one on a similar route and was brought down by the waist. My body felt numb. I'd been christened and the giant spotlight felt like it was off of me. I was really a Fighting Scot, alba gu bràth and all that stuff. Not even Ponce could hate on me now.

"Hermano!" Maez high-fived me on the sideline. "Getting it done." He was a good teammate, not a snake like Ponce and not uptight like Bustamonte. He enjoyed playing but seemed to have other things in his life. I was really starting to like Maez, but he wasn't all about football. I knew we couldn't get much closer because I was becoming all about football and almost nothing else.

The score was 35-14 at halftime, and the third quarter opened with Patterson picking off a Gaines pass and taking it back for a touchdown. It was 56-20 at the start of the fourth quarter when I noticed the Arcadia players holding up four fingers with their right-hands. With a pair of catches and a dirty uniform, I was in a good enough place to ask why.

"It's what a lot of teams do when the fourth quarter starts," Fred said with a smirk. Some of our guys were letting out small laughs as well. "It's their way of saying the quarter belongs to them. It's stupid but, whatever, it's what they do. I can guarantee you we'll never do it because the whole game is ours, not just a quarter."

"You get it, Handsman?" Pineapple said. "Why take one slice of pizza when you can have the whole f-bombing thing?"

With a thirty-six point lead, the officials started a running clock and Coach Piccou began pulling starters. Good thing I was among the last to leave because my third catch of the night was a nineteen-yard touchdown pass on a corner-route from Billy Hudson with eleven minutes to play.

Running the pattern into the end zone, I turned and saw the ball already in flight. It didn't come to me, I came to it, and my hands gobbled it up. The stadium felt like it exploded, but it really didn't. The explosion took place in my head and joy ran through my entire body, but reality came in mild applause. The fans knew it was another score in a game long decided.

"Handsdrade!" An alumnus named Horse, about as tall as a jockey and as heavy as Pineapple, yelled and put a fist to my shoulder and a slap to my butt as I returned to the players box. Mildly mobbed as the band played, I came to ask the question again: why would anyone want to play volleyball?

"Alright, Handsman!" Lena said, coming to me with her camera in hand. She was shooting yearbook pictures. I pulled my helmet off and our faces grazed as we embraced.

Almost everything for me was about football.

"Hold it!" Another girl with a raised camera said, and she snapped a picture of us.

"Send me a copy," I said. "It's my first touchdown." If I died now I would have been content, but death wasn't close. A touchdown is an elixir for an extra hundred years of life.

Thanks to the offensive line, none of the Arcadia defenders got near our backfield. Bustamonte made several great catches, and Edwards rushed for over a hundred yards, but the media only had eyes for our quarterback and his seven touchdown passes.

"You had a great night. Tell us about it," Charles Chanos, local cable sports reporter, asked. He put a microphone next to Fred's mouth and a bright light in his eyes. "You already have ten touchdown passes on the season. How many do you think you're going to throw this year?"

"We played great tonight," Fred said. We were huddled in back of him. "Jack Gelbaugh, Edgar Escandon and the defense give our offense the freedom to do what we do."

"Your defense was great tonight, but take us through that first half when you threw those touchdown passes. They just kept coming one right after another; did you see something in their scheme?"

"It all starts with Pineapple and the offensive line," he said. "And then when you add a receiver like Bustamonte, the best in the valley, we're a tough team to stop."

"Fred, how far do you think you can take the team this year?"

"I can't take the team anywhere, but together the Fighting Scots are going to go a long way. Don't doubt us!" He raised a fist and yelled into the camera, "Alba gu bràth!" We cheered and ran to the locker room.

The on going disaster of the booster club cost us another team party. Maez went home, Ponce went somewhere with Mike Miranda and Billy Hudson while the rest of us went to Alfredo's for tacos. Time and touchdowns melted all tension between Bustamonte and myself. I was grateful as we talked as teammates and fellow receivers about the game.

Getting home, the house was quiet. I went to bed, but I hardly slept. Instead, I fever dreamed about the football game. I kept running the corner-route over and over, and over and over I kept catching the pass for a touchdown. No depth of sleep could give me the sound of the crowd or reconstruct the feeling of my teammates and Lena congratulating me. I just kept looking to my left to nod at Billy Hudson and then taking off when the ball was snapped. Over and over, all night, it was the best.

On Saturday morning, Dad beat me out of bed and was in the process of cleaning house. Everything smelled of bleach and he was running a duster for cobwebs in the corners of the walls. Every few weeks he had a morning full of energy and then a few days later he was back to normal. A big smile was on his face this morning as he agreed to pick me up at Jack In The Box when I was done with film.

At film, we were told we sucked, but the coaches praised me. They liked my three catches and touchdown but were really happy with the way I ran. Basler tossed me a glazed donut. "You earned it, Handsman," he said.

"Handsdrade," Piccou called out. "That's how you do it! Keep running those routes hard, sharp. Coach Jackson, do you think we've we found a slot receiver?"

"Let's see how he does against Pomona this week before we name him All CIF," Jackson said.

From the desk behind me Fred-X slapped his hand on the top of my head and shook it. "Told you."

"Shake?" Pineapple tapped me on the shoulder and offered a hand of congrats.

I took it, he slow grinned, and I'd been slimed again.

On Sunday, I sat in the last row of pews towards the center aisle. My performance against Arcadia cured my compulsion to pray at the altar, and Lena added a thumbs up to her smile when she exited with the children's church kids.

"Now it is God, it says in Second Corinthians chapter five verse five," Pastor Domres preached, "who has made us for this very purpose and has given us the Spirit as a deposit, guaranteeing what is to come. So what is this scripture saying? It is telling us we were made for this time, for this moment. So often we are caught up in tomorrow and yesterday, but it is today that God requires obedience from us. Today he requires our faithfulness. Folks will say leave me alone, let me live my life...And I will say this to the believer, the believer, the person that claims a relationship with Christ,...you should desire no life apart from the will of God."

After service, I moved my eyes around the packed foyer to get a glimpse of Lena. People were talking, shaking hands, and making plans for lunch. I only stayed to see her, but it was fruitless.

"There you are, young man." It was my old friend from the week before with the thick hair and glasses. "Good to see you again. I read online you scored a touchdown."

"Yeah, I got lucky," I said. The old guy was far from cool, but it was flattering that someone else knew I scored a meaningless touchdown in a blowout of a game.

"I think you're the only teen from this church playing football," he said. "I'm trying to get the Pastor to brag on you some."

The idea of my name being mentioned in front of a packed church with Lena in it did thrill me.

"I don't know your name, sir," I said, "but thank you."

"I'm Richard Umphries, and I remember your dad too. You tell him I said, hello."

WEEK THREE

Read The Blitz
By Grip Teague

Well, what do you know? The Downey fans are upset again. All the good summer feelings down the 605 must have disappeared after last week's loss to La Serna dropped the Vikings to 0-2...I told all of you to keep an eye on Shane Delfman at the start of the season. Now I'm telling you to keep both eyes on the San Dimas quarterback. Spread, wishbone, bone-spread, whatever you want to call that crazy offense of theirs, Delfman is running it to perfection. This is why I have the Saints number one in their division, Pomona number two, and West El Monte Poly number three. Which means this Friday's game at Alonson Stadium off of Flair Drive is going to be a big one...He plays for a bad Pasadena Marshall team but remember the name, Charlie Wong. He's a defensive back, and he's all class on and off the field as his 4.2 GPA indicates. This kid could be running the country someday...I like Maranatha against Charter Oak and Del Chance this week. Minuteman

Jake Sharper is more like a split-second man with the ball...Calvin Greene, Calvin Greene, Calvin Greene! All I'm getting in my message box is stuff about Calvin Greene. Note to Paraclete Fans: If you want me to talk about Calvin Greene, find some way to get me his stats. I'm in the dark here. Hook this old guy up.

66 "They don't respect us," Bustamonte said, swiping through Grip Teague's column on Monday.

"Who gives a f-bomb what Teague thinks," Fred answered back. "We ain't playing Teague this Friday. We're playing Pomona."

We were in the film room and Coach Piccou started the Pomona highlights against Chino. The staff pointed out the Red Devils ran the same offense we did but their quarterback Jackson Johns was more runner than passer. Their defense was scary. Tank Davis was going to be a nightmare and the secondary looked like they had a dozen Mike Pattersons.

"Do you guys want to know how good you are?" Coach Piccou said. "Because you're about to find out."

That night I downloaded the picture of Lena and me from the Arcadia game. We faced the camera, she had an arm around my back, I had an arm around her's, and if a lawyer was making a case, I could have been convicted as being her boyfriend.

My investment in football was paying big dividends.

On Tuesday, Trudy Shields came to watch practice and write a preview for Friday's contest. Number two against number three sounded volatile, like playing with matches next to a gas truck. The first team to ignite it wins.

It was no surprise she wanted to interview Fred. In the locker room Pineapple claimed Shields was his woman and began calling down curses on his quarterback.

"Mr. Pretty Boy quarterback gets to talk to all the chicks, get all the attention." Pineapple whined. Of course, as always, he was naked. "Shields should be in here talking to me. I'm the one that makes him look good. Plus! She's on my list! Fred knows she's on my list. He should be sending her to me!"

"Cover your junk man," Fast Eddie said, "and write a letter."

"What list?" I said. "I keep hearing about your list."

"This f-bombing list, Handsman!" Pineapple held up a yellow legal pad. A list of names he referred to as his 'To Do List' was written on it.

"She's on the list?" I said. "Do you really think you have shot with her?"

"You're missing the point, Handsman," Fast Eddie said. "Pineapple's list is not just a list; it's all of his greatest dreams and ambitions."

"She's here," Bustamonte said, taking a seat and stripping off his shoes. "Did you see her?"

Fast Eddie cleared his throat. "Oh, yeah."

"I still haven't seen her," I said.

"Would you?" Bustamonte said to Edwards.

"Would I what?"

"Shields."

"Oh, about five times," Fast Eddie said.

Coach Jackson came into the locker room and ordered every-one to hurry and get dressed.

"Why can't you tell her to talk to us?" Pineapple pleaded. "We're the ones doing all the blocking."

"You're a disease to the eyes, Pineapple. Put some clothes on. People are sick of seeing you naked," Jackson said. "Bustamonte! Fred says he won't do the interview without you, so don't waste time combing your hair. Everyone else, let's go!"

Out on the practice field, I expected a little blonde cupcake with debatable curves. Instead, I saw a tall, African-American wom-an, with non-debatable curves, whose body fulfilled the Olympian ideal.

"Look at that," Edwards said.

"What is she doing covering high school football?" I said.

"Now you know why Pineapple is moaning," he said into my ear. "Faaa..."

"About five times," I said.

Three days later the Pomona Red Devils arrived with a fan base equal to ours. They were twenty-five miles away and brought half their city with them. Arcadia, the week before, was five miles up the road and all they brought were a handful of people looking like they'd rather be at Starbucks.

They were faster, but we were more efficient. In the first two games of the season, the argument was easy to make for Gelbaugh, the defense, and Bustamonte as being contributors to us being unbeaten. Against Pomona, the only thing we had going for us was Fred-X. He kept us in the game when we should have been blown out.

Except for a few costly comments to Gelbaugh over the summer, I realized I had zero experience talking trash. Gilliam Gilliam, the linebacker from Downey, at least waited until I was flat on my back before he got in my face. The Red Devils defensive backs started talking the moment they hit the field and never shut up. Triay, from Alhambra, insulted me in a normal everyday tone. The Pomona guys announced loudly to the world what I was lacking and what they were going to do to me.

Stephon Stukes, the defensive back opposite me, threw everything my way, verbally, to get a rise. My mom was this, my dad was that, I was really a girl, my girlfriend was really a guy, my dog hated me, I was ugly, I was a wimp, what time was band practice, did the team still know I wet the bed, and I was so pretty I should have been a volleyball player.

Everybody got the treatment, but I didn't know how to answer. With Gelbaugh's reaction fresh in my memory, I decided the best thing to do was keep my mouth shut. The way the game broke down, I should have bought dinner afterward for our middle linebacker for literally drilling the safety lesson into me.

Edwards got into a shoving match when they came at him for being one of only two brothers on a team full of whiteys. Bustamonte got into a back and forth when they told him he had no game. Pineapple got into several shoving matches because he could only protect Fred on every other pass play against Tank.

So who kept their mouth shut? Me, out of fear, and our quarterback because he was focused only on the game.

Fred-X started early with me. Thirteen catches and four touchdowns later, my uniform was filthy, and we were down 55-46 in the fourth quarter. The ball kept coming and I kept catching. I was the guy they hadn't game planned for and Fred exploited it.

My standard dream was a three touchdown performance, but tonight I had four. The real world didn't slip away, it just boiled itself down to the hundred yards of grass I was playing on. I'd spent the whole night getting knocked around and mangled. Twice I was wrecked like a race car unable to come out of a turn but felt more powerful each time I stood backup.

The first blast came on a slant-route across the middle. The ball was high and I was hit low. I cartwheeled through the air and landed on my feet. That part happened so fast it was fun but when the strong safety tattooed me between the numbers a fraction of a second later, it wasn't. Breath vanished from my system and while it was a truly horrible feeling, I knew, thanks to Gelbaugh, I wasn't dying.

And I held onto the ball.

The second hit came after I caught a flat-route and skirted by a defender before a linebacker crushed me into the Pomona sideline. Their reserves let me roll all the way to the bench. They didn't put a hand on me but rode me all the way back on the field with encouraging words about staying the f-bomb out of their neighborhood.

"Robles? Robles!" Fred-X yelled at our right tackle. "You going to live?"

"Yeah," he said panting for breath.

"So shut the f-bomb up and stop groaning!"

"I hurt Fred," he said.

"No kidding Fat John, you think any of us feel good right now?"

There were hurts on my body, I knew, I wouldn't be feeling until the next morning, but something else was taking place. As I kept taking hits, catching passes, and trying to block, I realized I wasn't just having fun playing football. I was falling in love with the contact, a strange discovery no one clued me in about.

The Handsdrade from Week One was still hiding under his bed, but this one by the fourth quarter would have played defense or returned punts. Something had kicked in. I was craving the opportunity to deliver a blow with a lowered shoulder and eager to take another hit to prove my worth. Every time I collided with another jersey it took me deeper into the game. I learned about the 'suspension of disbelief' in English class and tonight I was living it out.

Mom or Dad could have had terminal cancer, terrorists could have been blowing up New York, flesh eating zombies could have been eating people in the parking lot, but it wouldn't have mattered. The only priority was the f-bombing football game, and everything after the game was a decade away. Its consequences were in another dimension of time and space. Might sound hyperbolic, but it was true. The game was sucking me in. All that mattered to me was soaking up the glory and getting even with the mother-f-bomber who hurt me or a teammate.

When a pass was dumped off to Edwards out of the backfield I felt a twinge of anger. By now, even Fred-X should have known I was always open. I was rational enough not to say anything, choking all neglects down, but I began to believe there wasn't anything I couldn't catch.

We called our last timeout with 2:39 to play, down by nine. Gathering at the numbers on the field, we were exhausted. Water bottles were being passed around. Even without energy, everyone cursed because we knew we were in trouble and everyone had their opinion why.

"Robles!" Coach Von Huson yelled. "If you can't do it anymore, let me know because Cardenas is ready to play!"

"I can play Coach!" Fat John said.

"Then make a play! You gotta make plays! Knock somebody on their butt a few times and the pain will go away!"

Fat John grunted and put his helmet back on. He looked more tired than hurt. When knocking heads on every snap three-hundred pounds was a lot to haul around in a football game that had turned into a track meet.

"We're going to get it done," Basler said to him with a punch to the pads. "We're going to get it done." When I saw Basler use his left instead of right-hand to punch Fat John, I knew it was because his wrist was hurting.

"They're going to be so closed down on Handsdrade on the post," Jackson said to Fred, "you're going to get Bustamonte solo up the sideline. He's going to be in single coverage. If we get it quick enough, we might have a shot with an onside kick."

"He's been in single coverage the whole second half, but he can't catch the f-bombing ball," Fred said. "Give me something with Maez."

"F-bomb you Fred!" Bustamonte said, his helmet parked on his forehead and hands on his hips. "Put it where I can catch it!"

We put our hands together for a break and Coach Von Huson stuck an angry finger into Pineapple's chest. "Pineapple! That's your offensive line and Ritter's our quarterback! You gotta keep Tank out of there!"

Pineapple matched up well with Pomona's Tank Davis size wise but was outclassed athletically. When Tank was stopped, it was because Pineapple guessed right, dropping into pass protection but guessing was all he had. Davis had already received three Division-one offers. He was big time.

We came to the line of scrimmage with Bustamonte and I setting up on the left. Stukes was across from me again. Deep and behind him was the free safety, who drilled me after the cartwheel.
I'd already had a great night and knew Coach Jackson was right.
The safety was going to come with me to the middle of the field.

"Oh look at this! Look...at...this!" Tank said as he set up outside
of Pineapple. "I'm getting so fat tonight they ain't going to let me
back on the bus. Positively f-bombing obese! Pineapple, what you
got left over there for me to eat? F-bomb! I guess I'm going to have
to take some more of that quarterback of yours."

Telepathy wasn't necessary to know Pineapple was screaming
murder in his head. Fred needed to get in and out of the count before our left tackle false started or had a stroke.

Basler snapped the ball. Tank tried to leap frog over Pineapple
but didn't make it and went end over end to the ground. Stukes
jammed me inside, but I made my cut and saw the ball flying in
Bustamonte's direction.

He dropped it. Trying to gather it between his arms and chest
the ball ricocheted off his pads to the grass. A groan went across
our side of the stadium. Bustamonte got up, adjusted his jersey,
and came back to the line of scrimmage. The advantage of the no-
huddle, I learned, was you didn't have to go back and immediately
face your teammates after a drop.

"F-bomb you!" Pineapple said to Tank. "Is that all you got?"

"Don't get cocky, Pineblubber!" Tank said.

We went with the same play, with one difference. The ball was
snapped and I came down the line of scrimmage and threw myself

into Tank as Fred-X scrambled left. Pineapple finished the Red Devil off and Bustamonte held on to this one to set us up at the Pomona nineteen.

As we raced down field Tank wasn't saying a word because he didn't have the oxygen inside to get anything out. Fred-X caught the hike and hit me on an out pattern at the thirteen. I got out of bounds to stop the clock with 2:07 remaining.

On second down, I went in motion from the left to the right. I prepared to sell a slant back inside and then break for the corner. Fred was going to boot right and hit me on the run, but Basler's snap sailed and Fred chased it down at the thirty-five.

The clock kept running and we were facing a third and twenty-six. He signaled with his hands and waved us quickly back into position without wasting a word or moment cursing our center.

Fred hit me in the flat and I was able to get to the twenty-three before going out of bounds.

A voice came from somewhere telling us we needed to kick a field goal to make it a six point game and then go for the onside kick. Smart thought, but we didn't have a kicker. Piccou and Jackson didn't waste any time.

I saw what they signaled in, and then I saw Fred-X shake his head. He hurried us into formation. The coaches yelled and he waved a right-hand at them without taking his eyes off the defense.

The snap came out high again. Later, on film, I'd see Fred-X leap into the air and catch the ball with one hand. Just before Tank drove him into the turf, he quickly lofted it down the middle of the field to me on the go-route.

I had two safeties on me, but I was six-foot with long arms, and just enough juice left in my legs to knife between them and grab the ball at the four for a first down. The crowd cheered, but its effect on me was zero. The field and the stadium were connected by soil, steps, bolts, screws and fences, but being buried into blades of grass was like being on another planet. I heard the cheers but relished the catch much more.

With 1:25 to play Fred-X came right back to me on a fade in the corner, but I couldn't get to it. On second and goal, Tank blindsided him. Since I was a football player now, and no longer a normal person, I didn't fear for Fred's life as much as I did for him holding onto the ball.

He did.

At the fifty second mark, the ball was snapped on third and goal. We broke into our routes. Fred raced up the middle and leaped from the one. On the other side of the goal line, a tandem of linebackers helicoptered him around in the air before he landed for the score.

It was now 55-52 with thirty-seven seconds to play. Pineapple helped him up, the stadium rocked, but we didn't celebrate. There was no three-point conversion. We were going for two and would still be down by one if we got it.

We didn't. I was open. I had Stukes beat on an out-route, but Edwards caught the pass out of the backfield and was blown up by Tank.

As the special teams guys talked about the onside kick, Fred and I were on one knee hauling in breaths and exchanging glances. He didn't congratulate me on the catch and I didn't congratulate him on the touchdown. We were wrecks. The glance alone said we'd done our jobs and unnecessary words were a big expense at the moment. I'd already reconciled I'd be sore tomorrow, but Fred was going to be lucky if he could walk.

Pomona easily recovered Bustamonte's lame onside kick. Concerns about going back out on the field melted with the Red Devils running out the clock in a victory formation. We lined up at the fifty to shake hands.

After all the things Stukes said earlier, I could only imagine what he was going to say to me now. The coaches ordered us to be classy, to not start anything in front of our fans, and, for Coach Piccou's sake, not in front of the administration.

Stukes slapped his right-hand against mine but didn't let go. His left-hand patted the top of my helmet.

"I'm going to get my butt chewed off in film because of you," he said. "Good job."

"You too," I said, not knowing what else to say. Welcome to football, where there were always lessons to be learned. This one being the four quarters were played like four chapters in a book, and, once it was closed, we resurfaced into reality. The suspension of disbelief eroded. We lost, my muscles were starting to complain, and the thought struck me there were only seven weeks left in the season.

Chanos, even in defeat, needed something. He got his camera, microphone, and light in our quarterback's face. Fred took off his helmet and wiped some blood away from his lower lip.

"Tough night out there Fred, what happened?"

"Pomona played great, and I just have to do a better job," he said.

"Tank Davis was all over you," Chanos said. "Were there some breakdowns on the offensive line?"

I knew the answer before Fred opened his mouth.

"You know we're a bang bang offense, and I wasn't getting the ball out quick enough and it put a lot of pressure on our line," he said. "Give credit to Pomona's secondary. It was tough."

There was a little less wattage, but the smile remained sincere.

"You had some drops tonight, were you..."

"It's football," Fred cut off the third question. "Nothing is ever going to be perfect. I'm not worried. We're going to be alright."

Tank Davis came out of nowhere and put a fist to Fred's shoulder pads, and then he and Pineapple hugged like they were brothers.

Football, I shrugged and turned for the lockers, was like being at Disneyland for the first time. All of it was amazing.

The team party was happening at Bobby Lucia's house. It was my understanding more than just the team would be there, which I hoped meant Lena, so I showered. The team wasn't particularly big on showering in public, but modesty went out the window as far as I was concerned if I was headed to a social situation. Fred, Bustamonte, and Pineapple showered as well, but no one else. So we were fresh when we got to the team funeral slash party.

A win would have made it a great gathering, but the loss just left us all in different groups, complaining about everything and everyone else. Lena didn't show so I drifted around looking for Maez, who was easy to be around but couldn't find him. When Grip Teague and the Bald Guy came on, we gathered in the living room.

According to Grip, I'd set a school record for receptions in a game.

"Alright, Handsdrade!" Dan Feliz said, losing the facade of mourning we were all expressing at the moment. I pointed a finger back at him and turned it into a thumbs up to convey thanks and that he had a great game too.

Bald Guy: Fred-X has a fleet of big time receivers in Bustamonte, Andrade, and Maez.

"F-bomb, wait until next year," Ponce said from the back of the room.

Grip Teague: You know what they call Andrade?

Bald Guy: What?

Grip Teague: They call him *Handsdrade*.

Bald Guy: I like that. That's cool.

Seeing this with the rest of the team, I was careful not to smile even though one was begging to get out. When they started talking about the problems we were having on the offensive line and on defense, I heard it but I was relishing and digesting what they'd said about me.

Pomona's Jackson Johns, who I hardly noticed during the game, looked great on the highlights. Several times he escaped Gelbaugh and Escandon to make big plays. Then they showed Fred and the out of this world plays he made on the run, mostly to save his life.

When they showed the shot of me cartwheeling through the air and then getting smashed by the Pomona free safety, whose name I learned was Devin Young, the room laughed, cringed, and applauded.

"Great catch, Handsman," Bustamonte said and I got warm inside because I knew how much all of this meant to him, how much he wanted to be the guy making plays.

When the party ended Pineapple, Basler, and Bustamonte took me home. It was a direct shot, but I eventually got there after we illegally cruised a few neighborhoods. The three seniors didn't stress about the driving curfew we were breaking. Instead, they talked about needing to find the right girl, beating Arroyo in two weeks, and kicking the snot out of Ponce and Billy Hudson.

"I hate those guys," Basler said from behind the wheel.

Sitting in the back seat, I listened, happy to have been invited.

My left eye opened to the bedroom the next morning, but nothing moved without bartering a grimace in exchange. The picture of Lena and I from the Arcadia game stared back from the nightstand.

"Oh...I'm gonna die."

The right side of my face was embedded into a pillow. From shoulders to the backs of my legs, everything wrung whimpers of pain out of me. It felt like I'd been frozen overnight.

"Why on earth would anyone play football over volleyball?" I whispered as muscles cracked back into small action. The last I remembered was being dropped off at two in the morning. Somehow, because I don't remember, I reached my bed and stripped down to my boxer briefs.

Tilting my chin to get a glimpse of my toes, they were there and wiggled pain free. I bit the bullet and got out of bed like any other day of the week. It worked, but my body howled. Staggering to the dresser, I looked at myself in the mirror. There was a light bruise on the top of my right shoulder. My left pinky was swollen. A deep purple contusion was just above my stomach and a little below my heart. It was the spot the Pomona safety hit me in after my cartwheel.

Grip Teague said his name was Devin Young.

Replaying the catch over in my head, I smiled at my reflection in the mirror. I held on to the pass. Like a highlight film, the next memory went to the catch landing us at the four-yard line. There was a dark spot on my left shin to memorialize it.

The body loosened, but what it really needed was an extremely hot shower if I was going to make it to film. Flexing my hands and fingers, I held them up to the mirror and I felt pride surge by the pain to the rest of my body.

"You can play," I said to the mirror. The reflection smiled back without disagreement.

The memory of getting into my bed and stripping off my clothes was vague, but not the recap on the webshow we watched at Lucia's pad. Grip Teague and Bald Guy showed our highlights and said it was my coming out party. I set a school record with sixteen catches. They knew who Handsdrade was.

Intoxicating might be too big of a word, especially since I didn't know what it was to be buzzed, high, wasted, or drunk. Yet, the word fit perfectly because the positive linking of my name with football was euphoric. My body hurt, but nothing had ever felt so good swimming between my ears and through the chambers of my ego.

I wanted to win, but the idea of being a star was better. Who would underestimate the volleyball player now? Nobody. I was getting smarter about the game, I was getting taller, and my hands felt like they could catch a nine-millimeter spit out of a Glock.

Was it possible I was even better looking after getting beaten up the night before? I never looked like this after a volleyball game, but right now, with all the bruises, I wished Lena could see me.

Happy, when I should have been upset about the loss, rational thinking, thankfully, still had a perch. I couldn't let anyone know because the priority had to be winning. It couldn't be about how good I felt after making sixteen catches.

School record by the way...

"If they only knew how selfish Handsdrade was," I said to myself in the mirror. I put an index finger to my lips and smiled at me. "Ssshhhh!"

Outside of my bedroom, away from the mirror, the coaches could do the praising from here on out.

🍥

"You all suck!"

Coach Piccou opened with it. Coach Jackson reaffirmed it. Coach Gugliotta closed with it. The affirmation I gave myself in the mirror didn't make me feel so bad now because no one was praised for their performance. Not even Fred. No donuts were being tossed around as rewards.

"No one is saying it, but I know what you're thinking," Piccou went at us again. "You're thinking it's the offensive line's fault. Well, the offensive line was good enough for us to put 52-points on the board against Pomona. So you're probably thinking it is the defense's fault because it gave up 55."

I thought it was the defense's fault.

He stopped and stared at us in the film room. The blinds were pulled, the lights were out, and we sat at desks, looking at Coach Piccou who was spotlighted by the digital projector.

"Pomona beat us! You get it?" He said. "They didn't beat our offense or our defense, they beat us!" He pointed towards where most of the offense was sitting. Fred was in front of me, and Bustamonte was to his right. "And I'm going to say this...You aren't as good as you think you are, not one of you. Pomona right now is better than you. Live with that and then think about this: you might not even make it out of the Mission Valley League alive if you don't tighten things up."

When we were dismissed, Fred ordered the offense to stay.

"I got to play better," he said. "I have to make better decisions and better throws. We can't lose games like this. We need to help our defense out by playing better."

Everyone agreed they needed to do the same, including Bustamonte. I went along and told them I did too. We came out of the meeting vowing to study the game film posted online and come back Monday working harder than we had before.

Truth was I didn't know if I could play any better. How can you improve on sixteen receptions and four touchdowns? I threw my body around like I never had before, I'd even made strides blocking. What more could I give?

No one hung out. Everyone took off. I walked down Campus Avenue toward the Flair Drive exit. Dad wasn't expecting me to be home until after lunch, so I was going to Jack In The Box to wolf some food. If there was something else to learn about football, it might come to me after a Coke and five or six tacos.

On the edge of campus, Fred's four-door Frontier pulled up alongside me. I liked the truck and loved what was riding in the passenger seat.

"Hey handsome!" Lena Durkin hung her green eyes, dimples, and smile out the window. It was the look bringing me to church each week and would again tomorrow. "Do you want a ride home?"

If Lena had known what she did to me every time she looked my way, she wouldn't have called me handsome. In the looks department some would argue for Desi over Lena, but it wasn't the decider for me. Desi had a great body, I knew first-hand, but I longed for Lena because she was a good person. Desi was someone Pineapple put on his list. Lena was someone you kept forever. I know it sounds awful, but truth is supposed to be a virtue, right?

"Come on man, get inside, I'll take you home," Fred said, leaning over to be seen.

"No, I'm cool," I said. "Just thinking about last night." I lied.

"You can think about it all you want, but it's not going to change anything. Start thinking about South El Monte instead."

"I know."

"You sure you don't want a ride?" I shook my head. "Suit yourself then," he said. "Talk to you later."

Fred hit the accelerator. Lena, with the wind pushing the back of her hair, kept smiling. "You were great last night...See you at church!"

As they drove away, I realized I'd learned something more about football, another valuable football lesson. It was a hard one but made perfect sense underneath a soft Saturday sun. Never fall in love with your quarterback's girlfriend.

My body was still aching when I took my usual seat at church. I felt on top of things enough that no temptation seized me about going to pray. What was there to ask for after scoring four touchdowns and catching sixteen passes?

School record by the way.

Lena gave me her smile as she went out of the sanctuary with her tribe of kids. Fred never came with her, and if she asked me then I knew she asked him. I wasn't a fool, I knew when I came to church I was supposed to be thinking about God and contemplating his works and the giving of his son and the whole whatever. In reality what church really did was make me feel hopeful about Lena.

"We all got strength in our hands. We got strength in our thoughts. Strength in our friends, children, and family. We do right? I mean...at least until we get tired, sick, or old," Pastor Domres preached.

It was okay, I wasn't feeling much from it because an idea about helping Lena next week with the children bubbled like brilliant gold.

"At least until time and/or circumstance robs us of these things...Second Corinthians chapter one verse nine says, 'Indeed in our hearts we felt the sentence of death. But this happened that we might not rely on ourselves but on God, who raises the dead.'"

I side stepped through the crowded foyer when it was over to get to the children's department and came across Lena holding a clipboard as the parents signed their kids out. She made eye contact with me and sighed a smile.

Another gush rippled through my body.

"Hey," I said masking the thud my heart took from her sigh. "I was thinking if you weren't doing anything we could get some lunch?" It didn't feel like I was asking her out on a date, but to my ears it sounded dangerously close and I tried to walk it back. "I just wanted to kill some time before the Rams game today."

"I wish," she said. "I got homework and then Fred's parents invited me over for dinner."

The smell of Old Spice came to my nostrils and a hand clamp down on my shoulder. I knew who it belong to immediately.

"Hello, young man."

"Hey Mr. Umphries, how are you?"

"I want to invite you to lunch with me and my wife."

The Umphries took me to Coco's and were very kind. They shared about seeing us as a family come into the church years ago. They also said they were sad when they found out about the divorce.

"I wish life could be perfect for you son," Mr. Umphries said. Much cooler than I first thought, he probably had a good run as a 'cool guy' in his day. Now he was an older version of a hipster. "As beautiful as it can be, it's still a killer."

WEEK FOUR

Read The Blitz
By Grip Teague

Guilty...I'm just as bad as everyone else for not talking about Arroyo quarterback Connor Stone. The junior threw three touchdown passes last week and has surprised everyone with the way he's running the Knights' offense. I blame Bald Guy...If you were wondering what was going on at Bishop Amat on Friday night, we were as well. On Sunday, the mystery unraveled. Former Arcadia running back, Jefferson Pham, is now a former Bishop Amat running back. Pham played two games for the Lancers but was a no show for Friday night's contest against Crespi. Sunday night we received word Pham transferred to St. John Bosco and will sit out the rest of this football season...It's early, but we are being told to expect weather this weekend...Duarte is off to a nice start... Be sure to vote in our poll to see who had the biggest hit of the week: San Dimas linebacker "Bazooka" Joe Natalia or Pomona free safety Devin Young...It may be smoke, it may be mirrors, fate or just great defense, no matter, West Covina has scored 22-points total this season and has allowed only 11. Bulldogs linebacker Courtney Graye? Six sacks, two interceptions, and a fumble return for a touchdown...They are very young (my kiss of death, not the HC's) and what they wouldn't give for a quarterback...

Through Sunday night I was a topic on the boards, but by the time Monday morning hit the discussion moved on to other things. When I read Grip Teague's column I was stunned to find no mention of me. It all centered on Jefferson Pham and the Arroyo's Matt Burns, who was featured in the 'Player Spotlight' in the right-hand corner of the webpage. Burns returned a kickoff for a touchdown against Baldwin Park. I thought back to my game, did the math--sixteen receptions, four touchdowns--and immediately felt ripped off.

Whatever I did against Pomona didn't matter anymore. We lost.

I passed through the trainer's room before practice. Dan Feliz was sitting back on the table while Sondra taped an ankle he turned Friday night.

"When did you get hurt?" I said. He never left the game or said a word about his ankle.

Sondra carefully continued to wind tape around black and blue skin.

"In the second quarter chasing Johns," he said letting out a wince. "I was hoping I wouldn't get one of these this season. It's such a hassle."

"It would be less of a hassle if you stopped moving," Sondra said.

"Sorry."

"But you never came out?" He shrugged back at me as if there was no other option. "How long until it's better?"

"January."

"That sucks."

I went into the lockers and ignored another naked, genital scratching, march around the room by Pineapple. Peeling off my shirt, it occurred to me Feliz would be playing with a bad ankle for the rest of the season. Taking another survey of the bruises I was collecting from the first three weeks, there were long lingering splotches of plum and purple all over the front of my body. I didn't know what was on my back.

We all had something hurting. Bobby Lucia had a bruise running the length of his left shin, Basler had his sore wrist, and Bustamonte's back was darkened with a deep bruise behind his right shoulder. Fred scratched and bruised all over, put an ice pack on his left shoulder after every practice and game. No one complained, and I hoped I could do the same as the hurts accumulated.

The game plan called for us to pound the ball. A storm was coming Friday. Late September was early for weather in Southern California, but we prepared for it. Part of the preparation was utilizing Edwards and the running game more if the weather turned bad. Passing would be difficult. Fred was five-nine, five-eleven if you talked to his dad, and he had the kind of hands a five-nine guy should have. They weren't tiny, but they weren't big. A wet football was going to change how we did things.

"I agree," he said in the Monday's meeting to Coach Jackson. "Let's pound it."

"It might mess with your numbers," I said. "Grip's got you on track for 50 touchdown passes."

"All Grip's tracking is his next pizza," Fred said. "You ever wonder why all the sportswriters are fat? Because they sit, eat, and talk about us. That's all they do."

"Trudy's not fat," Edwards said.

"No," Fred said. "Trudy's different. In another year or two she's going to be working for a network, so she's not like the rest of those guys."

"That's better," Edwards said.

"I thought Trudy was Pineapple's woman?" Fred said.

"Trudy's on Pineapple's 'To Do List,'" Edwards said. "I just dig her, but you're cool, you've got Lena."

"Yep," he said without passion. "I've got Lena."

Lena was the only thing I knew about Fred that didn't come across as golden to me. He never spoke bad about her, never tried to convince us he was getting something sexual out of her, he never treated her poorly in public. He was just unenthused, and how could anyone be unenthused about Lena Durkin? She was crazy about him. She came to all the games, made him cookies, let him spend time with his friends, and never complained. It was torture for me to see.

The only reporter to show at practice during the week was Benny from the student paper. He took a picture of Piccou and Fred. A year ago he came to volleyball practice and took a picture of the team. Big stuff when I was a sophomore, but now, as I anticipated daily mentions on real sports sites, Benny was small.

Fred didn't have to give Benny any time, but he did. He didn't just answer his questions; he talked to him as if he were Teague or Bald Guy, treating him as if he was somebody important, making him feel important. Outside of throwing touchdown passes it was probably the thing Fred did best. I knew first-hand.

Friday night at South El Monte the rain wasn't heavy but steady for the whole game. The Eagles stadium is nicknamed *The Swamp*, and I didn't know why until the rain began to collect in puddles on the field. They were 0-3 and not expected to give us much of a problem.

They didn't.

We cruised to a 41-7 victory, and the only thing keeping us from cracking fifty again was the rain. Fred went thirteen of nineteen for 203 yards and a pair of touchdowns. I caught four of those passes and took one in for a score. I also took a helmet to the outside of my right thigh, just above the knee. The joint sill flexed, but the muscle above it was cursing me.

Fast Eddie's 215 rushing yards and three touchdowns easily made him the star of the game, but when the fourth quarter ended there was no camera crew and no reporters. Not even Benny. He had the best game of his prep career, and there wasn't anyone there to talk about it.

In the locker room, Fred-X praised Pineapple's offensive line. Gelbaugh threw a towel at him. "What about some love for the defensive?"

"Good game Dan Feliz!" I said. The linebacker played the entire game ignoring the pain in his ankle. He returned a thumb's up.

"It was South El Monte, man," Fred said.

"What about me?" Fast Eddie said.

"You get first pick of the donuts tomorrow."

The team party was at Hector Cardenas' house. A backup lineman, he was well liked for a sophomore. Cardenas played and acted like someone who was just happy to be on the team. Unlike me, a junior, who tried to give off the vibe I always belonged, he asked all the questions I never had the guts to.

The food was good. It wasn't just pizza and soda, but pizza, chicken, potatoes and ice cream. Everyone came except for Maez and Bobby Lucia, who said his leg hurt after the game. The rain eased to a sprinkle, but the wind remained and the power blinked twice before staying on for good. Scores of games were discussed: Pomona, San Dimas, and Arroyo won. West Covina won its fourth game, but all the guys were talking about the comment on the WestCo thread that said Billy Hudson would be the Bulldogs' quarterback next season.

"I didn't write that," Hudson said, defending himself. "Anyone can put anything they want on those boards."

"Coach is going to be hacked when he reads it," Basler said.

"I didn't do it!" Hudson said. "F-bomb!"

"Hey guys," Cardenas appeared at the buffet table waving his hands in front of us. "Easy on the cussing, my folks don't like it in the house."

"Can we cuss outside?" Pineapple said.

"All you want."

I didn't blame Edwards for getting a spot on the couch to watch Grip Teague's show. He was certain to be mentioned, and he was. In the final five minutes a hand off screen gave Teague a note.

Grip Teague: We got some details from West El Monte's win tonight at The Swamp. Fast Eddie Edwards rushed for 215 yards and three scores. So it was a big night for him and the Fighting Scots.

Bald Guy: Not a surprise, Edwards is an important part of that team. A good rebound for West El Monte and that brings us back to Pomona, no letdown with the Red Devils tonight.

Grip Teague: I should say not...

That was it.

The clock said 4:17 when I woke up to the tightening of the muscle in my right thigh. My neck was sore from sleeping wrong, and I hobbled to the bathroom. The bruise looked worse now than it did earlier. It loosened as I walked and I didn't think it was going to hold me back unless there was another game to play this weekend.

At my bedroom door, I heard something. It was coming from the living room. I recognized the sound, but for the briefest of seconds didn't know who it could be. Opening the door and taking a step towards the dining table, I knew it was my father. He was crying.

Eyes adjusting to the dark, I drifted into the kitchen to get a better look and I saw him kneeling, boxers only, crying into the sofa cushions. I could only assume he came out here to keep me from hearing him.

Unless news came that some unknown sister or brother of mine died, I knew exactly why he was crying. It was because of Mom. I hated seeing him like this. Confident and strong was a much better look for a man. If he was this weak in front of her then I understood why she left him.

Sensibility said I should go put a hand on his shoulder, but instead I went back to bed, knowing I had nothing to say he wanted to hear.

Fred brought donuts to film, gave Edwards first choice, served the offensive line, and then gave the rest of the box to Gelbaugh and his henchmen.

"Okay, before we get started," Coach Piccou said. "I was at the hospital with Bobby Lucia last night and he's got two fractures below his left knee. He's wrecked for the year."

Lucia was a cornerback, and I hadn't noticed his absence from the meeting. He'd been lifting and working since December and only got to play in four games as a reward. I didn't ask, but it was an unfair aspect of football. Talent, no talent, you could work hard, but there was no guarantee something wouldn't randomly snap and burn down all your dreams.

"If you think about it, drop him a line. He's very upset," Piccou said and then motioned for the film to roll. "Off the top...you guys suck."

"Mr. Andrade!" Mr. Umphries said as I came through the church's glass doors. "I finally saw your game against Pomona last week on my computer." He gave me an okay sign and smiled. "You might be making me a football fan again."

"Thanks," I said. He was becoming cooler by the week.

"Now get to church."

The worship music was playing as I slid into the back surrounded by people I didn't know, but it didn't matter. I kept scanning the front to get a glimpse of Lena, but too many heads were in the way.

Pastor David prayed. Offering plates were passed around, and I thought about putting something in since this was the only place I could come to see Lena without Fred being in the way. A buck was fair exchange for the opportunity to breathe in Lena's Royal Jasmine. I let the plate pass because I wasn't sure how into this whole church thing I was.

When the kids were dismissed for children's church there was no Lena.

A husband and wife came in late, smiling, and asked with their eyes if I could scoot down a little bit on the bench. I did, coming closer to a middle-aged woman wearing too much perfume. I didn't know what it was, but it certainly wasn't Royal Jasmine. Sandwiched between strangers, with no sign of Lena, I had to act like I came to hear the sermon.

"Throughout the New Testament we are called to repent," Pastor Domres said. "To turn around but before we will do that it seems we must know that there is something to turn around from. Confession of our sinfulness and our deep need for God becomes the turn around point. This confession of sin is not you confessing your sins to me...I'm a sinner too. Confess them to the Lord. Without Christ, we are not okay and to say that we are is not okay."

I wanted to break out, but I was trapped. I daydreamed about Lena being sick and me bringing her soup. Demonstrating by the act, I had deep passion and concern for her. It was a great diversion, but Pastor Domres kept hammering into my thought stream.

"This isn't hard, this isn't like graduating from West Point, and it's certainly not rocket science. The scripture is clear in First John, one-nine: 'If we confess our sins he is faithful and just to forgive us our sins and cleanse us of all unrighteousness.'"

When I got home Dad was still sleeping. I nuked a pizza, turned on the Rams game, and then heard the notification from my phone.

Lena Durkin:
How was church today? I was sick.

I stared at it. Checked it again an hour later, then two hours later. Why would she text me if she didn't like me? After several hours I deemed sufficient time had passed to respond.

Dale Andrade:
Great...How are you?

I stayed awake until two in the morning waiting for a response she never sent.

WEEK FIVE

Read The Blitz
By Grip Teague

I got two words to start off with: Shane Delfman. What more can you say about the San Dimas quarterback? Not much...West Covina pulled out another victory over the weekend, but until they straighten things out on offense I have a feeling we are looking at a one and done come November...If you get a chance click on Bald Guy's link to the interview he did with Jefferson Pham and why he bolted out of Bishop Amat. Curious to know what others think, I thought some of the shots against the Lancers were a bit cheap...Another week, another thread of Billy Hudson transferring out of West El Monte Poly. We've heard Cal High, West Covina, and Diamond Ranch; where will it be next week? "Billy's not going anywhere. He's happy and the family is happy at West El Monte." His uncle, Clint Hudson, told me by phone on Sunday afternoon...The El Rancho athletic department shared that D.K. Germany has received an offer from Dixie State in St. George, Utah...Under the radar because he does not play for a great team, but did you catch Anthony Ciccone's performance for Rosemead over the weekend? The linebacker/fullback was in on twelve tackles, three sacks, and he rushed for 150 yards and a touchdown. Now I know what you were thinking, defensive stats are kept by stat-girls who love to make their boyfriends numbers look good, and, for the most part, you're right. In fact, I made three tackles over the weekend for two different schools. In Ciccone's case, I saw the game film; he was awesome. The numbers are legit. How on earth did he get away from Flair Drive?

Catching four passes bugged me until Monday's practice when Fred encouraged everyone about the win. His numbers were good for Fred Ritter but hardly satisfactory for Fred-X. Meaning they weren't great, he didn't get any press, and no one in the media seemed to care. The South El Monte game was being treated like a throwaway.

We were in the film room or team room--it was called both--on Monday. The coaches were running late. I had an idea, and the veterans confirmed it, there was going to be a pep talk before we started 'Arroyo Week.' It was going to be about us keeping focus, sportsmanship, and staying off the message boards.

"Tell me the winning doesn't feel good?" Fred said to Gelbaugh. "Numbers, stats, it doesn't matter. It's the winning that feels good!"

"Winning feels good!" Gelbaugh shouted back.

"Are you preaching, Fred?" Pineapple said.

"I'm just saying the winning feels good!"

"Amen, brother!" Pineapple said and the rest of the team joined in. "The winning feels good!"

"It's about winning, it's about team, it's not about stats...It's about knocking teams on their butts!"

So we waited for the coaches and fed off Fred's sermon on the gospel of winning football. It felt good for some and made others feel like giants. I went along, but shame crept in. If they could have read my thoughts, what would they think? I was happy after the loss to Pomona and upset after the win against South El Monte. All because of how many passes I caught. I was happy with the win...I guess, but four catches made me feel average and Ponce-like.

The door opened and the coaching staff came in with Athletic Director, Bryan Crumsey, and Vice-Principal, Pam Padilla. They were all wearing lecture faces, ready to share stern warnings about keeping our minds on the game and remembering we were representing West El Monte Poly.

Piccou ordered us to be quiet.

"I added Arroyo to my 'To Do List,' Coach," Pineapple said rubbing his hands together. "I'm ready for a little boom, boom, bash!"

The team laughed, but Piccou didn't, and it was our signal something was up.

"Quiet down," he said. "We have things we need to talk about."

"It's Arroyo week Coach?" Pineapple said. "Time to get rowdy."

"Carl," Crumsey said straight to him. "I need you to chill."

"Carl?" Edwards and a few others repeated. "Carl? Pineapple when did you become Carl?"

Pineapple looked at Coach Piccou and the rest of the staff with his mouth open. His eyes appeared lost. Hurt? I wasn't sure.

"Carl?" Dan Feliz said. "Pineapple is the dude that walks around the locker room naked. Who the frick is Carl?"

Half the team laughed, the other half waited. Pineapple didn't make a sound. Crumsey shook his head and Vice Principal Padilla's vibe went from serious to angry. Instead of being warned, I got the feeling we were going to be yelled at. We'd done something.

"Gentlemen!" Crumsey called out. "We need your full attention." This time, we quieted. "Vice-Principal Padilla?"

"Thank you," she said. Padilla, middle-aged, thin, and not bad looking for having gray in her hair, always seemed to be talking down to you. "As you know, we have a code of conduct policy here at West El Monte Poly, which insists on respect being a two-way street between student and faculty. So it is with great sadness an issue with the football team has come to light and needs to be addressed." She paused briefly then continued. "West El Monte Poly strives to respect races, ethnicities, faiths and genders of its students, but it has come to our attention Carl Bartholomew has been on the receiving end of slurs and racial epithets from the coaching staff and his teammates. This is a clear violation of our code of conduct. A code of conduct all of you, including the coaching staff, agreed to and signed when joining the school's athletic program."

"This why you called me into your office this morning?" Pineapple said. "You didn't tell me it was about the team." His voice rose. "I told you I've been called Pineapple by my family since I was a kid."

"I smell something," Gelbaugh said.

"You need to keep quiet," Crumsey said.

"Coach, I didn't complain about anything," Pineapple said, starting to shake and obviously wanting out of his seat. "I swear it."

"I know you didn't son," Piccou said and received a sharp look from Padilla.

"So you are saying because we call him 'Pineapple,' who happens to be one of my best friends, that we're being racist?" Fred said understanding something sooner than the rest of us. "Wow, I think the problem's yours instead of ours."

"Listen up," Crumsey said. "Coach Piccou has something he needs to share."

"You're saying that us calling him 'Pineapple' is the same as someone calling me the N-word?" Edwards said. "That's f-bombed in the head."

"You're making it sound like I complained! I didn't complain! I told you that's my name!"

"Who the f-bomb complained?" Bustamonte said. "Who the f-bomb..."

"...The next player who talks will be suspended for Friday night's game," Padilla said cutting Bustamonte off. "Now, Coach Piccou has something he needs to share."

Piccou produced a sheet of paper in his hands. "I have to share something with you guys, and it's tough enough, so please do not interrupt me." He then rubbed the growth on his chin in anxiety.

A sick feeling swept over us. There was the accusation of us insulting Pineapple, who was beginning to tear up, and now we were certain we were losing Coach Piccou.

"West El Monte Poly has strict rules respecting the dignity of all of its students and I have violated this policy by joining in with racial slurs and stereotypical references to one of our players and I need to apologize publicly..." Piccou paused and cleared his throat. "Carl Bartholomew, although it was never my intention, I have insulted your heritage and cultural background with insensitive and poorly chosen remarks. To you, and before your teammates, I apologize with deep regret and sincerity."

Coach Piccou put away the paper, put his head down, defeated.

"Because of the seriousness of this matter," Crumsey spoke quickly. "West El Monte Poly feels it has no alternative but to suspend Coach Piccou for one week. In his absence, Coach Jackson will lead the program."

"This is the stupidest thing I have ever seen," Edwards said.

"You are suspended for Friday's game," Padilla said.

"Okay," Edwards answered. "Then f-bomb you."

The moment was insane and, in the insanity of the accusation and suspension, came Fast Eddie directly cursing at Vice Principal Padilla. I saw her eyes grow large and everything in her body wanting to lash back.

"How about if I call you a racist for suspending a black student?" he said to her. "Yeah, you don't want none of that."

"Edwards!" Coach Jackson yelled and shook his head at our running back.

Crumsey's words brought relief. I thought Coach Piccou was about to be fired. A week's suspension was terrible, but it wasn't a suspension for the rest of the season or a dismissal. Someone complained, and again the administration backed Piccou into a corner where he was forced to apologize.

"Coach Crumsey," Fred spoke with no rage. "You introduced Carl as 'Pineapple' at a pep rally last year. How come you didn't get suspended? Benny wrote in the school paper that the most valuable player on the team might be Pineapple Bartholomew. Did he get suspended?"

"Gentlemen," Crumsey said ignoring him. "We understand that you are all very supportive of your coach, but I ask your loyalty to him be shown by effort in the classroom, the athletic field, and in fair treatment with all your fellow students. We ask that you do not take this to social media. An email has been sent to all your parents and we would like to close this matter now."

Pineapple rose out of his chair, went through the faculty members, and out the door. Outside we could hear another trashcan being destroyed. Piccou took an initial step but then waited for Padilla and Crumsey to go through the door first.

Bustamonte waited until they were gone and then stood in front of the team. "Okay, who is the mother-f-bomber who complained?"

Practice was canceled.

In the locker room I learned it was possible for someone as big, tough, crazy, and funny as Pineapple to cry. He sobbed on the floor by his locker, swearing over and over he never said anything.

"My parents call me Pineapple," he said. "I wouldn't f-bomb Piccou over like that…" He balled.

A level of pity took me, it took all of us. Pineapple might have walked around naked far too much, but we loved this guy and knew no one, outside of Fred, and maybe Gelbaugh, was as committed to the team.

The pity, radicalized by our anger, soon changed into how we could help Coach Piccou and screw over the administration. I felt like the fraud in the room: I was the guy who loved his stats more than he loved winning, so I kept quiet.

"Let's win it for Coach," Fat John said. "That's all we can do."

"Let's all wear black wristbands for him," said Dinh Lee.

"Black wristbands?" Feliz said. "Coach didn't die."

It was quiet for a second and Basler looked at Fast Eddie. "I can't believe you just said, 'f-bomb you' to Padilla."

"I was already suspended. What does it matter?" Edwards said. "Sometimes when you're a brother there are things you can say and get away with," then he pointed at our center, "but not you, my fat white friend."

Basler smiled.

"I'm going to call Grip Teague," Gelbaugh said. "Him and Bald Guy are always looking for stuff to write about. I'm gonna give it to them."

Coach Jackson came out of the office angry. He stood in the center of the locker room. I didn't know how old he was. His head was always shaved so there was never discernible gray, but whenever he stopped playing football, he certainly didn't stop lifting weights. The guy was granite.

"So you're agreeing with this?" Fred said to him. "I can't believe it, Coach Jackson, you know this is bull."

"I'm going to say this once. Piccou had to eat a lot of garbage to remain your Coach and not let this season be lost," Jackson said. "He probably should have told them what they could do with all of it, but he didn't because he believes in you guys. So stay off the message boards. If you care about Coach Piccou and keeping this season alive, stay off the boards. They'll suspend anyone who talks to the media about it, and it could lead to Coach getting fired. And you can thank Crumsey for it only being one week. Padilla wanted Piccou gone, but Crumsey put himself on the line for all of us and persuaded Principal Mathers to make it just a week. It's only one week. You can all suck it up like men for one week."

"Coach Jackson," Edwards said. "Calling him 'Pineapple' is not the same as calling you, Patterson, or me the N-word."

"It don't make any difference because we don't make the rules," Jackson said. "We just follow them. It's one week and then it'll be over. Don't stir the pot. If you take your focus off the field, you could get your butts kicked by Arroyo Friday night."

Jackson punctuated his leaving with a hard shove of the double doors and the sound of the same abused trashcan being kicked over on the other side.

Except for Pineapple's crying, there wasn't another sound.

"Hey! Moanin' Samoan," Fred said to him, "I don't care how much you cry about it. I'm still going to call you Pineapple. I mean it, so don't punk out on me."

Pineapple gave a tortured smile and then went to Fred and hugged him. Gelbaugh joined, then Edwards, and all of us. The more we pressed against him, the more he cried. It reached a point where his body shook before we released our hold.

"You all know, right?" He asked us again, wiping at his eyes and nose. "I didn't say anything. Padilla called me into her office and asked me if I was offended by being called Pineapple. I told her no and she didn't say anything else."

"We know," Feliz said. "We got your back."

He wiped at his eyes again. "I got to call my parents."

"Use mine," Edwards gave him his cell phone and Pineapple went through the double doors to make his call outside.

"So what do we do?" Feliz said.

"You play without Coach and me, and you beat Arroyo," Edwards said. "We just get on with the rest of the season."

We wandered back to our lockers and started to undress, but Fred stayed in the center of the room. He looked to the floor, then to the ceiling, going over things in his mind, and shook his head.

"You talking to yourself Fred?" Basler said, kicking off his cleats. "You freaking about Estrada and Ruiz?"

"If we don't go to Grip Teague or post anything on Facebook or Twitter, the school is going to issue a statement about why Coach Piccou was suspended for Friday's game," he said. "I mean, they have to right? Everyone is going to notice when Piccou is not on the sideline at Arroyo." We nodded. "It's going to come out eventually and people are going to believe he was racially insensitive towards our Pacific Islander teammate…"

"I believe he prefers to be called Polynesian-American," Edwards said.

"…Or whatever the hell they decide to call him this week."

Fred wasn't giving us new revelation, but repeating facts. All of us standing at our locker or sitting on the short benches in front of them watched him reason it out and hung on his words like he was George Washington. A Fred moment was about to morph into a Fred-X moment.

"So would you rather be thought of as someone pathetic and win a championship or would you rather not win a championship and let people know you had integrity? That your coach wasn't a racist and that you stood for what was right?"

"They didn't call Piccou a racist," Edwards said. "They implied he made insensitive remarks."

"And the difference when it leaks out?" Fred-X said. "This matter won't end on its own. Somebody in this room is going to leak it out or their uncle will. Padilla doesn't like Coach and wants to get rid of him and if no one stands up for him he's going to get screwed even more. The media is going to start linking in Coach Paleo, the letter about Piccou cussing too much, the hassles with the booster club presidents. They're going to take this dude down."

My eyes darted around for Billy Hudson, but he, Ponce, and Miranda cleared out when practice was canceled.

"What are you talking about?" Bustamonte said. "I don't understand."

"What I'm saying is how tough are we?" Fred said. "Are we tough enough to risk our season to prove Coach Piccou is a good man and not a racist? Are we tough enough to do that?"

"Are you saying we shouldn't play?" I said. "That we won't play unless Piccou is back?"

"I'm saying we get ready to play and we play, but go see Grip Teague, call Trudy Shields, call Chanos and tell them what happened. Tell them why and if the school suspends us, they'll know from us that we don't think our coach is a racist or made racist remarks. How stupid are they going to look when Pineapple refutes everything they are saying about Piccou?"

"Can they suspend all of us?" Fat John said.

"They can do whatever they want," Fred-X said. "But so can we and maybe we can embarrass them real bad by supporting Piccou."

"Big gamble," Gelbaugh said. "Let's do it."

"The question is," Fred-X said. "Do we have the sack to do something like that or is our season more important?" He paused for a second, slightly shook his head. "I say we force them to f-bombing suspend us."

"You need to think about this Fred," Edwards said. "You've already gotten some letters from colleges. What's going to happen if you don't play the rest of the season? No offense, but I think you need to throw every one of those fifty touchdowns Teague is talking about. Piccou has all the time in the world, but we only have this season."

"That's true," Bustamonte said. "If Padilla and the administration kill our season that'll be it for us."

The double doors opened back up and a less emotional Pineapple came back in with Edwards' cell phone in hand. "I just talked to my dad. Padilla called him this morning and asked if they were offended. They told her there was no problem and that it was my nickname since we came from Samoa."

"And she still went through with all of this?" Bustamonte said. "What a hag."

"Bruja," Maez said.

"What do you think, Fred?" Feliz asked.

"F-bomb them, I'd rather play football at Citrus College next year than have the world think the worst of Coach Piccou."

We fed the story to every reporter we could on Monday night. Got on the message boards as ourselves to voice protest. Fred and Pineapple went on Grip Teague's show Tuesday. The story was blowing hard, but we heard nothing from the administration. We spent most of the practices waiting for Padilla and Crumsey to show and say we were suspended, but they never came.

Grip Teague, Bald Guy, Chanos, and Trudy Shields, without working in concert, set a narrative making Pineapple the pawn, Piccou the martyr, and Padilla the dirtbag CYA Vice Principal who had it out for Coach. Pineapple's parents, when interviewed by Teague, mentioned legal options due to the stress and anxiety it had caused for all of them. Our goal was to make the administration look bad, especially Padilla, and it was working.

None of it would have happened without Fred. Bustamonte and Basler's parents initially balked at the idea, but they came around when they realized Fred, who had the most to lose, was all in. I knew he couldn't walk on water but if somebody in the San Gabriel Valley had a shot it was Fred-X.

Grip Teague: BG this is exactly the kind of thing teams try to avoid and especially the ones with a chance to go far. Bad mojo at West El Monte Poly.

Bald Guy: They've suspended Skip Piccou and, according to Fred Ritter, they have suspended Fast Eddie Edwards for talking out of turn, and right now Ritter and the rest of his teammates are facing possible discipline for speaking to us. We've reached out to Athletic Director Bryan Crumsey, but thus far there has been no response.

Grip Teague: So do the actions of the team, by speaking to us, help or hurt?

Bald Guy: I believe it hurts right now, for this week, but, in the long run, it will bring this team together. And when you think about it, even though West El Monte is not commenting, the idea of suspending Piccou for calling Carl Bartholomew 'Pineapple' is ridiculous. I was on the sideline last year and even the administrators were calling him 'Pineapple.' So this makes me think it is more of a personal issue between the administration and Piccou.

Grip Teague: It's hard to imagine Principal Mathers, who's been around a long time, having an issue with Skip Piccou.

Bald Guy: It's not Mathers. Everyone knows he's a short timer getting ready to retire and take the golden handshake. He's a great guy, but old. One of the best people you'll ever meet, but he's not very engaged. Crumsey has always been stand up, but VP Padilla has the biggest hand in what is happening at West El Monte these days. She's the heir apparent when Mathers retires at the end of the year. At least that's what everyone believes. So I think it's probably more her in this issue than Mathers. In her view, it's probably preventive maintenance.

Grip Teague: You mean cleaning things us before a bigger problem develops?

Bald Guy: Yep. I don't agree with this at all, but Padilla's an educator and she knows there's always a lawyer out there looking to make a buck when he see's the slightest opening. Take some action now and you have plausible deniability if, or when, something hits the fan later.

◈

"What do people say about me, Handsman?"

We were at The Boat in San Gabriel on Wednesday after practice watching a recording of Fred being interviewed by Chanos in the school's parking lot. Lena and I were saving tables while everyone else ordered.

"What do you mean?"

"What do they say about Fred and me?" She was staring at him on the screen as he spoke. Then she flexed a softer version of her smile. It gave me a shiver even if she came across as somewhat sad. "Do they think I'm having sex with him or just some stupid girl who lives for him and nothing else?"

Even beautiful people can have bad days.

"Why would you say something like that?"

"I don't know," she said. "I really love that guy, but I worry about him."

It was quiet for a moment, and I questioned myself what the point was of even dreaming about Lena. She might have been smart, she might have been stupid, she was certainly gorgeous, but she was obviously clueless about what I felt for her.

Then she turned and smiled at me in a painful way. Every smile she gave me, whether intended or not, was immersed in cruelty. "Well?"

"I've never heard anyone say anything bad about you," I said. It was true. If someone had a problem with Lena Durkin, they had a problem with life. "Everyone thinks you're great."

"What does Fred say about me?"

"Fred never says anything bad about you."

"Does he ever talk about me?"

There were many ways to lie at this juncture. I could say Fred said terrible things about her and, hopefully, be the one to pick up the pieces when she broke into tears. I could say he always said wonderful things about her and display a wonderful grace like Sydney Carton on the way to the guillotine. Or I could tell her the truth, which was he never talked about her.

Fred never spoke about Lena. He wasn't selfish, but anything between him and Lena he held back from the guys. He'd become my friend, took care of Pineapple, and he was watching Piccou's back, but Lena was like furniture. Arm candy for school functions, the default when something required him to be in a couples capacity.

"Don't worry about it," she said smiling at my hesitation. "I know where I stand with him when it comes to football and the future." She looked towards the ordering area and the soda fountain. The guys were loading trays. "Do you ever wonder why I'm good with being fourth or fifth?"

"You're not fourth or fifth," I lied. She was more like forty-fifth with Fred after the team and coaches.

"I'll tell you why, and it's not because he's the quarterback." A tear streaked out of the corner of her eye. "Because when we started dating last June he made me feel like anything was possible. I'm not playing games at church. I believe in Jesus and I also believe he brings people into our lives to help us see things we couldn't see before. That's who Fred was this summer for me."

"Not anymore?"

She stared at me without a smile and then rubbed out the tear clinging on her cheek. The guys reached us and our conversation ended as the ongoing, now to me so trivial, discussion of Padilla, Pineapple, and Piccou started up again.

"Fred, I want to say something," Gelbaugh said. He pointed to the large flat-screen where the interview with Chanos played. The sound was too low to be heard over all the talking in the restaurant. "I just want to say, that you are the best quarterback in the San Gabriel Valley." The guys concurred with nodding heads. "But you are one ugly mofo!"

Fred fired fries at the middle linebacker. "You want a piece of me, holmes?"

"Run on home, little Freddy," Gelbaugh dismissed him. "You don't want any of this. You better save what little you got for Ruiz and Estrada."

"Those boys ain't touching Fred-X on Friday night," Pineapple said. "Fat John and I are shutting them down."

"Shutting them down!" Fat John affirmed.

Edwards's suspension being upheld was unjust. Fred wanted to make it an issue, but Edwards told them to let it go. He munched his burger and laughed with the rest of us. Fast Eddie had an address of questionable origin and didn't need any spotlights or web threads pointed his way.

"I feel bad, dude," I told him.

"I don't need any questions being asked," Edwards said, his ASU cap turned around. "You know what I mean? I pushed it a little bit with Padilla. I'll sit this revolution out, Handsman."

An hour later everyone was leaving, and I was getting a ride from Lena and my quarterback. Fred followed the boys into the bathroom. I waited outside on the benches and scanned the boards on my cell phone.

Grip Teague had published a blurb that the school district was going to look into a possible overreaction by the West El Monte Poly administration. That sounded like a victory to me.

"Do you want to know why I asked you all those questions?"

I looked up from my phone and Lena was standing over me in the dark. She was wearing jeans and a ski sweater. Her eyes seemed to glow. I could make out her dimples in the shade of the night. If it had been somebody else, if it had been Desi, it just would have been too dark to see. No shadow was ever too dark to hide Lena.

"You don't have to tell me," I said, closing out Grip Teague on my phone. "Unless you want to."

"Last summer," she eyed the door to make sure she wouldn't be interrupted, "we talked forever about what we wanted to do and where we wanted to go. I didn't want to go anywhere, but then he talked about the idea of leaving and going someplace new. I didn't think I could, or was even ready, to leave home but the more we talked the more I believed. Fred got me to thinking about bigger things, things I would have thought were impossible for me. Then I started looking at colleges for nursing and realized it was really possible. I'm not that tough. I needed him."

"That's awesome," I said in the most plastic of voices. "So you're going to go away for school too?"

"I am." She put her eyes back on the door and then back to me. "But Fred's not."

"Of course he is," I said. "He's going to play football."

"Fred's a great guy," she said. "I mean, why would he risk everything to help Coach Piccou? But..."

"Because he's Fred-X," I said.

"Did you know about the Machados and the Bartholomews going through a tough time last year? They didn't have any income or even money for food." I shook my head at her. I didn't know Machado and just met Pineapple this spring. "Coach Piccou took groceries to their houses and never told anybody. He did it because he's a good man. Fred only knew because Pineapple was at his house when his parents called to say what Piccou had done. Now Fred's risking a lot to help Piccou; how could I not love a guy like that?"

"I don't know," I said, waiting for her to explain why Fred wasn't leaving, but I let it go when everyone came out. Lena turned to them and forced a smile. Then we all left for home.

B.L. Bergstrom Stadium, the home of the Arroyo Knights, was older than dirt. It received a minor upgrade every other decade but still looked like it belonged in the previous century. The grandstands were big, metal, and far away. A running track and course-ways sat crowds further back creating a buffer, between the players and noise.

Rain was a possibility, and the temperature when we went back into the locker room before kickoff was fifty-eight degrees. Balmy to someone from New Hampshire but it was stone cold to me.

Coach Jackson had us stand around him before we went back to the field. Coach Piccou always had us sitting as he gave us some sober business like directives about not quitting and having each other's backs.

"Tonight, fellas, it's all about what you want to do," he said. "That's a good football team, but they can't beat you unless you decide to let them beat you. So what do you want to do? Do you want to be what West El Monte was or do you want to be what West El Monte is today?"

Hands started clapping and mine joined in. To my left was Dinh Lee, his face painted blue, to my right was Dan Feliz and his face was painted blue. The entire defense had gone to the blue.

"So make it happen," he said. "Make it happen. Make it happen to them! Alba McF-bombing gu brath!"

We got in our pairs, took hands, and marched out of the locker room and onto the concrete where the clacking of our cleats served again, at least to me, as a drumbeat to war.

We kicked off and the ball flew down the center of the field to Arroyo's Matt Burns, who ran straight. Accelerating past the twenty and then the twenty-five, no hand touched him. When he hit the fifty the cursing started on our sideline and he was gone. Ninety-eight yards later, the Knights led 7-0. Their fans cheered, their band played, and Fred looked at me and let out a laugh.

"What's so funny?" I said. I knew he cared, but I couldn't figure why he made it seem like no big deal. This was game five of the ten we were guaranteed and panic found a foothold inside of me.

"Did you really think this was going to be easy?" His smile pushed my panic back down.

Burns' touchdown was bad, worse was Gelbaugh coming off the field holding his right-hand. A dislocated index finger lying across the knuckles of the soul of our defense made the seven-point deficit shrink by comparison.

"I'm gonna have to pop this back into place," Sondra said.

Gelbaugh nodded.

"It's going to hurt."

Gelbaugh nodded.

"Do you understand?"

"I know," he answered calmly. "Just do it."

I thought about looking away but didn't. A silent, painful, shudder worked through his body as the finger and joint resumed proper relationship. I didn't play volleyball long enough to see a dislocated finger, but I knew for sure no one I played with would have been so eager to pop it back into place.

"Now tape it," Gelbaugh said to Sondra.

"What?"

"Tape the f-bombing thing!" The madman shouted.

We got a good return on the ensuing kickoff, and five plays later, (which included my seventeen-yard catch on a dig-route) a scrambling Fred-X found Bustamonte for a thirty-eight-yard score to tie the game.

Pineapple's well intentioned promise of them not touching Fred went unfulfilled.

Arroyo's Chao Estrada and Miguel Ruiz were jacking everything up. They were relentless. Without the threat of Fast Eddie in the backfield, it was an all you can eat buffet on Fred. He started taking shots in the first quarter and it never stopped. He got hit low, high, crunched and sandwiched.

I caught three passes in the first half, but it was the third catch on the last play in the second quarter, fluttering out of Fred-X's hand when Ruiz hit him, that nearly did me in. I charged back for the ball and when I leaped to take it out of the air Estrada bulldozed me. I hit the ground, the air stayed inside of me, but in front of my eyes stars flashed.

A bell rang, or something buzzed to indicate it was halftime. We were trailing 21-14. Slowly collecting myself, I returned to the land of the living and followed the like colored herd to the locker room.

"You cool?" Sondra asked running alongside me. "Something had to hurt after getting hit like that. You feel sick or anything?"

"I'm cool," I lied. "No problem." Football had become a routine, almost involuntary and reflexive. Run the play, catch the ball, get hit, curse, get up, go back to your side of the scrimmage line, get the next play, and do the same thing all over again. My days in helmet and pads were under a year, but I'd figured this out. I imagined how ingrained to people like Gelbaugh and Fred it was.

"Okay," she said. "Let me know if something changes."

"You can't play scared, guys," Coach Jackson said to us in the locker room. "Play nervous, that's fine. You should be nervous. This is a big game, but you're looking scared out there. When you play scared you get hurt and we lose."

My body, after assessing the first half hit count, felt like it was already Saturday morning. The stars had gone away, but everything attached by skin, sinew, muscle, and tendon hurt. I gulped it down like bad medicine.

Pineapple, rocking slowly back and forth, was trying to get a handle on whatever was hurting him. Feliz was getting his ankle reinforced with tape. Gelbaugh fixed the tape holding his index finger to the middle finger. Bustamonte stood like a rock and his hair was perfect.

Coach Gugliotta cursed the defense for not doing a better job, but it sounded like required rhetoric. He was just trying to get more out of them. The problem tonight, we all knew, wasn't the defense but the offense.

"We know they're physical, but so is Gelbaugh and the defense," Jackson said. His tone was different. Usually, his halftime rants as the offensive coordinator questioned our manhood, our heart, and our ability to walk and chew gum at the same time. With his head coach hat on, Jackson was Mr. Relational. "We're giving as good as we're getting, except you can't be afraid. You can't be afraid of them, you can't be afraid of losing, you can't be afraid of them taking a Mission Valley crown that should be yours. You have 24 minutes to make it happen, but you can't do it if you're afraid of what might happen. Again, whatever is going to happen, you make it happen. Make it happen to them! Fellas, it's time for us to deliver a little boom, boom, bash!"

"We're not losing this game," Fred said, strapping his helmet back over his sweat drenched head. "Not after this week, not to these guys."

The team rose, and like the power of surf coming in from the sea, it took me with them. I hurt, but I wasn't hurting like Gelbaugh or Pineapple. I wasn't getting racked on every play like Fred.

We marched in pairs to the spot underneath our goal post and began to get the edge in attitude we were lacking in the first half.

"Sons of Scotland, what will you do with your freedom?" Fred-X shouted. "Will you fight?"

"Yes!"

"Will you fight?"

"Yes!"

He raised his fist and we shouted with him. "Alba gu bràth!"

We charged to the field, losing, hurting, dirty, and people cheered us. I saw faces I knew, with names I didn't, looking right at me and encouraging me. I put the pain aside. I put Lena aside. Surrounded by these guys I'd only known for a few months, I realized they were depending on me as much as I was depending on them. I put my three catches aside. The shame of my selfishness, so far undetected by my teammates, died in those seconds before the third quarter kickoff. I felt the liberty to just play football.

The odd quality, I realized, was I wasn't on the outside but the inside. I was numbered among the select valiant attempting to make victory happen. If I'd been part of something of nobler purpose in my life up to this point, I failed to remember it. Football, because it demanded so much, always delivered pride to me.

This was the first time I felt the burning desire to win. It was liberating because I didn't need to worry about making another catch. I only needed to win. The problem was so did Arroyo.

The wind picked up. It turned colder and a dampness, like an opening act leading to a bigger show, tipped us off a real drenching was close. The weather changed, but nothing changed for us on offense.

I caught a couple of passes in the flat. Bustamonte caught a hitch and later got smacked on a failed bubble screen. This was the sum of our offense in the third quarter. Fred didn't have the time to look at any of us downfield. Arroyo's defensive game plan was nearly perfect. Ruiz and Estrada kept him hemmed in and number fifty-six, too fast for the middle linebacker spot he was playing, spied in the center of the field.

"Who the f-bomb is this that guy!" Matt Grieb, our roundly built left guard, said between breaths.

"A f-bombing freshman," Basler answered in one of our rare huddles.

On the flip side, Gelbaugh was making miracles happen. He plugged holes, chased down runners, and backpedaled into coverage. Feliz grunted with every step he took, but he kept playing. Dinh Lee was knocking away passes and sacrificing his thin body to stop the running game.

I hated coming to the sideline when the defense was on the field. Standing, drinking water, or worse sitting, the pain in my thigh and shoulder multiplied. A soreness was getting stronger at the lower end of my left rib cage where Estrada had blasted me. On the field, there were other things to worry about, but at least we were moving. Standing still, the San Gabriel Valley never felt so cold.

"We've got to figure something out," Fred said. "Gelbaugh is out there kicking butt and we're not doing anything!"

"What can we do?" I said.

"We got to get a running game," he said as Arroyo punted and the ball deflected off the shoulder pad of Lee, who was in because he had sure hands. The ball caromed to our nineteen before being recovered by the Knights.

"F-bomb!" Gugliotta howled.

We were in serious trouble. Three plays into the fourth quarter, Burns broke a Patterson tackle and scored on a slip screen. It was 28-14, Arroyo. The rain arrived and the fans, who didn't leave, turned silent.

Bustamonte lined up deep for the kickoff, and Fred went to Coach Jackson for a discussion. I was pacing behind the bench near the cheerleaders, my body was killing me, and I needed to move. If I didn't, I was going to freeze from the inside out.

Jackson and Fred yelled, but it wasn't like they were yelling at each other. They cursed, Jackson asked him if he was crazy, and Fred-X grinned at him nodding and hopeful. Where he acquired hope for us with less than ten minutes to play and down two touchdowns, I didn't know.

The kick was squibbed and Bustamonte fielded it at the seventeen. Cutting left he eluded one tackler and hurdled a second to gain thirty-yards of real estate before landing at midfield. Fred clapped his hands at the offense as we left the sideline.

"We got to score on this one, guys," he said as the refs spotted the ball, "or it's my butt."

He barked the signals and sent Bustamonte in motion. The ball snapped and Fred-X gave it to him on a Jet Sweep, but instead of running wide, Bustamonte planted and cut directly for the line of scrimmage against the grain.

We ran this play earlier in the game. It was designed to go wide, but Estrada blew it up. This time, Arroyo over pursued and Bustamonte went forty-yards, through reaching arms, to the Knights thirteen.

Racing to the line of scrimmage, everyone was out of breath except for Fred-X. Ruiz and Estrada were sucking air. I was sucking air when the ball was snapped and Bustamonte ran the same exact play the way he'd run it before. He was tackled inside the one.

Fred-X hurried us again and took the ball on the first sound. Running behind Pineapple, he crossed into paydirt. He cursed as we tried to congratulate him and ordered us quickly to the line of scrimmage. Then he handed the ball to Mike Miranda for two-points to make it 28-22.

We had a game again, and people were looking for ways to hang on as the conditions worsened. Umbrellas, trash bags, even seat cushions, were being used to blunt the falling water.

"We're going to get one more possession," Coach Jackson said to the offense as we grouped around the benches. The rain was pushing harder. If I wasn't so scared of losing, I would have enjoyed it. Who didn't like to play in the rain? "Just one more and we're not going to be able to throw the ball in this." He wiped at the water collecting on his face. The band started to play then gave up. We tightened our huddle. "We're going to run Gun-Power, and we're going to run it with Fred-X."

The offensive linemen nodded their heads as if they'd been told steaks were on the grill. Drive blocking was always preferred to pass protection. "Yes!" Pineapple screamed. "F-bombing Christmas!"

"They're going to be all hopped up to close us out." Jackson started again. "So we're going to stay in the spread and run Power with Fred. Pineapple," Coach Jackson calling Pineapple by his preferred handle made our left tackle perk up even more. "We're going to move you to left guard and you're going to pull and lead Fred-X!"

"F-bomb yeah!" Pineapple said.

"Grieb, you're going to slide over to left tackle," Jackson said. "We're going to find out how tough and how much character each one of us has. One possession to live. Hands in!"

He counted one...two...three; "Alba gu bràth!"

Gelbaugh and the defense had been awesome all night, but they had spent most of it on the field, and it was catching up with them. Arroyo ran for a first down on its first play from scrimmage. Then their quarterback, Connor Stone, picked up nine more on a bootleg. The clock continued to run and our coaching staff began the discussion of when to use our last two timeouts.

Burns ran a Jet Sweep to give his team a first and ten at our thirty-eight. Our defense had lost its legs, and a pair of dive plays showed it was losing its strength. With 5:02 to play, the ball was on our twenty-six and the Knights went for the kill.

Gugliotta dialed up a blitz for the defense and the gimpy Feliz, ignoring the play-action, went straight for Arroyo's Stone. Getting his hand just high enough, he tipped the ball.

Burns had Lee beat, but Lee reacted to the wobbling pass and picked it off at our seventeen. He should have celebrated with a cartwheel, but all he afforded himself was a small smile as the defense mobbed him back to our sideline.

"It's all us now, baby," Fred-X said, clapping his hands. "It's all us!"

Running back onto the field, a hand reached out and grabbed me by the front collar. It pulled and turned me face to face with Gelbaugh. His helmet was off and his face was streaked a psycho blue from his war paint.

"What?" I said.

He stared at me, grinned, slowly nodded and let go. Too scared to rationalize what it was all about then, it came to me as I rejoined the offense. The dude was affirming me. My mind didn't take it as an 'or else' look but an 'I believe in you' one. Adrenaline surged. The cold eased.

Pineapple was banged up, everyone knew it, and he played it all the more by hobbling onto the field and into the left guard spot. The appearance was he couldn't go at left tackle against Ruiz and the coaching staff was trying someone else. It was a great sell.

The snap came and Pineapple nimbly stepped around Basler and led Fred-X across the line of scrimmage. Estrada and Ruiz pushed upfield. The Knights' linebackers had dropped and the safeties were deep, so Pineapple had a full head of steam when he demolished the first defender coming into his sights. Fred-X picked up eighteen on the play.

Next play was the same, Gun-Power, and Fred-X, running out of the shotgun, went twelve-yards to our forty-seven. Next play, Gun-Power: he went seven yards before Burns came up to lay a big hit, but instead got crushed by Fred-X and another eight yards were gained.

Arroyo called timeout, and Coach Jackson came out to meet us at the numbers.

"What do you like?" Jackson said.

"Gun-Power," Fred-X said, rotating his left shoulder to loosen whatever needed to be loosened. He was in pain.

"You okay?" Jackson said.

"Fine Scottish weather," Fred-X said.

"I'm serious!"

"I'm good," he said.

Jackson looked over to the Arroyo side. The rain fell sideways and the wind was against us.

"Gun-Power," Jackson said, "but see if they move Estrada inside. If they move him inside, audible to the Jet Sweep. Bustamonte, you turn that corner. You got enough fuel to turn that corner?"

"Always," Bustamonte said, barely above a whisper. White wisps of breath could be seen exiting our mouths now.

The timeout ended, and Estrada was still lined up at left end. The Knights pulled their strong safety into the box and I knew Fred wanted to throw the ball because we had single coverage on the outside. It might have been fine Scottish weather, but there would be no passing through it.

We ran Gun-Power through the right side of the line and picked up six more yards. Because they had made the adjustment, this was probably the most demoralizing play of the series for the defense. They couldn't stop us. We lined up again, and Fred picked up another five yards as Pineapple heaped carnage upon carnage. The Knights freshman middle linebacker might have been fast, but he wasn't going to win a collision with the Moanin' Samoan.

There had been some early trash talking, but the elements and exhaustion extinguished most of it. If anything, with each play as we crashed into each other, our respect was growing. They'd shut down our offense, and we showed we could do other things. I didn't hate Arroyo, but the way I was feeling about them right then I would have used a baseball bat on every one of them to get the win.

Bustamonte and the rest of us kept running our routes, trying to sell the pass. It was a long shot, but if we could get them to believe just a little bit, we knew it could buy Fred and extra-yard or five.

"It's the same freaking play!" The Arroyo coach screamed at the top of his lungs. "All they're running is Power! They're just running Power! You know where they're going! Stop it!"

We ran it again for five more yards. Now we were at the fifteen with 1:09 remaining. I could taste the touchdown. We were going to win this game. They couldn't stop us, we couldn't stop ourselves, Fred and Pineapple were like a snowball rolling downhill, getting bigger and more dangerous as it advanced.

Bustamonte set up to the left. I lined up in the slot on the right and noticed something missing. Estrada had moved inside. Click. The audible came, and instead of selling a pass route I drove into the defensive end. Shocked, he backed up and we both crashed to the ground as I saw the back of Bustamonte's number eighty-six run by me into the end zone.

Tired or not, this time we exploded. The emotion was bigger than the hurt. Everyone climbed onto Bustamonte, the coaching staff raised their hands to signal touchdown. Pineapple took a knee, made a fist, and screamed something loud and incoherent to a Polynesian god that might have existed.

The moment felt like it had no sense of time attached to it, but it was just a few seconds. Had to be because Fred-X took control. He called a timeout and started pulling us away from Bustamonte.

No flags were thrown for our celebration, but the lead official pointed to Jackson and told him it was close. Where Piccou might have said something back, Jackson nodded and huddled us at the numbers.

"Shut up and listen," Jackson said. We pushed tight into each other. "Gun-Power, but Bustamonte you're going to be in single coverage. Sell the slant, run the corner. Handsdrade, run the in-route and be there in the back of the end zone."

I loved it. I was going to catch the game winner, but Bustamonte shook his head.

"What?" Jackson said.

"Fred-X gets the ball." Bustamonte wasn't deferring because of fear--everyone knew he wanted the ball all the time. After all, he was always open, but the arrogant Bustamonte put the team first. "I go with you jefe," he said to Fred. They reached out hands and clasped.

"Gun-Power, then," Jackson said with no dissent. "If Estrada drives inside, pop it around right end. Handsdrade, you and Bustamonte get him to paydirt."

I lined up in the right slot, but tighter to Fat John than usual. Bustamonte was outside of me by two arms' lengths. Estrada was back inside. The middle linebacker and Burns were behind him. They were ready for Gun-Power and they were going to get it because there was no turning back. We weren't going to change and they knew what we were going to do.

I prayed I wouldn't blink. I wanted to honor Gelbaugh for believing in me. I was ready to go through a brick wall for my team.

When the ball was hiked, Estrada pushed up field to pinch the gap. The defender on me pedaled back on the snap, so I went after Burns. Driving my shoulder into him I saw his eyes grow large as he fell back, and then I heard our fans cheer.

Laying in the mass pile of limbs, flesh, and equipment I caught a glimpse of Fred-X with his arms raised and the ball in his right-hand. Our best player had given us a 30-28 lead with less than a minute to play. Like the Colossus, we studied in WHG, he never looked so tall, so super human.

The offensive line picked him up and carried him to the sidelines. Horse, completely drenched, pointed two index fingers at me and hammered both my pads. "Way to go Handsdrade!" He said with elation in his eyes and then raised his arms in victory.

At the sidelines, the cheerleaders joined the fray as did all the hangers on. Security had melted with the rain, and the players who used to play, the parents who had worked their way down to the field, all of them were reaching to touch Fred. I couldn't tell if they were saying thank you or were just hoping the feel of his uniform would change their lives. Rain continued to fall, but tears were on so many faces. Basler and Pineapple embraced like brothers returning from war. Fat John came and put arms around both of them. I was happy, but I wasn't crying. Whatever was calling up that particular emotion in my teammates was older and before me.

I worried about Gelbaugh and the defense having too little left in the tank to stop Burns and company. The kickoff was squibbed and fallen on inside the Arroyo thirty. The rain wasn't only falling on our side of the field. What hampered us would hamper them, and it did.

Stone's first two passes were incomplete, one was knocked down by Patterson.

"Eat'em!" Pineapple screamed from the sideline. "Gelbaugh! Eat'em!"

On third down, when Stone tried to scramble, Edgar Escandon dragged him down in the mud and the clock ran out.

Football was awesome.

Message Board Friday Night:

"I'll tell you West El Monte won that game because Piccou wasn't coaching."---Cool Jets

"They won that game because of Fred-X and OC Jackson."---Kansas

"They got lucky against Arroyo, but they won't be lucky against San Dimas. SD will kill them."---Sunshine

"Fred-X makes a better running back than quarterback. Piccou needs to start Hudson."---Dooin-Bruin

"Fred's a helluva a running back. Hudson is a great passer. State title with the two of them on the field at the same time."---MaxAtax

"Gelbaugh is a beast!!!! What a great game by the defense"---Wolfman

"Keep talking your ***DELETED***. The Fighting Scots are going undefeated in league!"---Big Tony

"Doesn't this just encourage the West El Monte administration to do more to get rid of Piccou?"---Bad News

"Piccou is gone after this season."---Jorge Grande

Billy Hudson's parents hosted the team party. Pizza, sodas, some laughter, Grip Teague & Bald Guy on the flat-screen, and a big helping of exhaustion defined the fiesta. The drama of the week had taken its toll. We loved Coach Jackson, we were very happy to be getting Piccou and Fast Eddie back, but our tank was empty.

Edwards was the only one who was ready. He laughed out loud, moved about the room, clean and healthy. The rest of us, even those who showered, still smelled like we had been scrubbed with grass and mud.

I wouldn't have traded places with him for the world. The Arroyo game was going to be something that stuck with me forever. Fast Eddie had his games to remember, but this one, even more so than the Pomona game, was mine.

Was I still selfish? Absolutely. Had it been bedded down?

Yes,…Temporally.

A cramp at the bottom of my right foot woke me on Saturday. When I reached for it the muscles across the top of my chest protested strongly. Swinging to my feet I walked it off. Catching a glimpse of the hand-some dude in the mirror, the reflection reminded me the season was half way through. My bruises were starting to layer and overlap.

"It's worth it," I said heading for the shower. "It's so worth it."

Coach Piccou returned for film study. He told us he was happy to be back, to keep our mouths shut on the boards, to show re-spect to Vice Principal Padilla, and even though we beat Arroyo we shouldn't be too full of ourselves because we didn't play that well.

"There were times I thought you just flat out sucked," he said. "I know everyone is kissing your behinds right now for winning and overcoming the drama, and we're in here passing out donuts, but you play like that in the playoffs and you'll be turning in your gear the next day. By the way, do we have an offensive line? Pineapple, I think Ruiz and Estrada put you on their 'To Do List'…several times."

"You're supposed to say; 'about five times' coach," Edwards corrected.

"About five times then," Piccou said.

This was the guy we fought so hard to get back?

Nobody complained.

I messaged Lena on Saturday night that I could help her on Sunday morning with the kids. She wrote back saying I was sweet, but the church had a screening process new workers had to go through before they could work with the children.

Lena Durkin:
You're still going to come, right?

Dale Andrade:
I'll be there.

Twelve hours later, I got my smile from Lena coming up the center aisle.

"Like the old preacher said a long time ago," Pastor Domres said from the pulpit. "If nothing in this world satisfies us, it is because we were made for another world. In a very clear manner, the scripture makes it plain to us that we should always be content with what we have, but never content with what we are."

I heard it like I hear traffic: I wasn't listening. Instead, I plotted on how to avoid Mr. Umphries and get some time with Lena.

When asked to stand for closing prayer, I darted out of the sanctuary to avoid my old friend and fan to head for the children's department.

"I'm sorry," an older woman said to me. "She had to leave early."

Politely, I thanked the woman and asked myself what I would have said to Lena if she had been there. Didn't really know what I expected. Sometimes just seeing her walk down the center aisle at church or stick her head out of a car window was good enough. It had to be because it seemed it was all I was ever going to get.

WEEK SIX

Read The Blitz
By Grip Teague

Good News & Bad News: The best thing about this time of the year is everyone is into or getting into league play and all the talk about weak schedules goes out the window. If you don't win in league then everything is lost. The drag? It's Week Six...Charter Oak has not confirmed if it was an offer, and we have not heard anything from Del Chance, but message board threads are talking about him being offered by Azusa Pacific. As par for the course, APU has no comment on the situation. If true, this is the second D-two offer for an area quarterback. Last week Dixie State offered El Rancho's D.K. Germany...Be sure to vote in our poll for best defensive player of the year so far: Courtney Graye (West Covina), "Bazooka Joe" Natalia (San Dimas), Jack Gelbaugh (West El Monte), Tank Davis (Pomona) or Arroyo Defensive Twins Chao Estrada & Miguel Ruiz...Word out of Downey is linebacker Gilliam Gilliam is gone for the year with a knee injury...Speaking of injuries: Cathedral's Julius

Morales is back this week for the Phantoms as is Los Altos quarterback Jeremy Chandos...A bad season for Monrovia gets a little bit better with Dominic Townes now eligible to play. The Wildcats play La Canada on Thursday...Latest stat check shows Maranatha's Jake Sharper is on pace for a 2,000 yard season. The Minutemen get Valley Christian on Friday night...

Our bodies were mending at Monday's practice. We were getting Rosemead at home this week and Coach Jackson said our first ten plays would be scripted. This meant no matter what the defense showed or did we would run the ten plays regardless.

He installed a game plan to grind Rosemead down. Fast Eddie, with fresh legs, was scheduled to get the ball on eight of the ten plays. The strategy was based on our threat of killing them by air would cause the Panthers to play back and open the door for us to run. Disappointment settled over me about the limited targets I'd get.

Fred raised his hand at the team meeting. "Doesn't this seem like the perfect time to get Gelbaugh some reps at fullback?"

"It would," Jackson said. "but we can't burn him out. Coach Gugliotta needs him on defense."

"Keep your f-bombing hands off my defense Ritter," Gugliotta said.

"Fine, fine," Fred said. "Whatever you say Coach."

After practice on Thursday we all took a knee and Piccou gave us his thoughts on Rosemead. "I'm telling you, don't take the bait. The stuff is already popping up on the message boards and Ciccone is going to try to get you to take a swing," he said.

Anthony Ciccone played varsity for West El Monte Poly as a sophomore and junior but transferred to Rosemead in January. Of course, like everyone else, he said it was because of an address change. What it was really about was getting kicked off the team by Coach Piccou. I learned in football an attitude towards rookies, opponents, or even the administration was one thing, but giving attitude when the coaches ordered you to do something was a major no-no. This is who Ciccone was.

"Is he that bad of a guy?" I said to Fred. I remembered seeing Ciccone on campus the year before and was told he transferred because he was high strung and couldn't get along with anybody.

"He's just gets too wired up and won't listen to anything or anyone," Fred said. "He's on meds because he's got some sort of alphabet syndrome, Special Ed guy."

"They expect us to pass so we're going to run. We're going to run right at Ciccone and make him too worn out to start anything."

"What if he starts something?" Basler said.

"I would prefer you walk away. The last thing we..." Piccou smiled, pressed his hands against his chest, "...the last thing I need after being suspended last week is for you guys to get into a brawl with a former teammate."

Afterward in the locker room Pineapple wasn't just walking and scratching, he was doing something worse: dancing.

"See this Handsman...?" He gyrated his lower half with his arms held out wide. Everything flopping and flying. "...These are the moves you need if you're going to score at homecoming...Yeah... Mmmf..." He clapped his hands. "Work it...Get the groove...yeah... Mmmf...I'm feeling it...You feeling it?"

"I'm feeling sick," I said just out of the shower and dressing at my locker.

"Dude, you ain't a brother," Fast Eddie said, backpack hanging over his shoulder and heading to the double doors.

"Samoans are the African-Americans of the South Pacific!" Pineapple answered back loudly as the doors opened and shut. He kept moving. "Fred-X! My man! Have some!" He raised a hand for our quarterback to high five.

"I don't think so," Fred said in disgust. "I got to get a penicillin shot for my eyes just for looking at you." He went to rinse. "Handsman, watch my locker."

No one liked standing wet and naked while trying to work a combination lock. This might have been why Fred had my locker put next to his. Though I preferred to think he did it to keep his favorite receiver close.

Pineapple plopped down on the bench across from me, his wet butt making gross smooshing sounds. Opening his locker he pulled out a pen and began writing a name on his 'To Do List.'

"Who is it this time?" I said finishing with my socks and fastening my shoes.

"Maybe you," he said without looking. I got closer and saw the name he was spelling out.

"Sondra?" I said. "You're putting our team trainer on the list? She's like fifty years old!"

"Forty-one," he said.

"And you're hot for her?"

He leered and nodded.

"I don't know what to say," I said. "Why don't you add Padilla to your list?"

Pineapple pointed to number nineteen. "Already did."

"Padilla? After all she did to you?"

"My list is all about business boss," he said.

"You're a sick, sick mofo Pineapple," I said slamming my locker. Several envelopes fell out of Fred's. Picking up three, I began to put them back inside when I noticed a whole stack. Quickly I counted nine letters from different schools. Norwich, North Central, Carleton, and Iowa Wesleyan were some of the names. A large paperclip held them together. Thumbing through I saw nothing from USC, UCLA, San Diego State, or even Azusa Pacific.

Something began to reek like a busted sewer line. "Pineapple did you rip one?

"Yeah," he said. "I call that, 'Crushed Pineapple.'"

When the season first began I was told to take a nap before getting dressed for the game. To relax, listen to some easy music, and drift into a blissful doze. This was impossible at the beginning. Trying to relax before a game wore me out. So I paced and tried to act cool. Six games in, it was still a struggle, but I did feel better knowing I wasn't the only one who stressed.

In the trainer's room, Sondra was taping Mike Patterson's ankles. Like always, his earbuds were locked in, and he was grooving to whatever he always grooved to. He was a good player, but as a teammate he didn't connect with anybody, not even Fast Eddie.

We made eye contact and he gave me the tilt of the head.

"You getting taped Handsdrade?" He said loudly through his music.

"Nope," I said. "Just excited."

"Butterflies," he said holding his stomach. "They're always jacking me up. You have a good game tonight, Handsdrade."

"You too."

I passed into the locker room and some of the guys were starting to get dressed. Toilets were flushing from down the hall. Fast Eddie was asleep. Bustamonte was carefully laying out all of his duds. Pineapple pulled up his pants.

Then Kiel Basler walked by our lockers wearing nothing but a baseball cap. "What's up guys?" He said.

"What are you doing?" Bustamonte said.

"What do you mean? I'm just getting dressed before the game," Basler said. He turned to make sure we were exposed, fully, to all his nudity. Then he put his foot up on a bench the way someone might put their shoe on a car fender to tie it. "Is something wrong?"

"Basler, cover your junk!" Fred said, coming into the locker room.

"I don't know what the problem is," Basler said. "Pineapple, dude, you don't have a problem do you?"

Pineapple opened his locker, pulled out his yellow pad and added Basler's name to his list. "I don't have a problem at all big boy."

It was a nice night. The temperature was someplace in the sixties and not expected to dip. Bad Rosemead team or not, their fans traveled well. Our fans were also out in force. I was happy I didn't have to imagine what an empty stadium would look like. I mean, after all, it was part of the football package right? There were supposed to be fans, but I was told at some schools the marching band outnumbered the people in the seats.

The Panthers, facing their supporters, were doing a loud war dance out on the edge of the sideline grass. ESPN has something like this on all the time before college football games--the players chanting and repeating unrecognizable words to get psyched for a big game.

"What the heck are they doing?" Jesse Maez asked.

"It's the Haka," Fast Eddie said. "You've seen it before."

"Yeah, I just never seen Ciccone trying to move like he had rhythm," Maez said.

"Is that him out there?" Fred said.

"Number forty-nine," Fast Eddie answered. "The one who looks like he's having a seizure."

"Hey, Pineapple, how come we don't do the Haka?" Bustamonte said.

"Because I'm f-bombing Samoan," Pineapple said. "Samoan's do the Siva Tau."

"Then how come we don't do the Siva Tau?"

"Because we're f-bombing sons of Scotland."

Rosemead won the toss, took the ball, and opened with a thirteen-yard run from Ciccone for a first down. When Dinh Lee took him down by the ankles, the former Fighting Scot jumped to his feet and indicated first down. On the next play he hammered into the line and picked up eight more.

According to the websites, Ciccone was six feet and two hundred pounds. Of course, West El Monte's game program listed Fred at five-eleven so truth in these matters was irrelevant. Ciccone did have decent size, but he wasn't Jack Gelbaugh as a linebacker and he wasn't much more than an average running back.

Fred, Fast Eddie, and myself were standing next to each other on the sideline as he pounded into the line for another first down, then was stopped after six more yards as Rosemead got inside of our forty.

"I thought running the ball was our game plan tonight," I said.

"It is," Fred said. "I think Mead took Ciccone off his meds for this game."

"He's all amped," Fast Eddie said. "Trying to play good soldier."

Each time Ciccone was tackled he sprang up and gave the ball to the official.

"Maybe I should say something about his mom," Fast Eddie said. "Coax him into a flag."

"No man, let it ride. In a minute he's going to crash and burn on his own," Fred said. "Just watch." Then he slipped through the ranks of the rest of the team and stood next to the offensive line where Coach Von Huson was giving final instructions.

Fast Eddie and I shouldered closer together. On the next play, Edgar Escandon got a hand up as Ciccone went by and popped the ball free. Dan Feliz recovered and Ciccone screamed at the top of his lungs in frustration. Teammates stayed away from him.

"How did Fred know?" I said.

"He knows Ciccone," Fast Eddie answered and we went onto the field.

We lined up on offense, Basler snapped, Fred gave it to Edwards, and our offensive line plowed the road. On our fourth play, from twenty-nine-yards out, Fast Eddie cleared the line of scrimmage and went into another gear for a touchdown. On our next possession, he went the distance from sixty-two-yards.

My first catch was a go-route and no pass I caught since the spring was any easier. I coasted to the end zone. Edwards added another touchdown by way of Fred-X and we led 40-7 at halftime.

In the locker room, the coaches avoided railing against us and focused on everyone being efficient. Coach Von Huson was talking to Hector Cardenas who would replace Basler at center in the second half.

"Make the adjustments, make the calls," Von Huson said. "Be smart out there."

"What if they...?" Cardenas asked a string of questions before Pineapple and Basler jumped in to help the sophomore out.

Coach Jackson worked with Fred and Hudson. Gugliotta was encouraging the defense to keep things tight and Sondra was looking at Dan Feliz's ankle. The receivers just sat and waited to go back on the field. I was happy I got the touchdown, at least, but few of us were excited. Bustamonte, Maez, and myself didn't speak to it, but we knew there would be very few opportunities in the second half. It was like spending an entire week getting ready for a party and then leaving a half hour into it.

Catching two more passes on the first drive of the second half, I was barely touched going out of bounds. We moved at will and there wasn't a word out of Ciccone. We all expected so much more. He was panting for breath from chasing Fast Eddie and doing everything he could in a game where he was outmatched.

From the Rosemead twenty-two, Mike Miranda took a swing pass to the left from Fred-X and cut in and then out as Ciccone zeroed in. It was Miranda's second move that forced Ciccone to plant awkwardly. Something in his leg gave and he went down in pain.

The game stopped. The officials sent us to our sideline. We took a knee. This was a ritual never explained to me, but something we did when someone was injured. I understood the obvious, that it was done to show respect, but no one ever shared where it came from.

Both trainers came out, then the coaches. We all knew it was serious when a motion was made by Crumsey to roll in the ambulance. Ciccone's mother came onto the field.

"F-bomber is hurt big time," Pineapple said.

"No one touched him, right?" Coach Jackson said and everyone shook their head.

"Miranda broke his f-bombing ankles with that move," said Ponce.

"I saw him coming in at an angle," Miranda said to all of us, "so I just made the break outside."

"It was a good move," Fast Eddie said. "Stuff happens."

As they loaded Ciccone onto the stretcher and then into the back of the ambulance, everyone applauded. Ciccone's mom, weeping, gave Piccou a hug. She said something, he nodded, and then they parted. Coming back to our side of the field, I saw Piccou wipe at his eyes.

When play resumed Fred-X used a bootleg play to score and then the starters were done for the night. Billy Hudson closed it out by sticking to Coach Jackson's script and added another touchdown on a short pass to Ponce. The final score was 54-10.

After the game, there were no new bruises or pains which started to become a sign of honor. Nobody smacked me and I felt cheated. An insane part of me considered rubbing Gelbaugh the wrong way at the team party so he'd light me up.

Grip Teague: Whether he gets his fifty or not, Ritter is having a terrific senior season and is showing he's not only the best quarterback in the San Gabriel Valley but is also going to play on Saturdays next season.

Bald Guy: I'm not arguing he's a great high school quarterback, but we've seen a lot of great high school quarterbacks over the years and they just don't have the physical skills to play beyond this level.

We were in Lena Durkin's living room, spread out on couches, chairs, and carpet. I leaned next to the hallway entrance watching the show. They knew Fast Eddie scored three touchdowns, two of them on long runs, but all they talked about was Fred-X.

Grip Teague: Where do you see him playing?

Bald Guy: I know I'm going to get yelled at for this. I can see our message board now.

Grip Teague: That's right, I'm tweeting this the moment you say it. So where's Fred-X playing next year?

Bald Guy: You tell me where you think he'll be playing next year and then I'll answer.

Grip Teague: Don't turn this around. I'm his number one supporter.

Bald Guy: Where is Fred-X playing next fall? Come on, I want to tweet out your answer.

With four catches, including a score, my totals through the first six games were: 32 receptions with seven touchdowns. We all dreamed, but some dreams give no indication of coming true and others arrive before you know it. I thought I might be able to play football and I was. Yet, averaging five grabs and at least one touchdown a game wasn't enough. I was irked as I watched the show. Would anything ever be enough?

Grip Teague: He's going to play Division-two. Now he might not play next year, probably redshirt but I could see him playing at Azusa Pacific.

Bald Guy: So you think Ritter has got the arm to play D-2?

Grip Teague: Yeah, he's got a really good arm.

Bald Guy: He does. Good but it's not great, and everybody at D-2 has a great arm. I don't think he's big enough or quick enough.

Grip Teague: You're a dead man.

Bald Guy: I'm not expecting any invites to the West El Monte team banquet.

Grip Teague: So what you are saying is…?

Bald Guy: I say if he gets a good Division-three package he should take it.

The guys yelled at Bald Guy's face on the flat-screen. Fred didn't say anything, kept smiling, sipping his soda, but I assumed he was dying inside. The conversation avoided the most pressing part of the equation; Fred was expecting to play Division-one football. Now the men, whose job was to watch football, were in a consensus he'd be lucky to play Division-two.

If it worried him, he didn't let it show. He'd prove them wrong. He was just one of those guys who could make anything happen. He could pull a rabbit out of a hat without starting with a hat or rabbit.

"All that matters is that we play and win," he said.

"Like sons of Scotland," Pineapple said.

"Like sons of Scotland," Fred said.

"Alba f-bombing gu brath to that," Gelbaugh chimed solemnly in.

The highlights played on. Pomona looked better than when they played us. Tank Davis, who would be playing some place special next year, was making a case for playing on Sundays in a few short seasons. San Dimas, running the Spread Bone, was thriving with Shane Delfman at quarterback. A clip from the Dominguez game featured its quarterback, Alec Jammon, surviving contact with a linebacker, bouncing, spinning, and then throwing a sixty-yard rope for a touchdown.

Grip Teague: That's why Jammon is Oregon bound.

Bald Guy: And that's the difference between a great high school player like Fred-X and a guy with next level talent like Jammon.

Pineapple cornered me in the kitchen when the party was dialing down. There was no alcohol at our team parties, everything was strictly monitored, but it never kept Pineapple from acting like a drunk when he was tired. Inebriation for him came with physical exhaustion. The combination of humor, parading around the locker room naked, and the spending of maniacal energy on the field always left him a mess after a game.

Some people got grumpy, but Pineapple laughed at everything. He also took the time to let everyone on the team know he loved them. With a paper bowl on his head he had my back to the pantry door in the kitchen. Working in my zero zone, he began sharing how much he loved me.

"I wasn't sure about you, Handsman," he said. "I thought you were the biggest little wuss I ever saw...I mean the tallest little wuss I ever saw...Whatever...you were a wuss..."

He stared straight at me to convey sincerity. I stared back over his shoulder to Lena and Fred on the other side of the sliding glass door. They were on the patio, her arms were around his neck, and she kissed him. Fred gave little response.

"...You are a f-bombing football player. You're great...You're gonna be great...You see most of these guys don't know the secret, but Fred and I do. It's work man, you gotta work to be great...Wusses don't want to work. Ponce doesn't want to work, neither do a lot of those f-bombers..."

Fred didn't take her arms away in anger or push her away. He pulled them down slowly and folded them in front and then kissed her on the forehead. I put my eyes back where they belonged when he came through the door.

"We gotta go," he said, walking into the kitchen. "Give Handsdrade a kiss and say goodnight."

"You know I love you," Pineapple said. "I should give you a big wet one right on the lips..."

"I'm cool," I said.

"Alright," he said and slapped me across the cheek. "I'll owe you the kiss."

"Put him on your 'To Do List,'" Fred said going into the living room. "Time to skate."

Pineapple's eyebrows rose. He smiled and pointed at me. "Already have," he said and then broke out laughing.

Yes, there were times I missed volleyball.

Lena on the other side of the sliding glass door had her hands on her hips. The porch light on her and I knew she was crying. Then she caught me staring and pushed out a smile.

I waved back and motioned for me to come outside with her. This would be a great opportunity to get closer. To be the ear she bended, the friend she relied on, to perhaps confess my feelings, I could talk with her on the patio glider until the sun came up…but she shook her head for me not to come. It was the only hit I took in Week Six. Not one bruise I collected thus far into the season hurt as much as her shaking me off. Nodding like I understood, I took it as time for me to skate as well.

Dad was up early again on Saturday, but there was no smell of bleach and no sound of him cleaning.

"I'm going out to breakfast," he said. "You want to come?"

I was blurry eyed after being up until four. I said no.

"I'll see you later then," he said and was out the door.

Maybe he had a date, maybe he was going to go out by himself, I didn't want to ask because I didn't want to know. By himself it was certainly going to be pathetic. If I were with him while he was teary-eyed in public, it would have been even worse.

After the donuts were flung by Fred to the stars of the game we sat for Saturday morning film as a 5-1 team. We knew what was coming.

"You guys suck." Piccou shook his head at us. "You're thinking you won 54-10, but when you look at this film, add up all the missed assignments, all the arm tackling, the lousy route running, and even the quarterbacking then you know we got issues. Coach Gugliotta, we're going to need more from this defensive unit if we're going to compete in the post season."

"F-bombing right about that." The defensive coordinator agreed.

The meeting continued and I schemed for a moment to casually ask Fred if everything was good with him and Lena, but couldn't build the courage. Best to let things stay on football and get back to being hacked about getting only four catches against f-bombing Rosemead.

"If you guys think about it, I know some of you are still friends with Ciccone online," Piccou shared as we were wrapping up. "Send him a note. His ACL is blown and he couldn't stop crying last night."

"So you saw him?" Fred said.

"His mother asked me to come after the game, so I went," Piccou said. "Hey, we know the guy is different, but imagine someone as high strung as Ciccone being unable to walk for two months? There aren't enough meds on the planet to calm him down from that. This is going to be tough on him and especially his mom. There's no dad around to help him or her out." He paused, I saw his throat bob up and down, as he struggled for composure. "I swear if any of you ever run out on your child, don't you ever say you played football for me."

Later that night I toyed with messaging Lena, but the head shake she'd given me hurt more than a bad dream involving Gilliam

Gilliam. I should have been grateful. I was healthy, I was playing, and I was playing on a winning team, but it wasn't enough.

We'd won, I played well, and the girl I was going to church to be around didn't really want me around. Doom built as I came to understand this wasn't going to play out like a movie script. I wasn't going to end up with the female lead. Instead, it felt like something out of Shakespeare.

I didn't bother to get out of bed on Sunday morning, but Dad did.

WEEK SEVEN

Read The Blitz
By Grip Teague

Is there a bigger game this coming weekend than Pomona and San Dimas? Seldom does a regular season game have league, playoff, and championship implications, but this one does. Experienced Red Devils quarterback, Jackson Johns, versus the talented but inexperienced Saints quarterback, Shane Delfman. San Dimas playmaker, Eric Johnson, going against Pomona's Devin Young and Stephon Stukes. "Bazooka" Joe Natalia, Tank Davis, this is the football apocalypse...Cathedral guard Josiah Chavez (formerly of West El Monte) has been offered by Idaho State...West Covina has officially confirmed Courtney Graye's offer from APU...The story of Charter Oak quarterback Del Chance being offered by APU has died. No one officially has said no, but after all this time no one has officially come out and said yes. It's not happening...La Mirada's Kennedy Jaynes leads Maranatha's Jake Sharper by one yard to take the rushing lead. Sharper was held to just 16 yards in the Minutemen's 21-0 loss to Valley Christian on Friday night...Finally, we caught up with El Rancho's D.K. Germany: "Other schools have said they're going to make offers, but if they don't I'm proud to go and play at Dixie State. They'll always have the advantage of being the first school to offer me."

At school on Monday I spent the day trying to convince myself I was mad at Lena, anything to avoid falling into the trap of thinking about her. I knew if I opened the door to some dream or hopeful fantasy connection in a misty meadow, I would try to rationalize away her shutting me down at the team party.

After fourth period, I came out of the administration building onto the school's lawn. A breeze blew from left to right and carried my eyes with it across the grass to the direction of the tennis courts. There, on the curb outside of the courts, Lena walked in white jeans and a yellow blouse with a sheet of paper in her hand.

I didn't know where she was going, I didn't know what she was doing, but it was as if everyone else was gone. I could see only her poetic walk. My brain relented, my heart softened, and baseline reason reminded me again, at least for now, she was still the love of my life.

On Tuesday, we went to work on the game plan for Mountain View, a program that had experienced extreme highs in recent years, but many bad ones over the course of its history. This was one of those bad years.

Bad or not, Fred worked harder than he worked all the days before. This, in turn, provoked better efforts out of the rest of us. The team may have wondered about the burst of energy, but they didn't ask and pushed through the rest of the day as if it were Arroyo week all over.

Distraction landed when Grip Teague's column was read in the locker room after practice. Teague tossed up another blurb about Billy Hudson's complaints and how he might transfer at the end of the year. None of that was new, neither was the argument being advanced that West El Monte Poly would be better off with Hudson at quarterback and Fred in the backfield with Edwards.

"You really think you're better than Fred?" Bustamonte said.

"I didn't tell Teague anything," Hudson said, loading his bag. His denials were becoming more common than Pineapple's naked parades around the locker room.

"Let it go," Basler said.

Everyone knew it was either Hudson's uncle or dad. I didn't like Hudson, but it wasn't him.

"Does anyone in here think Hudson should be playing quarterback?" Bustamonte said, looking around the room.

"I do," Fred said coming into view. "I think he should be the starting quarterback next year."

We laughed and Hudson began to storm out when Fred grabbed him by the arm.

"Everybody listen," Fred said. "Don't hassle Hudson on this. Teague needs clicks so he's trying to create controversy." Then he looked directly at Hudson. "Don't worry, I got your back and so does this team."

Hudson nodded.

"Now go before I make Pineapple kiss you."

Hudson broke a tiny smile and went out the doors

"Guys, we've already had our drama this year," Fred said. "Let's not go looking for anymore."

On Wednesday, I got home from practice and was hit with the smell of bleach and Dad cleaning the house. He was dusting shelves. The kitchen and dining room floors were freshly mopped.

"So when is Mom coming?" I said. He only did serious cleaning when he'd had a tough night or when Debbie, my mom, was coming by the house.

"She called this afternoon and wanted to have dinner with you," he said. "She'll be here in about an hour."

"Are we eating here?"

"She didn't say anything about me. I think the two of you are going out."

"So why are you cleaning?"

He tossed a used wipe into the waste can and put his hands together in nervousness. I knew my question disarmed him. If he was trying to impress her with a clean house, it was too late. I could never understand why he felt the need to impress her when she was the one who left us both. I didn't hate my mother, but I did hate the weakness my father showed when it came to her.

"I thought it would be nice," he sat down at the kitchen table. "I..."

"...Never mind," I said. There was an urge inside me to say something positive to Dad, but I couldn't cough it up. Twenty minutes later, as I was doing math homework, he knocked on my closed bedroom door to say he was leaving.

"I think you'll like Robert better the more you get to know him," Mom said. Robert was the jackwagon she moved in with after splitting from the house. We were in Arcadia, eating at Wood Ranch. The food was good and the atmosphere was light enough for her to pass on the news of her engagement to be married.

"You've been living with him for four years. Why are you getting married now?"

"Because we both feel it's time."

"So who is going to tell Dad?"

"Your father and I are divorced; he has no say in this," she said.

"Do you know Dad cleaned the house for you today," I said. "The other night I found him kneeling by the couch crying in the dark."

"What was he crying for?"

"Why do you think? It's been four years and you're still killing him. I don't know why, but he can't let it go." I didn't go the distance with my thought about it being tough to pull the knife stuck in your own back out. "There must be a reason."

The waiter brought us our food. We made small talk between stretches of silence. Off in the corner I saw someone wearing an Arcadia varsity jacket. No one else was. I couldn't wait to get mine with a football insignia, couldn't wait for people to know I caught passes from Fred-X.

"I wanted to tell you about the wedding," she said. "I also wanted to ask if you would consider coming to live with Robert and me."

I shook my head. "I don't think so."

"We're getting a bigger house in Glendora. It's really a mansion. His youngest son, Greg, is moving in. He's in junior high, and we thought, you know, maybe you could become brothers. Look after him a little bit. It would be good for you to have a sibling."

"I don't need a brother," I said.

"Well, you can play football in Glendora," she said. "Robert says they play much better football there."

"F-bomb Robert," I said, "and f-bomb the idea of moving in with you guys. Who the f-bomb is he to talk about West Poly? Have you even seen me play?"

Who the heck was Robert to talk about my team? My guys. I always hated Robert, now I hated him even more.

"I would prefer you wouldn't speak to me like that," she said. "Have you even invited me to see one of your games?"

She paused. The brief silence worked to lower the escalation of our voices.

"You've been with your father long enough. It's time for you to give me a chance to make a real home for you." She tilted closer to me and lowered her voice even more. "Besides, I don't think it's good for you to spend all your time around him. He'll just bring you down with his depressive attitude like he did me."

"Oh my god." He loved her and she hated him; it was exhausting.

"That's why I left. You know that. I shouldn't have to go over this every time we're together. I didn't need all that come down garbage with your father and I don't need it from you."

"He still f-bombing loves you."

"His pity parties are too much to take, and life's too short..."

"Unbelievable," I said and looked away.

"...And life's too short to play mama to the man that's supposed to be your husband."

We buffered a brief silence by letting waiters pass and a young family get seated in the booth across from us. A father, mother, two little girls, and it was all smiles. They sort of looked like we did once. They reminded me that our little family was never going to be together again and there was never going to be a family portrait hanging on the wall like the one in Fred's house.

I was so f-bombing sad and I didn't know why. Maybe I did, but it was too much to think about right now.

"I'm not moving in with you and Robert, and I'm not going to be someone's big brother," I said. "I'm going to keep living with Dad." A line from Pastor Domres sermon a few weeks back traced through my head about purpose, but I couldn't tag it. "Someone has to look out for him."

"Will you come to the wedding at least?"

"What does it matter?"

"You're my son," she said. Her voice was getting sharper. "It would be nice if a son came to his mother's wedding."

I thought back to the night she left and Dad sitting at the dining table at a loss to the reality of it. A slew of things came to mind about what I wanted to really say. She'd killed us, f-bombing murdered everything that was us.

"That's a hell of a lot to ask. Wanting me to go see you marry that piece of crap you left Dad for." I reached for my water and rested back in the booth. It got a quiet again.

"Dale," she started with her 'I love you' voice. "I wish this was easier..."

She talked and I didn't listen. She explained herself and I only thought about her being my mom. The one I was given, the one I was stuck with...And I knew I loved her too. F-bomb, this couldn't be the way it was supposed to be.

I swear if any of you ever run out on your child, don't you ever say you played football for me or played on one of my teams.

"...Can you understand that?"

"Whatever, I'll go, I guess."

After practice the next day, I rode with Pineapple, driving his mother's car, to Bergstrom to see El Monte play Arroyo. The Lions were still on our schedule and we were also interested in seeing how the Knights looked two weeks after losing to us.

Fred said it was good for us to go to games like this, but he told us to do it without our jackets and colors showing. I guess if you had a varsity jacket that looked like his it could cause a ruckus. My varsity jacket was stitched with a volleyball, I doubted anyone would have raised a protest or argument about it.

Of course, Fred gave us this advice and then decided not to show up. Bailing soon as practice ended, he even skipped the showers. I asked Pineapple what was up, and he said he'd tell me about it later.

The weather felt like late October should in Southern California. There was a chill to it, but no clouds in the sky and even a soul of average bravery could have handled the sixty-five degree weather with short sleeves.

First thing I picked up coming through the gate on El Monte's side of the stadium was, even without our colors, everyone noticed us. There were nods of respect, there were middle fingers, there were high fives, and there were other teams (most wearing their colors): South El Monte, Rosemead, Gabrielino, and Mt.View all had representation.

The second thing I noticed was the game announcer: **"Touchdown, Carter Ochoa"**...Then again, **"Touchdown, Carter Ochoa."** Arroyo slept walked through the first half of *The Carter Ochoa Show* and trailed 28-10 at the break.

I sat in the last open section on the south end of the grandstands. Pineapple was in line getting food.

"You guys are playing good ball," said a bearded dude with a bald head. Tattoos were running wild around his neck, down his shoulders and arms. His woman, wife, girlfriend sat back between his legs. She had a series of tattoos on her as well. I won't lie, they scared me. "The block you threw for Bustamonte against Arroyo when he scored was excellent. That's the kind of block a man makes."

"Thanks," I said. "We're you here?"

"I saw it online," he said. "You guys took the fight out of Arroyo. They've looked worn out the last two weeks."

The Arroyo band was playing and people were moving around. Pineapple came up the metal steps with a cardboard tray full of everything.

"Pineapple!" A small guy in a wife beater and black derby called over. "You going to share any of that you fat f-bomb?"

"Sure am Wuizar, I'm going to share some of this with you too," he said flexing the bicep on his right arm before sitting down next to me. "In two weeks I'm going to have me some Lion steaks!"

Boos came our way. When they cussed, cursed, or flipped off Pineapple it was like doing it to a cousin. Of the eight schools in the Mission Valley League, six were part of the district. Most of us grew up together, played Little League and AYSO against each other.

"Hey, mofo!" The small guy spoke again. His shoulder had a tattoo of a face with sunglasses and smoke hanging out of the corner of its mouth. "Where's f-bombing Ritter? I thought you guys couldn't do anything without his permission?" His friends around him laughed.

"He's out with your mama Wuizar," Pineapple yelled back. "He sent us a text to let you know she won't be home tonight."

Now the people in our section laughed.

"I see how it is," he said. "Maybe I'll see you after the game?"

"Come see me now," Pineapple said. "Nobody's going to stop you." He beckoned him with his hands to come. "I'll make some room for you right next to me."

"Man don't get into a fight," I said taking some of his popcorn. "We're playing tomorrow night."

"I'm not going to let that fool punk me," Pineapple said. "Wuizar went to Potrero with me and then changed over to Kranz. He talks a lot, but only does something when everybody's piled up and no one's watching." He gestured back over at him. "You coming Wuizar?"

Wuizar turned his attention back to the field.

"I told you he wasn't coming, f-bombing wuss. All talk unless he's got some homies around." Pineapple looked back up at him.

"You just let me know when you want to come man; I'll make you feel right at home."

The crowd jeered Wuizar and he raised high a middle finger to let everyone know what he thought.

"Hermano," the bearded bald guy full of tats said to Pineapple, "A piece like that will just try to hurt you. You gotta be cool."

"I'm cool, it's that fool," Pineapple said. His eyes kept covering the space of heads between him and Wuizar. I could tell he was playing with the idea of going after Wuizar now. "I don't mind it if somebody f-bombs with me, but when they start talking crap it pisses me off."

"Maintain," the bald guy said. "He's not going anywhere but la cárcel."

"La cárcel?" I asked.

"Prison," Pineapple said to me. "Who are you? Wait, you Machado's brother Benny?"

Pineapple and the bald guy traded hand slaps and a shake.

"That f-bomber still in Arizona?"

"Simon," Benny said. "Jimmy's f-bombing *La Ilorona*, crying and wanting to come home. I told him he could come home, but I'd kick his butt when he does."

As the conversation continued I discovered Benny played at El Monte a dozen years before. Caught a lot of passes and now was driving a forklift in a UPS warehouse. He knew all about us and was most likely one of the thousands who lived for prep football on the internet.

"Tell him I said to suck it," Pineapple said.

Benny smiled, nodded, and put his eyes back on the football game.

"You going to beat my El Monte team when you play them?"

"You should root for your brother's school," Pineapple said. "We got Fred-X."

"El Monte's got Carter Ochoa," Benny said.

Pineapple agreed. "F-bomber's good."

They bantered back and forth. They talked about Arroyo, Rosemead, and Anthony Ciccone's injury. By the time Pineapple got back to his food, I'd finished off half the popcorn and one of his hot dogs.

"So," I said wiping at my mouth. "You said you were going to tell me where Fred went after practice."

"F-bombing Handsdrade you ate all my food," Pineapple said, reaching for his Coke.

"You were f-bombing talking the whole time," I said. "What about Fred?"

"He went to workout."

"After practice?"

He slurped the drink through a straw until the remaining ice made static sounds. Then he belched. "Quarterback coach," he said double checking Wuizar. "He feels like he's got to do more work. Don't tell anybody."

Edwards was far to our right, talking with our guys. Bustamonte was at the top of the stadium, behind us, sweet talking some girl. If I craned my neck I could make out Coach Jackson on a bench towards the top in the middle.

"Really?"

Pineapple nodded.

We were sitting here, enjoying ourselves. Carter Ochoa was destroying the Arroyo defense and Fred was working to get his scholarship.

The Knights rallied in the second half, but El Monte beat Arroyo 34-24. On the way to the parking lot, I asked Pineapple about Benny.

"Was that guy a good football player?"

"Real good."

"What happened?"

"What do you mean what happened? He finished playing and that was it."

"Why didn't he keep playing?"

"I don't know," Pineapple said. "Maybe nobody wanted him."

Fred completed seventeen of eighteen passes in the first half for four touchdowns. Edwards scored on a long run and we took a 46-0 lead over Mountain View at the break. I caught the fifth Fred-X touchdown delivery with three minutes to play in the third and the offense was done for the night.

The clock was running and after one more defensive series, Gelbaugh and the rest of the starters were set to come out. In the Rosemead game, we were pulled at roughly the same time, but Ciccone and his Panther friends at least hit us for a while. View didn't, and I didn't like it. Two weeks in a row no one had hammered me. My experience was limited, but this wasn't football. Not when we were dressed for war and end up in a contest that was little more than two hand touch.

I understood what Coach Piccou was doing. The Vikings weren't going to challenge us and he didn't want anybody to get hurt. In the back of my head, I could hear the voice chirping away at me about the stats I was missing out on. Tonight was a chance to get seriously fat. The trade off for not getting hit was making catches and scoring touchdowns. I wasn't getting much of either.

Sucking it up, I tried to refocus my focus. Did I really want to be on the field with Billy Hudson running the show? Thoughts of playing with him next year were bad enough and it wasn't like he was going to share the ball. He'd be throwing to Ponce every chance he got.

Pineapple pulled off his pads and jersey, Bustamonte took to wearing a baseball cap to keep his hair under cover, and the rest of the veterans were doing something similar. The battle was over, but the voice kept on about my catches, the ones I needed to get now. I kept my gear on.

Fred worked on signals and encouraged his jerk backup. Patiently, with a team first mentality, Fred pointed at a laminated sheet to show the sophomore where the best opportunities were against the View defense.

I wanted to be Fred, I wanted to be great, but I wanted my touches all the time. I fully understood Bustamonte's argument about always being open. Didn't think I'd turn into something like this, but I had. The clapping sound of the ball coming into my hands was life giving and highly addictive. Of course I was always open, good receivers always are.

Behind our bench, Lena and a friend were looking at photos on a camera. She turned her head at that moment and caught me staring. I quickly moved my eyes back to the field to see Feliz close in on a tackle.

He planted, the bad ankle rolled, and the Mountain View lineman blew him up. For the Vikings the result was a touchdown; for us Feliz not only shredded his ankle but broke his wrist trying to fend off the pulling guard. Edgar Escandon later said he could hear the wrist snap.

When they got him to the bench, it was clear Feliz's season was wrecked. Gelbaugh lobbied Piccou and Gugliotta for the defense to have one more series to get some payback, but he wasn't let back on the field. It was no one's fault, the Mountain View guy didn't do anything dirty, and we couldn't risk another injury.

The Vikings scored another late touchdown and we won 56-16, but the good feeling we had in the third quarter was lost. Feliz wasn't Gelbaugh, but he was critical to the defense.

※

Grip Teague: Truth of the matter is, this is on Coach Piccou and his staff. The game was won and all of his starters should have been out. What was Feliz doing on the field?

Bald Guy: I'm reading the stuff on our message boards, it's getting ugly.

Grip Teague: What are they saying?"

Bald Guy: This is from Cool Jets: "The biggest problem for the Scots this year has been Piccou...Coach Jackson never would have let this happen."...And from Kansas: "Piccou is a poor game manager and the least prepared of all the area coaches and re-lies too much on Fred-X to save his butt."... Finally from Jorge Grande: "The West El Monte defense was bad enough. Without Feliz, they're a one and done in the playoffs. This is Piccou's fault for leaving him in the game too long. Stupid decision..."

Grip Teague: By Monday morning Piccou is going to be ac-cused of being the number one puppy killer in America...I know that sounds gross, but you know how these boards work.

Bald Guy: Believe me, I'm only reading what is okay to read. According to the stuff I'm seeing on the boards right now he's al-ready a bank robber, sex offender, thief, drug trafficker, pimp, puppy killer...Um what else...Oh yeah and the stupidest coach ever.

Grip Teague: I don't know BG, you'd like to think people would a be a little more tasteful.

Bald Guy: These are message boards, amigo.

We found out San Dimas beat Pomona 21-20 when we came through the doors of Fat John's house for the team party. Grip Teague's voice could be heard reading scores and giving updates. The Saints and Red Devils were the main topic.

Twenty minutes later news came from the hospital about Feliz. He was going to need surgery, pins, cast, the whole deal. We ate our pizza, drank our soda, and wished we had somebody to be angry with.

Gelbaugh left and the party was over. It was the worst win, but I wasn't sure if we were feeling bad about what happened to Feliz or for ourselves because we knew what it meant to lose him for the rest of the season.

I was certain we'd beat Pomona if we got another crack at them. We knew we could outscore them, but San Dimas had stopped them. Up to now, Pomona had not been held to twenty-points. If it made me nervous, I knew there were bigger football brains in our program having concerns.

"Guys," Fred clapped his hands together to get our attention. Everyone was following Gelbaugh's cue. "If there's a time for us to hang out together, tonight is it. This is football, people get hurt, but we don't honor them by getting depressed. We honor them by strapping it up and making San Dimas sorry for showing up to play us in the finals. Right? So next man up take care of business." He didn't scream or shout, he sounded like a teacher handing out a home-work assignment. "We are all still sons of Scotland. Alba gu bràth."

"Alba gu bràth," we answered in calm unison.

Saturday morning was subdued. Fred passed out the donuts. The coaching staff pointed out our flaws, but Piccou never built the energy to come out and say we sucked. For the most part, our execution had been close to flawless, but I was learning there was never a perfect game film. Something was always wrong, somewhere, and the coaches were sure to find out.

"Needless to say, Feliz is upset about missing the rest of the season," Piccou said at the end. "Be good teammates, let him know you guys are thinking about him. This was his third year on varsity. I'm bummed his high school career had to end this way."

We agreed, we nodded, we said we would reach out to him, but all I could think of was Gabrielino on Friday and another opportunity to build my stats. Dan Feliz was one of the best guys on the team, but he was gone and there was nothing we could do about it.

Fred and Gelbaugh understood it, and I understood it. Time for the next man up: sophomore outside linebacker Jaime Nguyen.

I slid into church without Mr. Umphries seeing me. During the pastoral prayer, I even offered a blessing up for Dan Feliz and for myself that I wouldn't get hurt. When an older woman led the children out I did everything I could to keep my eyes from searching for Lena.

"Isaiah chapter 32 talks about peace being the fruit of righteousness and the effect of righteousness will be quietness and confidence forever," Domres preached.

It occurred to me, as I sat there, that I had put Lena on lockdown for most of the week. I'd seen her on Monday and stole a glance at her on Friday, but that was it. Getting out of bed to an empty house on Sunday morning, I didn't stop to consider where Dad had gone nor did I think anything about Lena Durkin as I walked to church.

The only conclusion I came to was I liked the sound of Pastor Domres voice, even if I didn't pay much attention to what he had to say.

"It's archaic in some places to do an altar call. To invite people to repentance and restored life," Domres went on. "That's fine but my Bible doesn't call us to a shift of attitude, but to repentance. The worship team is going to lead us in song. This is your decision, not my decision for you. It's not my responsibility to count heads at the altar, it's your choice. If you need peace, if you need to be restored, I would be honored to meet and pray with you."

People got up, but not me. What for? Men, women, even teenagers began going forward to pray. Then I saw Dad step into an aisle on the right side of the sanctuary. Mr. Umphries went with him and they kneeled together. The question of how he got back to church eluded me for a few seconds and then I realized I saw it right in front of my eyes: Mr. Umphries.

With everyone's attention drawn forward, I went out the back. There was no way I was going to be part of that scene. I wasn't going to be part of the hugging, the crying, and the inevitable effort to get me to do the same thing.

I went through the foyer, then the glass doors, and down the steps. Lena wasn't worth it, having to sit next to Dad while he cried during the service wasn't worth it. My church days were officially over.

WEEK EIGHT

Read The Blitz
By Grip Teague

And down the stretch they come...If Arcadia loses to Muir this week, which they probably will, the Apaches can kiss the post-season goodbye...Bigger question is will Pomona rebound against Rowland?...Los Altos and Charter Oak will bruise each other up, you've got Jeremy Chandos against Del Chance. Should be good, should be close, but I like the Chargers...For kicks do you believe Gabrielino is going to give West El Monte any trouble? Can you say blowout? The biggest problem for the Fighting Scots is they only have two quality wins. Arroyo and the opener against Downey. Every other win has been of the cupcake variety, which won't get you any respect when brackets are put together... Maranatha's Jake Sharper has retaken the rushing lead from La Mirada's Kennedy Jaynes. Both players should be past 2,000 yards by the end of Week Ten...Does anyone remember when the Minutemen used to pass the ball?...Next Sunday night be sure to click on as Bald Guy will be doing his playoff breakdowns going into Week

Nine...Teams that will make it, teams that will surprise,
and teams that will be turning in their gear. It's always
a good show...Especially when he's wrong.

S o much was being made of homecoming and winning the big homecoming game, I didn't understand it. When I was a freshman I went to it and left halfway through. When I was a sophomore I stayed home and played the first person shooter game Fred's brothers were now obsessed with on my X-Box.

Now that I was on the team, I still didn't get it. More than anything else it was a distraction. The pep rally would be longer. Guys were scrambling for dates for Saturday night's homecoming dance, bouncing potentials off each other, discussing it over sips of water.

Fortunately for Fred, he had his. Pineapple scored a date with Mona Carrillo, cheerleader, number eleven on his list. Mona came with the essential curves and, according to gossip, a willingness to employ them from time to time. Our left tackle was very happy about this.

"That chick's got some nice hand warmers," he said to me at lunch on Monday. "You know what I mean?"

"No," I said. "What do you mean?"

He rubbed his hands together and reached out with them. I didn't get it at first, and then it came to me, he was talking about her chest. If Padilla had seen him she would have found an excuse to discipline him for his sexist behavior and suspend Piccou again.

The other distraction was the parade of former West El Monte Poly players who came to speak to us after practice Tuesday through

Thursday. What they said was good. The first guy told us to keep on fighting and never quit. The second guy told us to never quit and keep on fighting. The third told us to fight for each other and never quit on the team.

None of them talked about a great victory or big win because the teams they played on didn't win at all.

A win against Gabrielino was going to improve us to 7-1 and, better still, 5-0 in the Mission Valley League. Fred told us in the summer we were only guaranteed ten games. So, we didn't need anyone telling us it was an important game, we already knew it was important.

"Handsdrade!" Fred said, coming off the field from Thursday's practice. The rah-rah session with the alum was a yawning festival none of us would openly admit to. "What do you think of football? Glad you're playing?"

"Love it," I said. No lie. I'd lie about other things, but not football.

The winning was good, but I truly loved being part of something. It felt like we were one force moving forward together, almost unstoppable. Volleyball didn't give the same feeling; I never got to hear cleats marching and clacking over the cement while playing volleyball. It was corny, but it all jelled in my emotions as if something great was rising.

"Someone asked me about you," he said. "Do you know who James Splitorff is?"

"I don't know him, but I heard of him. Was he the one talking to you when we were throwing at Bonita this summer?"

"Yeah, he played receiver at Temple City and is on staff at Grandview State in Nebraska. He was talking to me online last night and asked about you."

"Really?" I was stunned. No one had mentioned anything about me playing in college. There wasn't stack of letters sitting inside my locker. "To play football?"

"He asked about your grades and says he likes your hands," Fred said. "Might not be a bad deal for you after next season."

"Would you go there?" I said. It would be cool having my quarterback with me out in Nebraska.

Fred turned to looked back at the field and then shook his head at me. "You know we get more attention here on Friday nights than Grandview does when it plays. There's no way I'm playing there."

It wasn't an insult for Fred to imply Grandview might be good enough for me, but not for him. He was Fred-X and on track to throw forty touchdown passes this season (down from fifty). I was only a first year receiver, finally putting my uniform on correctly.

Something in letterform would have been good, something I could leave out casually for teammates to notice. I pondered life in Nebraska and wondered if I could really leave if the opportunity came.

Cold, new people, and then the image of Lena Durkin dropped all over it. I'd be a thousand miles away from everybody I knew and from the girl I was desperately trying to not be in love with. What did it matter? The girl never flirted or gave me a flicker of hope, I was done dreaming about her.

...But not really.

"Do you think I could play college football?" I said.

"Why not?" He said. "You've got great hands and decent size." He stopped and looked around again. "Just don't say anything to Boosty about it."

"Are they interested in him?"

Fred shook his head. "They're passing."

"Why? He's great."

Fred held up his hands. "His hands aren't. Bad technique and they don't like the way he runs his routes. Don't say anything, I don't want him to lose focus."

"I won't," I said. Like Fred, Bustamonte desperately wanted to play college ball. I wasn't the hippest to how all the recruiting worked, but Grandview was a Division-three college. If Division-three colleges were passing on Bustamonte then he was going to end up at East Los Angeles.

"Of course, you know if you go to a place like Grandview," Fred said, "you'll have to forget about hooking back up with Desi." He laughed at his joke.

"Is that why...I mean..." I caught the foot just before inserting it into my mouth and saying Lena's name.

"Is that why you don't see me falling over Lena, telling her I love her and giving her a promise ring and all of that?"

"Yeah," I said, appreciating Fred-X the mind reader.

"I'm going to tell you something and I hope you believe me because I know you and Lena are friends," he said and then let some of the guys coming off the field pass by and go through the doors. "I don't use her. I'm not having sex with her and I'm not trying to get down her top or pull off her pants. I've respected her."

"She's never said..."

"I know," he said cutting me off, "I think Lena's great. I respect her and I think if things were a little bit different I'd really be in love with her, but the thing is, I'm leaving. I'm going to go somewhere and play football and if the worst happens I'll play Division-two, but that means I'm going to be leaving the state because I don't want to play at APU. How would it be if I got all serious and just dumped her?"

"She loves you," I said. A voice, sounding a lot like the voice complaining about not getting enough catches, said I should have lied to help my cause.

"I know she does," he said, "but I'm a football player first. I'm going to make it, I'm not going to be like Machado or even Splitorff, and you'll see it happen with Burns at Arroyo, and Ochoa at El Monte, they're not going anywhere. I am, and something serious with Lena right now won't help her or me. Imagine if something happened, if told her I wanted to marry her someday?"

I nodded and we went into the locker room. Pineapple was walking, talking on his cell phone, and completely naked.

How bad was Gabrielino this season? They were so bad I caught two touchdown passes in the first half, we scored fifty-six-points, and none of our starters played after we came out of the locker room for the third quarter.

"A little late to start thinking about safety, Piccou!" A voice yelled from our side of the stands.

Fred was nominated as a homecoming prince, but when they said he'd have to stay on the field during halftime he turned it down. Bustamonte didn't mind and ended up winning. With uniform on, hair perfectly combed and flowing back, he got to stand next to Desi.

They made a nice couple.

"We cool?" He said to me after on the sidelines.

"Don't even worry about it," I told him. "We're totally cool."

Billy Hudson was running the offense. He wasn't Fred. He acted like a leader and said things like a leader, but it was forced. Like he was reading lines out of a book titled: *How to be a High School Quarterback: In 10 Easy Lessons*. When he threw five touchdown passes in a game then I'd give him the respect that comes with throwing five touchdown passes in a game. Until then he was more of a scrub than I was.

No leading or rah-rah was necessary for a game like this. Get the play from Jackson, run the play, and get the next one. There was no strategy, the clock was running and even the Gabrielino parents were waving white flags.

Against Gabrielino, I could have played quarterback and the offense wouldn't have missed a beat. The Eagles were a playoff team a year ago, but graduation, transfers, and a bad coaching change late in July did them in before the season even started.

"No!" Jackson yelled to Hudson. The game was in its final minute. "Don't you change the play! Take a knee!"

Hudson changed the play and threw a deep pass with us leading 77-7. It fell incomplete and brought a loud chorus of shouts from the Gabrielino side of the field. Its remaining fans were angry and the Eagles coaching staff was starting to howl but calmed when they saw our staff's reaction.

"Get him out of there!" Coach Piccou shouted.

"Get in there and take two knees for me," Jackson said to Fred, who sprinted on as Hudson walked off ripping down on his chip strap. "What the f-bomb?" Jackson said to him as he went by. "Just to get your stats you're going to make us all look bad?"

"They were going to blitz!" Hudson said. "They weren't going to let us just line up in Victory."

"All you had to do was take a knee!" Piccou said. "So take a knee when we tell you!"

The Billy Hudson contingent in the stands rained curses down on Piccou.

I'd come to understand why people played football instead of volleyball, but after adding up all Piccou had been through, just in the time I'd been playing, I couldn't understand why he bothered with any of it. When something got screwed up in volleyball nobody was there to scream about it. If you screwed up in football there were thousands of experts in the stands and online to remind you how awful you were.

Fred took two snaps, the game ended, the Gabrielino staff understood and quickly took Piccou's apology.

"Piccou! You suck!" Came from our side of the field.

We sat spread out, couch and carpet, in the Ritter living room to see Grip Teague's highlights. It was okay, I scored twice while the game was somewhat relevant. My season totals were now thirty-eight catches and ten touchdowns.

With the lack of an upset around the valley or even a decent game, our passing on Gabrielino with a 77-7 lead made us public enemy number one on Teague's show and the message boards.

Grip Teague: It's like a political fumble. You want to know who screwed up, who knew it, and when?

Bald Guy: With all the heat Skip Piccou has taken this year from the drama around Pineapple Bartholomew to last week's injury to Dan Feliz this is just another distraction.

Grip Teague: By the way, you realize you violated the memo from the West El Monte administration asking us to refrain from using the nickname "Pineapple" in regard to Carl Bartholomew.

Bald Guy: You mean Pineapple? We're not supposed to use the word Pineapple?

Grip Teague: Yes, do not say Pineapple as it wouldn't be politically correct. So don't say Pineapple.

Bald Guy: Pineapple?

Grip Teague: Yes, don't say Pineapple.

Bald Guy: Okay, I won't say Pineapple. Question, though, do you really believe Piccou tried to run the score up on Gabrielino?

Grip Teague: I wasn't there, but no. Why would he? However, these people do: "...another night of incompetence from Skip Piccou and his staff"... "What horrible sportsmanship, remember West El Monte what goes around comes around"... "Disgrace"... "They've been running up the score all season just to get people to avoid talking about how bad they really are"... "They did it just to pad Fred-X stats"...

Bald Guy: For the record, I got a text here that says the starters had been pulled and Fred-X was out of the game. Along with...

Grip Teague: Don't say it.

Bald Guy: Don't say Pineapple?

For the next hour, Hudson defended his actions as he moved from room to room.

"They were going to blitz, what am I supposed to do?" He said. "They were going to hurt someone, so I changed the play."

We were in the kitchen, loading up our plates with more nachos as highlights of other games were shown and discussed.

"You're just supposed to f-bombing eat the ball," Bustamonte said. "You made us all look bad."

"Chill on the language, Mrs. Ritter doesn't like it," Pineapple said.

"To who, Gabrielino?" Hudson said. "We're not playing Gabrielino again."

"Just eat the ball next time, scrub," Fat John said.

"Or give it to Fat John, he'll eat it for you," Basler tossed in.

"With salsa, esé," Fat John said.

"My thing is if you're going to throw that pass at least complete it," Fast Eddie said. "Ponce was wide open."

Grip Teague: We need to clear up, again, something that has been going around the message boards. Fred Ritter, Fred-X, was not at quarterback for the Fighting Scots when they threw the late pass against Gabrielino.

Bald Guy: That's right, Grip, it was backup Billy Hudson, the heir apparent to Fred-X after this season. There seems to have been some confusion on the West El Monte sideline at the end of the game. I printed out this email that was sent to me by Billy Hudson's dad. Again, we weren't at the game, but according to the email...Hudson went deep after reading a blitz from the Gabrielino defense. Even though the game was in the closing seconds of a second half running clock, no call came in from the sidelines for the Fighting Scots to line up in the victory formation...Which most teams do when they a have a seventy point lead.

Grip Teague: This just heats up everything. One, you've got the offended Gabby fans. Two, you got the bad rap circulating about Fred-X. Three, Billy Hudson, and now, four, everyone wants to know what is going on with Piccou and the coaching staff.

Bald Guy: As of right now we don't have any complaints from the Gabrielino coaches...I just got this text from another area coach that said Piccou pulled his starters at halftime. He also doesn't believe a pass was called but that it was changed at the line of scrimmage.

Grip Teague: And with all this everyone has lost sight of this fact, West El Monte is now 7-1 and 5-0 in the Mission Valley League.

"Enough of these guys," Gelbaugh clicked off Teague's show with the remote.

"Come on, we're watching that!" Edwards said.

"There's one minute left and we got El Monte next week," he said feeding a DVD into the player. "We got to get ready."

"I'm not going to watch El Monte film tonight," Bustamonte said.

"You're going to watch this!" Pineapple said, standing in front of us. "We got to get serious."

The collective groan rose again as Gelbaugh selected and clicked play.

"Not *Braveheart* again dude," Basler said, "come on."

Fred stepped back into the living room with a fresh plate and looked at Gelbaugh with a smile. "We wearing blue paint to school this week?"

"Aye," Gelbaugh feebly attempted in a Scottish accent. "All week."

Saturday came and Piccou explained to us how much we sucked, but it was hard to make the case following a seventy point victory. Most of the guys were finalizing details for the homecoming dance.

"So you're really not going?" Fred said to me in the locker room. After our light run, my body was ready for another game. I hadn't been hit since the Rosemead game and had not been really whacked since Arroyo. "I thought you and Desi still had a little something going?"

"Nope," I said. "It's all good."

"Good for you," he said. "I'm getting there."

I didn't ask Fred what he meant but took it as meaning he and Lena were on the verge of breaking up. A twinge of excitement ran through me, but I checked it into place with a series of lies, to myself, about how I couldn't care less. I was now two weeks into being free of Lena contact.

Fred was in a hurry. I wasn't and planned to shower. He went out the double doors and Bustamonte came and asked me, again, if I was okay about him and Desi being named the homecoming king and queen. I told him it was fine. Since his initial cold shoulder when I first came out for football we'd become solid teammates. Except now it almost seemed like he was going over the top.

"Seriously, you and Desi are done?" He said as we went to the showers.

"Yeah," I said. "We never really were. Why? You want to ask her out officially?"

"Yeah."

"So ask her out," I told him.

"You don't mind?"

"Boosty, it's cool." I had to laugh at how far my relationship with him had come. Now he was Boosty to me. At the beginning of spring all he called me was white boy. "If anyone asks, tell them she dumped me for you. This way it looks like you stole her from me. Makes you look cooler."

"You're alright, Handsdrade."

"I can be."

Lena was walking through the school parking lot with me. Something got us both laughing and she leaned against a car door. She was wearing tan cords and a white blouse with an unbuttoned vest that matched her pants. I kissed her and she kissed me back. We seemed to smile at how long it took us to get to this point. We kissed again…

How or why I woke up at seven on Sunday was a mystery. I tried to return to sleep and crawl back into the dream, but the way was shut. Morning landed fully with its clarity and the memory began to erode. Mentally I saved her face, her smile, and the sensation of my arms around her.

I stared cooly at the knobs on my dresser, knowing I'd never again be back in that place. Then to the picture of us on my nightstand. Even the best of dreams were experiments in suffering.

After leaving the team meeting on Saturday, I watched college football, then a movie, and played Madden on my X-Box. I didn't miss going to the homecoming dance at all. A little soreness from Friday's game would have been welcome as an excuse to stay in bed, but I didn't have any. Didn't get the chance to inflate my stats, didn't get sore, practically a wasted weekend except for the dream.

I stretched getting out of bed, the shower was going in Dad's room. He was, of course, getting ready to go to church. If he hoped we were going to walk in as father and son then he had another thing coming.

The bruises on my body were a neat looking patchwork, but they didn't hurt unless I really pressed them. I wasn't sick and I was a starting receiver on one of the best teams in the San Gabriel Valley. I was the favorite receiver of the best quarterback in the valley, but I wasn't happy.

Her face, her smile, and the sensation of my arms around her in the dream came back to me. Was I really unhappy because Lena shook me off two weeks ago? Was it because Mom was getting married again? Was it because Dad was going back to church?

I should have been happy.

Getting back into bed, I waited for Dad to knock at the door and invite me to go with him. I waited until I fell back to sleep and a knock came at 11:45. The door opened and he stuck his head in.

"I brought home taco truck," Dad said. "You want to watch the Rams game with me?"

WEEK NINE

Read The Blitz
By Grip Teague

There is trouble in San Dimas. The Saints are being in-
vestigated to see if an ineligible player suited up for them
and it could cost them their season. More to come...MVL
title on the line this week. Might be a surprise to some,
but I'm going with Carter Ochoa and the El Monte Lions.
It's been a long time since West El Monte has been chal-
lenged. I think they're ready for a fall...We've confirmed
that former Arcadia/Bishop Amat running back Jefferson
Pham, who had enrolled at St. John Bosco, has now left
the state to move in with family in Arizona...After Jeremy
Chandos' performance against Charter Oak in Week
Eight we now see why the coaching staff wasn't devas-
tated when running back, Julius Morales transferred to
Cathedral in the spring...For the record Morales was in-
jured early and has received sparse playing time in the
Phantoms backfield...You heard it hear first, Mayfair
wins its division...Since beating Downey in Week Two, La
Serna has lost six in a row. How does that happen at La
Serna?...Paraclete's Calvin Greene has received an offer

from San Jose State...We love message board rumors...
Speaking of La Serna there are message board threads
on various sites saying Arcadia HC, Tab Figueroa will
be the next Lancers head coach...This might be news to
current La Serna head man Tom Crawl. We'll keep you
updated.

Monday started with news about Pineapple getting an offer from Humboldt State. A Division-two school offering a full ride. He'd had some letters from D-three schools, including Grandview, but this was his first legitimate offer.

"Bustamonte's mad," Fred said as we came out of the locker room for practice. He had a blue cross on his forehead. All the seniors did to signify the importance of getting ready for this week's game.

"Yeah," I said. "I heard he was upset about Desi not making out with him at homecoming."

"Desi?" Fred shrugged. "He's mad about Pineapple getting that offer."

"Why?"

"Because it wasn't him."

"Gentlemen," Nick Hudson (Billy's father) said, walking by us and into the locker room. Nick was an alcoholic thin man with some blonde hair up front and a lot missing in the back. I didn't know him, but his appearance and reputation made him seem like a real douche.

"What's he doing here?" I said.

"He's meeting with Piccou. Coach is still burned about what happened at the end of the Gabrielino game," Fred said.

"I'd be worried if I were you. If it goes his way you'll be playing running back."

"I think Hudson's going to transfer when the season is over," Fred said as we hit the field. "So you won't have to worry about playing with him next year."

"Really? Where?"

"I don't know, probably Cathedral."

Our cleats clacked on the hard ground going to the field. The sun was shining and the air was cold. It was so much better than coming out to practice in August. Coach Jackson and Coach Gugliotta were going to run the opening. Hopefully, Piccou wouldn't kill Mr. Hudson and join us before the day was over.

"You think Pineapple is going to go to Humboldt?" I said.

"Yeah," Fred said. "I think it's a great deal for him."

"Would you go there?"

"I'd have to see all my options first."

On Tuesday, Hudson was at practice and Fred was still the quarterback. Piccou, who had avoided beating up Mr. Hudson and getting suspended, was there barking at us. We were all there, but Bustamonte was out of it. He was short tempered and dropping passes.

"Are we cool?" I asked him during a water break.

"It's not you," he said and walked off.

When Edwards tweaked his right knee practice was halted for Sondra to take a look at it. Piccou called us all to midfield.

"You alright, Edwards?" Piccou said.

"Always."

Coach nodded and then looked at the rest of us. "Does anybody know when we're getting our championship rings?"

We looked around at each other.

"I said, 'Does anybody know when we are getting our championship rings?'"

"After we beat Pomona in the finals," Pineapple said.

"Really? I thought they were coming sometime this week because you guys are moving around here like you've already won something. Let me tell you right now, you haven't won jack...You don't even have a share of a league title yet."

It was rah-rah time again, but since it wasn't in the locker room or in the film room it came across as fresh. It was also a little scary because he was putting fear into us in broad daylight at the fifty-yard line.

"You think because you've got El Monte here at home this thing is over? We don't have Feliz, Lee is banged up, Edwards is lying to me about his knee being okay, and I got a bunch of backups who care more about their stats than team victories."

Part of me wanted to believe that was for Hudson and his group, but I couldn't stop thinking Piccou got a glimpse inside my soul. It was paranoia to assume people knew my thoughts, but it always worried me that they could. I fought to keep my thinking straight. Everything would get taken care of if we won. Fred would get his scholarship, Bustamonte would get something for sure, Pineapple might get a better offer, Gelbaugh would get some looks, and I'd be considered a good football player with D-three potential. Maybe I'd get some residual Fred-X praise from classmates when I walked the halls of the administration building.

"Unless something changes in the way of focus over the next two days, we're going to get our butts kicked on our own field. Then you want to know what happens? You're going to lose the coin flip for the playoffs because fortune doesn't favor the lazy and we're going to be playing our first playoff game in Paso Robles. They only do three things in Paso Robles: eat meat, make meth, and play football."

Wednesday's practice was better. Bustamonte's hands improved, but his attitude didn't. Fred worried about him losing it in the game and told me to be ready to pick up the slack. Music to my ears because a twelve catch effort would put me at fifty for the season.

After practice Boosty cleared out early. Not showering and, even more obvious, not spending a half hour grooming his hair before going into public. My hair was demanding attention and

Fred was combing his wet mop back in the mirror, when Gelbaugh came by.

"My house tonight," he said, the blue cross brightly painted on his forehead. "Be there." Then he walked off.

"Hey Gelbaugh, man," Fred said. "I'm with you, but I don't want to sit through *Braveheart* again."

"Be there!" The double doors kicked open and Gelbaugh was gone.

"How many times do you think he's seen *Braveheart* this year?" I said.

"I don't know, but I know how many times I've seen it. Dude watches it almost every night," Fred said. "He loves putting the blue paint on."

"You think he'll wear it on his wedding night?"

Fred laughed. "I wouldn't put it past him. I can see him coaching little Gelbaughs in twenty years and making them wear it."

Eight of us were at Gelbaugh's on Wednesday to watch the movie. Some guys worked their social media while it was playing, Pineapple fell asleep on the carpet, Gelbaugh and Feliz, with cast on his wrist and boot on his foot, stared at the flat-screen and mouthed the dialogue. Bustamonte didn't show.

"Did you ever talk to Boosty?" I said to Fred as another battle was taking place. A head rolled, blood spurted. Even after seeing it thirty times the battle scenes were still cool. "Did he say what's been burning his butt this whole week?"

Pineapple was balled up in a fetal position that looked way to awkward for someone his size. With eyes closed he yawned and issued some 'Crushed Pineapple' out of his backside.

"I told you," Fred said quietly and gestured his head towards Pineapple. "That's why."

"It's not his fault he got an offer."

"The clock's ticking," Fred said ending the conversation and turning back to the flat-screen.

The team was notified, by text, to report to the football room before school on Thursday morning. It was an odd time for a meeting and our fears were something else was coming down. Something bad. Maybe Piccou did punch Hudson's dad after all.

The coaching staff came in followed by Bryan Crumsey, but no one else. He closed the door.

"This will be real quick guys," Piccou said. "So listen up."

"Are you moving Fred to running back?" Pineapple said. We laughed nervously.

"Pine...Carl," Crumsey started and corrected himself. "If not we're trading him to Marshall." hanged mid-sentence. "Chill."

"Were going to give Ritter one more chance," Piccou said, "if not we're trading him to Marshall."

"I'd prefer Cathedral," Fred said.

I don't know how Billy Hudson handled all the indirect comments, but then again I didn't care. I was happy to see Piccou joking. Whatever was about to be shared wouldn't be devastating.

"Okay listen up," Crumsey said. "No one's done anything wrong, but we've had some complaints about the blue paint."

"We used the blue crosses last year," Gelbaugh said.

"Yeah, but things are different this year," Crumsey said. "A cross is cool if it's Ash Wednesday, but it's not Ash Wednesday, plus its paint not ash, and it comes across like you are promoting religion on campus."

"It's football," Gelbaugh said. "We're the Fighting Scots."

"We appreciate it, but we just don't want this to turn into a big thing," Crumsey said and then lowered his voice a little as if to make sure we were the only ones who could hear him. "And you know there is always someone out there looking to make a big thing out of something."

"So we're cool if we just don't make it into a cross?" Pineapple said.

"Yeah."

"Cool," Pineapple said. "You guys cool?" He looked at the team and everyone nodded.

It didn't matter to me, I wasn't a senior and had no intention of wearing the blue paint.

On Friday morning Pineapple, Gelbaugh, and Basler showed up with a blue Jesus fish painted on their foreheads.

"What do you think?"

Gelbaugh stood next to me at midfield as we looked at El Monte. The pregame warm-ups were going on. Through the bars of the mask, I could see blue covering the right side of his face and three lines of blue running horizontal under his left eye. The maniac look was accomplished again.

"I think we're going to win," I said, not knowing what he expected me to say.

"Dudes over there are hungry," he said then spit. "If we're going to win tonight, we're going to have to win tonight."

Duh? I thought, of course we were going to have to win.

"What I mean, Andrade," he said as if he was reading my mind, "is they ain't afraid of us and ain't going to roll over because we got Fred-X slinging it."

Piccou and the coaching staff gave us the same spiel every week. Even when we played Arcadia, Mt.View, Gabrielino, they told us no one was going to give us a win because they were afraid of West El Monte Poly. If we really wanted the win we were going to have to go out and take it. If we really wanted a Mission Valley League title we were going to have to go out and take it. If we really wanted a CIF championship we were going to have to go out and take it.

It moved me, for about a month, before I realized it was more of the same rah-rah. It ceased setting my blood on fire and became matter of course for the pregame devotional. Nobody respects us, got you, okay let's get on with it.

To have Gelbaugh voice concern about El Monte did get my attention. To this point, they looked like any other football team we played and beat. I never bothered worrying about other teams, not even Pomona. Nothing could shake the confidence I had in us.

Gelbaugh opened my eyes to the other end of the field and made me think.

Wearing white uniforms with blue trim and silver-blue helmets, they didn't seem to be interested in having fun as much as they seemed to be about business. They weren't laughing, they weren't high-fiving, they weren't smiling, and the growing legend of Fred-X wasn't overwhelming them with fear. They looked angry.

Number nine, Carter Ochoa, broke away from the passing drills and walked to his thirty-five and stared at Gelbaugh and me. His hands were on his hips as he gazed for a moment, and shook his head. Number thirty joined him and from film I knew it was Billy Camacho. Coach Jackson said he'd be the guy lining up across from me.

I asked Jackson how good Camacho was, and he said he was a lot tougher than Triay from Alhambra.

"F-bomb you Ochoa!" Gelbaugh screamed. "I'm going to f-bomb all of you up tonight!"

Ochoa and Camacho raised right-hands and made a chirping motions with their fingers.

"I'm going to kill that guy tonight," Gelbaugh said to me. "I swear, I'm gonna kill him. Huddle up!"

We gathered in the end zone, and what the pregame speech by the coaches didn't do, the gathering of our bodies, in full uniform, did. We started to heat up, we all started to get a bit of the Gelbaugh in us.

"You know exactly what you have to do tonight," Fred-X said to us under the goal post. "Stamp your will on this game. Give them a taste of Scottish steel. Alba f-bombing…"

"…Gu bràth!" We responded in unison and crashed through the banner the cheer squad put in front of us. We raced through the aisle of cheerleaders and flag girls and rallied on our side-line. I drifted from the pack and saw the Lions walk through theirs.

A Downey flashback traced across my thoughts, and the thin remnants of the bruise across my chest from Week One quivered. I didn't want to go through that Gilliam Gilliam hell again, but El Monte gave off the vibe I was about to. Fear ratcheted up not only in me but in the atmosphere. It was different tonight, different from the Pomona game. It felt like we had created something with every-thing in the universe riding on the outcome.

This was still just football, right? It was, but the rest of the world was condensing around us like it always did in the big moments and games. It condensed to the section of the city we were in, to the high school, to the stadium, to the field.

Carter Ochoa, the El Monte guy, stood five-ten, 185 pounds with a lot of muscle and a burst of speed. He played running back, safety, and never left the field. He wasn't just one of the best players in our league but in the division. Coach Gugliotta said he made Arroyo's Matt Burns look soft.

Their quarterback, Anthony Ledesma, was tall, six-four, with a decent arm and if Fred wasn't around he might have been out of the shadows and in the conversation as the best in the Mission Valley League.

The Lions won the toss and took the football. Many teams deferred to the second half when winning the flip, but against us they took it. Word trending around the message boards and the weekly previews was to limit our offensive touches early and frustrate us.

It worked.

Ochoa returned the opening kickoff to his thirty-nine. He then went five, six, five, eight, and fifteen-yards on five successive runs. The cursing started immediately, but Piccou, feeling the administration's squeeze, kept his tongue on lockdown.

Gugliotta ordered the defense to fill the box. Tom Preece, our strong safety, came forward alongside Gelbaugh. If we couldn't stop them on the ground we were going to be in trouble. The El Monte offensive line wasn't supposed to be great, but they were blowing us off the line of scrimmage.

"Can someone out there make a tackle?" Piccou said to Gugliotta before walking away from his defensive coordinator. He didn't like to interfere but even someone with pedestrian knowledge of football fundamentals, like myself, could tell we were reaching and not tackling.

On first and ten from our twenty-two, Ryan Torres scored the game's first touchdown. The Lions receiver shook Mike Patterson with one move, went to the post, and it was easy pickings for Ledesma with our safeties playing up.

Our first possession ended on a three and out. I caught a pass in the flat for two-yards and got smashed, not tackled, by a linebacker named Jared Jaramillo. The hit was good, but it wasn't the man-maker Gelbaugh gave me in August or the one I got at Downey from Gilliam Gilliam. However, it did mitigate the fear and put me more into the game. There was no more waiting for it to happen, it happened, it hurt, and it was time to get on with everything else. F-bomb it!

Holding penalties killed their next drive and ours, and we were soon forced to punt the ball back. The plan had been for us to never punt but neither Jackson nor Piccou liked what they were seeing. We were way out of sync.

"This is in front of our own crowd!" Pineapple said. "F-bomb! What the f-bomb are we doing out there? Punting twice in front of our own f-bombing crowd!"

"Make some f-bombing blocks out there and we won't have to punt," Coach Von Huson said. "In case you guys didn't know it the game has already started, so get your heads out of your butts and start hitting! I promise you'll feel better about yourselves."

They weren't doing anything different on defense than we expected, they were just doing it better. They swarmed in coverage and when Fred tried to scramble they assaulted him. It was as if they were playing with fourteen men instead of eleven.

After our second punt El Monte took over at its own thirty. We kept the box full and they kept blowing through us. They covered seventy yards in twelve plays without throwing a pass. Ochoa scored on a three-yard run and with 1:37 left in the first quarter we were down 14-0.

We were upset, but we weren't starting to panic. We knew what we could do. As long as Fred-X was at quarterback we were going to be okay. Our problem was keeping him on the field and our defense off it, at least for a few minutes to get some air. We needed to string some first downs together.

Gugliotta got Gelbaugh calmed down long enough so he could address the entire defense. I walked away, flexed my hands, and watched Bustamonte return the kickoff to our thirty-one.

"Let's go Scots!" Coach Von Huson said. "Pineapple, Basler, Fat John run the show out there! It's all you!"

A heartbeat later, Fred-X's pass went through Bustamonte's hands on a slant and into Ochoa's. The Lions standout returned it thirty-eight-yards to paydirt to make it 21-0 after the extra-point.

We'd had three possessions, we were down by three scores, and had yet to pick up a first down. The stadium went flat and was close to quiet. Sporadic hand claps could be heard, a sprinkle of encouragements, and the seemingly automated announcement of 'Piccou sucks!' floated down on us.

When I came to the sideline, the look on the faces was shock. They were beating us on the ground, they were scoring points on our offense, we were pathetic. We kept telling ourselves they weren't going to be able to stop us, but the scoreboard was showing something, painfully, different.

"Did we win this thing a week ago?" Piccou said. "According to the calendar if we want the league title we got to win tonight! Not tomorrow night! Not next week! Now is there anybody here that wants to play football?"

Only the defense seemed less discouraged by the third touchdown. Gugliotta kept instructing them through the pick and return by Ochoa. A safe guess would be they weren't even aware of it.

Then there was Fred, who told me about Bustamonte's hands before the season began, not laying any blame, not sulking. Instead he was talking to Jackson about what he saw.

"It's your eyes out there," Jackson said to him. "Tell me what you like."

They leafed through sheets of plays like someone might go through the New Testament for a particular scripture, knowing it's there but unable to find the correct chapter and verse. They kept searching for answers, for something that could beat the El Monte game plan.

We ran one play before the first quarter ended and then I caught my second pass for one-yard on the first play of the second. Facing a third and nine from our own twenty-four, Fred-X was forced out of the pocket and scrambled out of bounds for a three-yard gain. Any other time of the year Piccou would have had us go for it, but down by three scores, with no defensive answers, not happening. We punted.

Ochoa's third touchdown came at the end of a sixty-four-yard drive on an eight-yard run with 7:58 left in the half. 'Piccou sucks' chants became louder and the lid was just about closed on our casket. Mumbling stirred in the ranks of those with clean uniforms that not even Fred-X and all of his angels could get us out of this jam.

Down 28-0, Piccou called a timeout before the kickoff and gathered the team and staff around him.

"Forget the scoreboard! Forget it!" He said, walking a fine line between preaching football and surrender. "We are not going to win this game if you're looking at the scoreboard. We're going to win this mother-f-bombing game when we decide to play some mother f-bombing football! And yes I'm mother f-bombing cussing because I don't want you lose this game by not playing football and right now you are not playing football! So play some f-bombing football and if we win, we win. If we lose, we lose, f-bomb it!"

Pineapple and Gelbaugh screamed incoherently in support of Piccou. Froths of spit projected out of their mouths. They had the look, through the blue war paint covering their faces, of men about to die but with no intention of dying easy.

"Are you all in?" Piccou shouted. "Sons of Scotland, are you all in?" We closed in tighter and yelled. "Alba gu bràth!"

The motivation was good, but we needed something. Bustamonte gave it to us when he broke a tackle on the kick return and weaved his way into Lions territory before being chased out at the El Monte three. The play woke our crowd up, but not our offensive line.

Basler's first down snap launched over Fred's head and he recovered it at the thirteen. On second and goal, Bustamonte was tackled for a one-yard loss on a bubble screen. On third and goal from the fourteen Fred came my direction, but Camacho broke up the play.

Fred took a timeout to consult. They were going to give him the play with audible options if things looked different at the line of scrimmage. The break in action allowed the loudest voices in the stands to reach us clearly.

"Piccou sucks!"

"It'd be great to have a kicker right now! How many field goals have we kicked this year? Oh yeah, that's right...None!"

"Piccou sucks!"

"Hey, Coach! Why don't you try Hudson?"

"Hudson! Hudson!" A small section began to chant.

A larger section of the faithful met the challenge on Fred's behalf.
"Fred-X!...Fred-X!...Fred-X!"

Maybe it was going to turn ugly, maybe it wasn't, but the argument, at least, returned life to our fans.

"I hope if a fight breaks out in the stands Gelbaugh doesn't go up there," Basler said, flexing his right-hand.

"You okay?" I said.

"I'll be alright, it just hurts like a mother-f-bomber."

Fred came back and we huddled briefly before setting up in our regular package: Edwards at running back and four wide receivers with Ponce in the left and me in the right slot. My route was a fade to the corner. Bustamonte, wide right of me, was going to the post.

"Blue sixteen, blue sixteen," Fred-X said looking left, then right, then he changed the play. "Check...Check, red eleven, red eleven... Set!...Hut!"

When I heard the play being changed I was angry. I wanted the ball. Bustamonte could run with it, but he couldn't catch. The running game had done nothing, Fred couldn't find any running room, and I wanted a shot on the corner.

The ball was snapped. Draw play. Edwards scored untouched on a fourteen-yard run up the middle. The audible was brilliant because all the attention was on the receivers, Fred-X read the safeties and flipped the switch.

The pass on the two-point conversion was batted down at the line, but we felt hope and so did the crowd. Although it was still very clear Piccou sucked, those without an axe to grind had something to cheer about.

On the kickoff, Preece knifed through some blockers and flattened the Lions' Ray Medina on the return. The clash of pads and subsequent sigh of the fans juiced up our sideline all the more.

"Defense!" Fat John screamed as Gelbaugh and crew took the field. "Defense!"

Ledesma brought the El Monte offense out to its own twenty-seven. He used play action to Ochoa and tried to go long to Torres but the play was broke up by Patterson. On second down the ball was given to Ochoa, and Gelbaugh filled the gap to stop him at the line of scrimmage.

"Gelbaugh!" Fred-X said, cupping his hands around his mouth. "Gelbaugh!"

"Stop them here!" Gugliotta screamed, and the ball was snapped on third and nine.

I couldn't get inside the head of the El Monte coaching staff, but I'm sure they had to be thinking about getting out of the first half with a 28-6 lead. They also had to be wondering if Gelbaugh's stop of Ochoa was a fluke because that's what I was thinking.

It wasn't. Ochoa got the ball again on a dive and Gelbaugh bit hard into him for a two-yard loss. Seeing the Lions punt, to me, felt as good as us scoring. Knowing we could stop them meant Fred-X was going to be on the field. Nobody, not even Army Rangers, could stop us for forty-eight minutes.

We took over at our twenty-three and quickly found ourselves in a third and ten. A couple of first downs would keep Gelbaugh and the defense off the field until the third quarter. Another incomplete pass would put us behind the eight ball late in an exhausting first half.

The El Monte rush came hard, and Bustamonte was there to make a twelve-yard catch for our first, first down of the night.

Next snap Fred-X took straight up the middle for seven-yards to keep the clock running. On second and three from our forty-two, Fred had us run 'Trips Right Richie 798 F Swing.' A lot of words to have three receivers, on the same side of the field, run verticals and Edwards slide out of protection to catch a swing pass for nine-yards.

Careful to stay in bounds, Edwards landed us at the Lions forty-nine with just under two minutes remaining in the half. A quick pitch to Edwards on first down netted another eight-yards. Then a six-yard pass to Bustamonte got us to the thirty-five with fifty-six seconds to play.

On first down Basler snapped low and threw off the timing. Fred was tackled for a two-yard loss. A corner-route intended for me on second down was broken up. On third and twelve with thirty-seconds on the clock, the pocket collapsed around Fred.

Near the end zone, I saw him come out of it with defenders breathing down his neck. He lowered a shoulder to break a tackle and raced for the sideline. Two Lions closed in on him as he came to the first down marker.

He jumped with the ball out, the defenders launched, and he turned head over heels out of bounds for the first down. One of the members of the chain crew was wiped out on the play. The stadium on both sides erupted. If Fred was seeing stars, he didn't say anything. Coming back onto the field he waved us off as we tried to congratulate him.

"Not now," he said to Pineapple who wanted to hug. "Not now!"

We were at the twenty-one with seventeen-seconds left. Our trainer and the El Monte trainer were looking at the injured man. Fred's cleat had cut his face coming over the top.

We slurped out of the water bottles the girls brought us as Jackson gave Fred the next play. I still wanted to go to the corner.

With the right pass I knew I could beat Ochoa, but Bustamonte wouldn't shut up.

"Got to get me the ball they can't stop me," Bustamonte said and a part of me wanted to ask if he could catch the ball. "They can't stop me!" He drank some more water and spit it to the grass.

"I don't give a f-bomb," Pineapple said. "We just got to get a f-bombing touchdown!"

"Just get me the mother f-bombing-ball!"

The two began to jaw at each other.

"Let it go!" Fred yelled. "You want to get hot with somebody start with El Monte! F-bomb, stop acting like rookies!"

The ball was spotted and the chains were set. Fred barked signals, made his hand motions, and Basler snapped the ball.

Fred looked at me, he looked at Bustamonte, but before being crushed by a Lions defensive end he went to a wide open Jesse Maez in the end zone.

Again, without letting us celebrate Fred got us to the line of scrimmage for the two-point conversion. He fed the ball to Edwards, who slammed in behind a heavy breathing Pineapple to make it 28-14 at the half.

The locker room felt better being down by two touchdowns instead of four, but frustration hurt more than the pain. I felt fine but ached for the ball. This was going to be a night long remembered and I wanted my name mentioned as much as possible when it was retold.

Bustamonte needed to shut up and no one was shutting him up. He kept yapping about how El Monte couldn't stop him. The defense was exhausted. The blue paint on Gelbaugh's face was streaking down with perspiration, and I think tears, as he fought himself to keep focused.

Fred-X was on his back on the trainer's table. He'd been getting hit all night, but on the last drive alone he'd taken three deluxe bangs. Everything was working, but it wasn't pain free. Through the noise, I heard a groan escape as he put a hand to his shoulder.

Piccou's tone was not what I expected.

"They thought they'd won this game," he said. A grin rose on his face. "They had every reason to think they'd won this game, but I can tell you they're scared. They came out, built a big lead and we survived it. The momentum is ours. We have an opportunity to crush them in the second half. Make me proud, make West El Monte proud, make yourselves proud. Give yourselves a history and not something you wished had come true twenty years from now. Win this game. Forget about everything else and win this game."

I had to be the better soldier and forget about myself. There were moments I'd been able to do it, to forget about myself, and just play for the team. But how many nights do you get like this night when it feels the whole world is watching? Actions were easy to guard, but selfishness was always longing to surface.

They kicked away from Bustamonte to start the second half. Maez fielded the ball at the fourteen and moved all the way to our forty. On first down the pocket disintegrated but Fred escaped through the middle of the field for a forty-three-yard gain to the El Monte seventeen.

A Jet Sweep to Bustamonte fell apart and he was thrown for a five-yard loss. Getting up off the turf, he was about to slam the ball into the ground before Fred-X stepped into his face.

"When I complain about your lousy hands, you can complain about someone else," he said, grabbing hold of Bustamonte's face-mask and giving him a death look. "I'll kick your butt right off this field." Boosty gave him no protest. "Come on, I need you! We all need you Boosty!"

On second and fifteen from the twenty-two, pressure came up the middle. Fred, running to his right, was cut off. He turned his back to the goal line and spun back to his left. When he spun, I broke off of the out-route I was running and went towards the goal line.

Completing a 360 turn, he fired the ball high and I jumped along with Billy Camacho for the ball. My size was the difference and I came down with it. Only when I landed and saw the refs hands go up did I realize I'd scored.

"Handsdrade!" Faces in street clothes screamed in joy at me. Alumni with beards, bellies, and red faces, earned by too many beers, grouped hugged me as I came out of the side of the end zone. Horse and nameless others ushered me back to the team with praises and slaps to the top of my helmet. They knew who 'Handsdrade' was.

I saw Vice Principal Padilla, standing in back of the players box, giving applause. I hadn't seen her at a game all season. I was happy and shocked at the same time by it. I didn't know if she was there to give support to the team or if she was just jumping on the band-wagon. As long as she wasn't suspending anybody I didn't care.

We lined up for the deuce. Edwards took the ball behind Pineapple and got stoned at the one. It would have helped, but it didn't make a difference. We were one possession away from tying the game.

The loud button had been hit. People were screaming for us and pounding their feet into the floor of the grandstand. The band played the same ancient rock and roll song my grandfather listened to when the radio was still used for music. I heard my name, then I heard my nickname, and for a second I felt like Fred-X. Everyone was clapping, jumping up and down. It was electric. This was why Pineapple, Gelbaugh, and Fred had the look of men not wanting to die. To lose this game for them was to lose everything.

With 5:10 remaining in the quarter, leading 28-20, El Monte pieced together a dominant drive highlighted by the hard running of Ochoa and a catch and run by fullback Memo Rivera for twen-ty-six-yards. Ledesma finished the advance on the first play of the fourth quarter with a one-yard sneak.

Leading, 35-20, it was apparent the Lions weren't close to be-ing finished and there didn't seem to be a way to stop Ochoa. Gelbaugh, too exhausted to scream, vomited when the defense came to the bench. Edgar Escandon was on the trainer's table with Sondra looking at his knee. Gugliotta went to work searching for an anti-Ochoa formula on his dry erase board. Dinh Lee stood with his helmet off and pointed into the cluster of Xs and Os to empha-size what was happening.

I began to wonder if a school board meeting or Wall Street deal was ever this tense in such a compact space of time. The cheering reminded me, us, we were still part of the planet, but on the sideline by the time the fourth quarter arrived we were totally detached from matters of this world. It was the game and nothing else.

The defense was struggling, but the offense was clicking. After Maez brought us to the thirty-eight on the kickoff we went to work. Answering back with the kind of drive we were known for, it was all lightening. A twenty-yard sprint by Edwards on first down was followed by thirty-three-yard pass to Bustamonte. On first and goal from the nine Fred-X pulled the ball back from Bustamonte on a Jet Sweep going left and pitched right to Edwards who drew us closer when he beat Ochoa to the corner of the end zone. Fred-X kept the ball on the two-pointer to make it 35-28.

Crowd noise pushed in around us. From where I was on the sideline, I could see full stands, on both sides, but all the way around the playing field a ring of people had emerged. Trudy Shields was there. Grip Teague and Bald Guy were there. Chanos's camera man was working up and down our sideline.

El Monte got the ball back, and Ledesma hit Medina for a thirty-two-yard gain as the Lions crossed midfield. Ochoa added a twenty-nine-yard run to set up shop with a first and ten at our eighteen. No matter what Gugliotta schemed with his markers we couldn't get a stop.

I didn't know what was going to happen, but through football I learned something was always about to happen. I never knew how, but I knew it would come. We were a good football team and (I remembered reading in a Grip Teague column) good football teams made their own luck.

Ledesma dropped back on first down. Medina was open in the back of the end zone, but the El Monte quarterback threw instead to Torres on a crossing pattern. Gelbaugh arrived with the ball and

Torres was sent to the moon. The ball went straight up and began to descend.

Lee tracked it and grabbed the ball in the air. Ochoa leveled him, but we'd dodged a huge bullet with 6:16 to play and took possession at our ten.

The best feeling came over me when we came back to the field. Fate, the football gods or the Polynesian deities Pineapple pleaded to had written the script. The last pages were going to be about the next ninety yards and a game winning touchdown.

"You guys clear the path and I'll go to the house," Edwards said, clapping his hands as we rushed to the field.

"It's all you, baby," Pineapple said.

Then Fat John was hit with a flag for a false start and we were moved back to the five.

On first and fifteen, Fred-X checked down to Edwards. He reached our fifteen when Jaramillo came in from the side and dove at him low. Edwards's cleat caught, and I wasn't the only one that heard the symphony of tendons ripping and bone shattering in his knee. The ball flew out of his hands and after a scramble Torres recovered for El Monte at the 10.

Fast Eddie screamed and beat his arms on the turf as his left leg, awkwardly twisted, gave no sign of life. Trainers from both schools and Coach Piccou raced to him. I only stared at Edwards in his agony as the rest of his body flopped around.

My thinking was clear, there was no fog or hazed thoughts about this catastrophic injury. I was unashamedly concerned about us winning this game since El Monte had the ball again at our ten. There was a wrongness begging to be recognized inside me, but that was the world, a vast space away from this football field. This was the only place where anything mattered. Losing Edwards was a huge blow for us, so my thoughts were all about replacing him.

Pineapple made a move towards Jaramillo and Fred-X grabbed him before he could start anything. The El Monte linebacker's helmet was off and tears were pouring as he took a knee. His teammates huddled around him.

"You think he meant for this to happen?" Our quarterback said. Pineapple tried to move around him. "Look at him! Look at him! He's sick. There's nothing you can do. Eddie's gone…Pineapple, he's gone. We can't lose you!"

Pineapple, with his helmet off and blue face paint, either absorbed or streaked across his entire face, looked like a zombie, inhuman. Coach Von Huson came and helped get him back with the team and down to a knee.

It took twenty minutes for the paramedic's van to roll onto the field and get Edwards strapped in. It was time enough for his family to come out of the stands, for Piccou and the El Monte head coach Dan Valencia to connect, for sideline onlookers to describe what they saw, what they heard, and tweet it all out. I was on one knee with a water bottle, dreading the moment play would start again.

Twenty-five minutes after the injury, the official rotated his arm for the clock to resume ticking. On first down Ochoa ran for four-yards. On second down he ran for four more to create third and goal from the two. Everyone expected Ochoa to get it again, but he didn't. Ledesma faked the hand off and bootlegged right, but Jamie Nguyen, Dan Feliz's replacement, trapped him for a three-yard loss.

El Monte sent in its kick team. A twenty-two-yard field goal would finish us with less than four minutes to play. Gugliotta kept the defense in to guard against a fake. They might be able to stop a fake, but they were clearly too exhausted to spend a burst of energy trying to block the field goal.

When the snap went high the defense didn't have to get the block. The Lions kicker picked up the ball and lobbed a feeble pass incomplete and we were back in business. The only negative besides being down by seven-points was we were marooned at our own five with 2:44 to live.

Fred pulled us into a huddle before we lined up.

"Ninety-five yards and it is all there," he said. "Payback for Eddie, our defense doesn't have to go back on the field, and we're league champs if we do it right. Okay, you know the play: Trips Right Richie 798 F Swing. Maez, line up alongside Pineapple and sell yourself as a blocker. I'm going to you."

While we ran our routes down field, the ball was supposed to go to Miranda, in for Edwards, on a swing. Fred-X was certain Maez would be open off the line at the tight end spot.

The ball was snapped, Maez was open, pass was there, but he dropped it. Dropped it knowing he had thirty-yards of open country in front of him. It hurt and was compounded by a second down pass to Bustamonte that was too low.

"Don't think, Ritter!" Jackson said with one foot on the field and a hand covering the microphone of his headset. "Trust them. If they drop it, they drop it, don't try to be perfect!"

Fred tapped his helmet in acknowledgment.

The third and ten we were in was the biggest third and ten we'd faced all night. This time, Fred-X managed to get a split second longer to look up field and he found me. After El Monte's Camacho bought the skinny I sold him, I caught a corner-route for thirty-three-yards.

Two plays later on third and four Bustamonte had the ball go off his hands and we were looking at fourth down from our own thirty-eight. The sliver lining to the drop? Bustamonte kept his mouth shut for the rest of the game.

On another *biggest down of the night*, Fred-X found me on an out-route. I squeezed the ball for eleven-yards and a first down at the forty-nine.

Quickly lining up to the right for the next play, the ball was snapped. Fred-X pumped with shoulders, Camacho went for the out-route and I was open along the sideline. The pass was perfect.

I could see the ball and the threads spiraling to a meeting point with me and a wave of fear attempted to pulse through me. This torturing of myself, by myself, about what it would mean to my life if I dropped it.

On this night, the fear was overwhelmed by the faith of my quarterback. I was 'Handsdrade' and for the smallest fraction of the infinite moments of the universe I was the greatest pass catcher who ever lived. And my creator was the legendary Fred-X.

The ball came into my hands at the El Monte thirty-five. As I ran with it, I could see the faces and the bodies on the sideline raising their hands. Horse was there, Lena with her camera, Bald Guy, Trudy Shields all looking at me. Some were screaming, some were cheering, and some were marveling at the moment. There was no distinction to the noise, but only a swelling of power packing me deeply into the experience. I did not feel my feet touch the grass as I galloped inside the most perfect moment of my life. As if a dying man might see his entire life in a few moments, I saw my football life in the space of thirty-five-yards, 105 feet down the sideline where Fred-X threw the first pass I ever caught seven months before.

When the fifty-one-yard pass play reached the end zone, weakness came into me and it felt like, finally, it was my turn to cry. Did my dad ever have this moment? Did Bustamonte or any of my other teammates, besides Fred, have this moment? I raised my arms and the ball above my head and the noise became even more powerful.

Everyone congratulated me except for Fred. Pineapple, Bustamonte, Miranda, and Maez mobbed me, but my one alley of exposed vision showed Fred, calling a timeout, walking over to Jackson to see what we were going to run next.

The clock showed 1:46 to play. The band was playing, fans were still cheering, but our celebration ended as Piccou and Jackson began waving the entire offense over to the numbers. My elation drained when the reality of things settled in. We were still down 35-34

If we didn't convert the two-pointer, the chances of us getting the ball back were slim. An onside kick was risky and we didn't even have a real kicker on the roster, so we couldn't go for one if we wanted too.

"It be good to have a kicker right now wouldn't it, Piccou!" I knew it was impossible to distinguish anything coming out of the stands, but I was certain I heard it. It may have just been a replay of the countless other times I heard it screamed by what was certainly a Hudsonite.

With Edwards hurt, Bustamonte fading, and knowing I was going to be double-covered, I began to wish we had a kicker as well.

"Let's run Scram. We can put Handsman split left, drop Miranda into the right slot and empty the backfield completely. Why can't we do that?" Fred said.

"Because if we do they're going to double him and not buy the Jet Sweep," Jackson said. "This is what we're going to do, we're going to sell the Jet Sweep left..."

The play put me in at the tight end spot next to Pineapple on the left. Out of the shotgun, Fred would have Miranda to his right, Bustamonte in the right slot, and Maez to the outside, running a dig-route across the middle.

At the snap, Miranda would flare as a receiver to the right and Bustamonte would race left. The option was Fred's to give it to Boosty or not. My job was to pull from the left and run behind the offensive line to the right to be either a blocker or receiver for Fred. The play was all misdirection and tailor made for Fred-X.

"If you don't like it, you've got Maez on the dig. He'll be in single coverage because everybody is going to be moving with Bustamonte. If you don't like that Miranda will be in the corner, Handsdrade in the flat, or make the f-bombing play yourself."

It was a good call. There might have been a more perfect design to a play, but what this one did was leave it all in the hands of Fred-X. Multiple choices, multiple decisions the defense had to make and they had to make it against the best quarterback in the SGV.

That was it. Coach Piccou didn't give us any more rah-rah because we didn't need it. No need to motivate a team needing to go three yards for a win and a league championship. We were also too tired to yell Alba gu bràth again.

We settled into formation and the Lions defense set up across from us.

"Four-three, four-three blue twenty-five," Fred said as the defensive front was even. We were giving them a look we hadn't shown all night. They were assuming pass with Edwards out of the game. "Blue twenty-five...Pomona, Pomona..." Fred keyed us in that he was going to call for the ball.

The noise of the crowd went silent, a trickle of sweat streamed down around the back of my ear.

"Hut..."

There was no trash talk. Our defense had taken a beating, but so had theirs as we converted on every big down.

"...Hut..."

My heart felt like it was going to burst through my pads and jersey. It was like being in the open door of a plane and waiting to parachute out.

"...Hut!"

In my peripheral, I saw the ball zip back. Kicking out of my stance I went to my right and saw Bustamonte crossing in front of Fred-X. The outside linebacker chased after Boosty and was oblivious to me.

Fred-X tucked the ball. I switched to blocker and chipped the defensive end trying to get by Fat John. I landed with my face toward our sideline. I saw the coaches ready to jump. They extended to their tip toes, came back down and then launched into the air as the crowd went off.

Turning I saw Fred-X standing in the end zone raising the ball high with his right-hand. The band began to play the ancient rock and roll song again. He disappeared and then was raised by Miranda, Pineapple and Maez onto their shoulders. He kept the ball raised in the one hand as they carried him to the sidelines.

How could a person not love this moment? I wasn't Fred, I wasn't being carried off the field, but there was nothing not to love. It needed to be held onto forever. Yet, something in Fred's face wasn't registering. I wasn't sure if it was expressing gratitude or a little indifference. There should have been tears and shouts, but his smile was small in comparison with the moment.

They put him down next to Coach Jackson. They embraced, Coach Piccou ran a hand over his sweaty hair, and Coach Gugliotta preached to his huddled defense to keep everything in front of them.

El Monte tried a lateral throwback across the field on the kickoff and ended up stranding itself at the seventeen. Ledesma's first pass was incomplete. His second was picked off by Patterson and the Lions were done.

Running on the field with us, to clearly set up in the victory formation, was Billy Hudson. Fred was standing next to Jackson, holding his left arm. Hudson took two knees and the Mission Valley League crown was ours for the first time in school history.

After the victory all any of us really wanted was bed. We were happy we won but exhausted from the effort. Edwards went to the hospital in the ambulance, Edgar Escandon went for x-rays, and Fred left the locker room in uniform with his left arm in a sling. There were things about tomorrow we didn't even want to begin to consider.

Was there a team party?

Of course, there was, but how do you qualify a fiesta? Is it the celebration of an event? Is it the company of others? Is it both? The motivating factor for going to the party was respect. Jesse Maez's family was hosting the after party for the team. Catching a big touchdown made it a good night for him.

The spread was excellent and the Maez's house was welcoming. They had a big family room, plenty of space, and I found out why he never ate with the team or went out with us. Jesse Maez had a little girl.

"She's yours?"

He nodded as he held the sleeping baby in his arms. "She was born during dead period," he said with an attitude and look completely different from what I saw at school and on the field. "Her name's Jayleen." He rocked her in his arms as if she was a treasure.

"I didn't know," I said. "Congrats."

He shrugged. "I'm getting married after graduation. My dad said he'd let me play this last year of football and then I'd have to man up."

I didn't ask anymore. Maez had already started his life and I didn't know if the daughter in his arms was a bad thing or a great blessing. If it was a bad thing, I couldn't tell. He was happy.

"Did you see the text?" Maez said to me.

The first news about Edwards was by text from the hospital. The alphabet in his knee had been fully blown; ACL, MCL, all of it shredded. His season was wrecked.

I nodded from the kitchen table. My chair was turned to the television. The opening music for Grip Teague and Bald Guy's show was playing. Everyone found some furniture. Hudson and his crew were sitting front and center on the couch and floor. Gelbaugh and Feliz, off crutches, were against a wall on the other side of the family room near the fireplace.

"Gentleman," Maez's father spoke. "Have fun, but try not to yell too much, it scares the mija."

They began reading the scores. Pomona won again, as did West Covina, Bonita, and La Mirada. Downey was upset by Warren, then they read our score and declared us Mission Valley League champs.

Quiet applause worked its way up to loud yells. The baby started to cry and Maez left room with his daughter.

Grip Teague: I had a flashback during the two-point conversion at the end. It reminded me of that La Canada-Temple City playoff a million years ago when I was a hundred pounds lighter.

Bald Guy: Who was the Spartans' quarterback that night, Moore? But that was a pass wasn't it?"

Grip Teague: It was Moore, but, yeah, it was a pass. I'm talking about in terms of excitement. Tonight's game was just awesome. Makes me proud of my career choice.

Bald Guy: Well Grip, we've got film from this game that our guys are working on. This was an incredible win for the Fighting Scots.

Grip Teague: It was. Down 28-0, plus they lost Eddie Edwards to a knee injury in the second half, and come all the way back for a 36-35 victory. But stay tuned because we're not done with the West El Monte injury situation.

The highlights began to roll and I felt the elation of my touchdown catch. I kept the satisfaction of it tamped down, but it exploded through my whole body. Then they showed Fred's collision with Ochoa at the goal line that I didn't see. Ochoa took the business end of Fred's left shoulder as his helmet caromed off.

Bald Guy: That collision with Carter Ochoa might have given West El Monte a Mission Valley League title, but it also may have cost them their season. Because in all the chaos at the end of this

game, when the Scots came out into a victory formation Fred-X wasn't with them. Later he was seen leaving the locker room with his left arm in a sling.

Grip Teague: As if this game didn't have enough for us to discuss, now we got to speculate about whether Fred Ritter will be in uniform next week for the Scots.

Bald Guy: So before we get to all the heroics tonight, attention immediately turns to the most famous backup quarterback in the Southern Section: Billy Hudson. Hudson, of course, of the disgruntled fan base that has believed all season he deserved to get more playing time and now may get his chance.

"Hudson!" Ponce and Miranda began slapping the top of his head. He got a big smile across his face. If perception was everything, then mine was they wanted Fred to be injured. They were happy about this.

"What the f-bomb?" Gelbaugh said and a pause button was hit in the room. The chattering and joking stopped. It was beautiful because of how it made the Hudsonites feel.

"Chill Gelbaugh." A scared Ponce said. "We're just clowning."

"He's not your quarterback." Gelbaugh pointed to Hudson. "Your quarterback got hurt tonight." He began to move closer to them when Jessie's father stepped in.

"I understand," Mr. Maez said. "But it's not going to do you any good to get into a fight, especially here."

None of us saw Bustamonte cut out. Hudson and his contingent were picked up by their families. The looks they got were hard. If a civil war started I was ready to join in. Hudson was a piece of garbage.

Pineapple was my ride, and he was hanging in the family room with Feliz and Gelbaugh, so I waited. Maez came back, without the baby, and we brought him up to speed. We were the only ones left and the house was quiet.

It was always good to hear Gelbaugh's rage aimed at someone else. Sitting with the seniors gave me another surge of acceptance. Of course I missed Fred, but I was with the core of the team and they were my friends. Nearly all I hoped for when I came out for football had come true. What was left? A championship with Lena being the bonus? Lena, with a championship as the bonus?

There was a part of me that knew I would trade out my football family for Lena if the opportunity came. Doing what I was best at, I kept it to myself and went on with the surface conversation.

We talked and I became good with whatever the plan was going forward. If it meant killing Hudson, I was good. If it meant sharing the misery of Hudson leading us, I was good with that too.

"I want to crack that mother-f-bomber's knees," Gelbaugh said.

"Sounds good," Maez said, "do Ponce at the same time, but if Fred's out we'll be finished without Hudson."

"If Fred's out, we're finished anyway," Pineapple said. "Hudson's got nothing but an arm and I got no faith in him."

If the mood was sour now it was going to be worse at eight on Saturday morning when we met for film because Fred always brought the donuts. I made a mental note before going to bed to grab a couple dozen at the Donut Star to keep the beasts happy.

"So what are we going to do?" Feliz said and then looked at the cast on his wrist. "I mean what are you guys going to do?"

"I'm going to get a beer," Maez said getting up and going into the kitchen. "You guys want one?"

Pineapple shook his head and then looked at me. "We gotta go."

"You don't want a cerveza Pineapple?"

"Not when I'm driving home after curfew." Pineapple then pointed a finger at Gelbaugh. "And you don't f-bombing want one either."

Gelbaugh gave no protest.

Sleep came in stops and starts but by four-thirty I'd landed in some far away dreamland. There was a meadow, early morning mist, and Lena. Whatever happened next would remain a mystery as the buzzing of my phone on the nightstand pulled me back into my bedroom. Part of me hoped it was Lena confessing to the same dream, and another hoped it was Pineapple, or Gelbaugh, telling me they were in the process of dumping Hudson's body into Leg Lake.

"Dude, how was the party?"

"Fred?"

"Yeah," the voice said.

"Fred?" I said again, not sure if he was really calling me this early in the morning.

"Yeah, how was the party?"

"It sucked," I said. "What did the doctor say?"

"I'm out next week," he said with an easy tone. "My left shoulder is sprained. A bad contusion the doctor said."

"You wrecked for the season?"

"Heck no."

Three weeks had passed since I was this stiff getting out of bed, but every ouch screamed accomplishment. My right thumb was swollen, a new bruise was on the right shoulder as well, a red welt was on my left hip bone. Not to be forgotten, the old aches, across my chest and in my thigh, resurfaced to join the concert. We'd done something important, something never done in school history, and I was part of it. That was the rate of exchange and I was happy with the deal.

In only my boxer briefs, I came out of the bedroom and saw a dozen donuts sitting on the table.

"I figured you deserved a donut or two after that game you played last night," Dad said stepping into view with a cup of coffee in his hand. "You were great."

"Did you see the highlights?" I said.

"I was there. I was so..." He looked like he was about to get emotional, but shook out of it. "They call you Handsdrade," he stopped, looked away to regain some fading composure, and looked back at me. "I didn't know. I'm sorry, I didn't know how good you were."

He should have known, but he didn't, and I couldn't be mad at him because I didn't really want him around in the first place. I wanted distance from his hurt looks and Mom's hypocrisy. Football gave it to me, it was my world, my friends, my thing.

"I wanted to say something to you after the game, but didn't want to embarrass you, I know how you feel about that sort of thing."

"I'm glad you were there," I said and for some reason I really was. He hadn't been to a game all season, I didn't expect him to come at all.

Dad wiped a tear from underneath his eye. "I'm proud of you..." He put down his coffee. "You've got to get to film and I've got an appointment."

"Where are you going?" I said.

"Men's breakfast at the church. Richard Umphries invited me."

He gave me a long smile and I could see he was itching to hug me but resisted the urge. "I'll see you at lunch." Then he left.

"We sucked!" The team said in unison.

"Yes, you did," Piccou said.

If there was ever a week we couldn't disagree this was it. My football intelligence was barely approaching remedial, but the things Coach pointed out were obvious. He broke down the problems with our defense as being the most basic and fundamental. Situations where we would put ourselves in the right spot but either out of fear, fatigue or both, reached instead of tackled and pushed instead of blocked.

On offense, I looked really good. Of course none of the coaches mentioned it and, for reasons I could only guess, they skipped over Bustamonte's drops. Instead, they focused on the offensive line. Basler took a beating at center for his bad snaps and poor reads along the front.

"Robles, you got to help me out here," Piccou said repeating a clip where Fat John false started at right tackle. "You got squirrels in your pants or what kid?" A few laughs came. "Look at this, you're killing us and so deep inside our own territory. If you can't get focused on that part of the field then where can you get focused? I can't put a pizza in front of you on the field to get your mind right. You gotta start clamping down, son."

Piccou told us we were league champs, but only because the MVL seemed to be grading on a curve.

"We're league champs, we're going to the playoffs for the first time in school history, you got what you wanted," he said. "But you're going to have to take a look at yourself today and tomorrow to see if you want something more. To settle for what we already have is going cheap...and cheap is easily replaced and always forgotten."

The lights came back on and he closed his notebook.

"Now for the rest of it. Fast Eddie is done for the season, Escandon might be..."

Although I knew what was coming next, I waited in serious anticipation with the rest of the team.

"...And Ritter's got a sprained left shoulder. He's out next week. Hudson, you're going to be living with Coach Jackson this week. It's time for the next man up and I don't want any screw ups against Marshall."

That night I got a Facebook message from Lena. Just the little red notification on my phone caused my heart to speed. She thought about me, she wrote me, and I didn't even know what she wrote because what mattered was she took time on a Saturday evening to message me.

"Haven't seen you in church for a while, you coming tomorrow?"

It was tagged at the end with a smiley face. I studied it and reasoned my church days weren't quite over after all.

On Sunday, I left the house after Dad. When I got there he was in the front section of pews to the right. I was in my favorite spot in the back just to the left of the center aisle.

"The Bible pushes this narrative all the way through the Old and New Testaments. Sincere obedience to God and his words out weigh any birthright you believe might be yours," Pastor Domres said.

While I shouldn't have cared either way, Lena was kicking around between my ears. She didn't go out with the children, but I could see the back of her head in the front of my section.

"This is where our society has crossed itself up over the decades. We've moved away from entitlement by obedience, to being entitled because we breathe. You can find arguments these days of folks saying they didn't ask for anything, not even to be born, and that their needs should be met because of this."

I gave some attention to the sermon but what I was really doing was working out a game plan after the benediction. She'd reached out to me for the first time in two weeks. I was positive Fred was getting ready to break up with her. A million possibilities ran through my mind along with a warning to stay rational. Rationality told me I'd be a fool to get my hopes up again.

"Can I tell you something this morning? We are deserving of and entitled to one thing; death. But because our God's love is so big, so deep, and so tall for us he gave us his son while we were still sinners. We all deserve death, but he gives us life."

I stayed and waited because *rationality* didn't understand the power of Lena's face when smiling or the potency of the Royal Jasmine she was wearing.

We saw each other in the foyer.

"Handsman, awesome to see you," she said giving me her smile before administering the dreaded side hug. The kind of hug declaring openly your friendship and no intention whatsoever of anything more. "I haven't talked to you for a long time."

A snappy answer eluded me.

"Well, after that night at your house," I said reaching for maturity. "I figured you might have wanted some space." I loved the words the second they came out of my mouth.

"It really wasn't a good night," she said. "But hey, you guys beat El Monte."

"Yeah, we did."

Mrs. Durkin, the woman I hoped someday would be my mother-in-law, called her daughter. "Honey, they're expecting us for lunch."

"I've got to go have lunch with my grandparents."

"Yeah, I gotta go too."

She side hugged me again and that was it...But it was fuel enough to keep the dream alive.

WEEK TEN

Read The Blitz
By Grip Teague

The best way to start is to say they got off lucky. It could have been so much worse. San Dimas dodged a huge bullet today when CIF ruled they will only forfeit two league wins, (one of them being the 21-20 victory over Pomona) after a clerical error left an ineligible player in uniform for a good chunk of the season. What this does is give the Pomona Red Devils the Valle Vista League championship. A San Dimas win Friday night against Northview (hardly a cake walk) will put them back in the playoff dance. If they lose? Then turn out the lights. Frustrating part is the player in question (name is being withheld) never saw the field. It came down to when San Dimas HC, Ben Lincoln found out and when he reported it. "Not how we wanted the league title, but we're not going to turn it down," said Pomona HC, Hiram Thomas. "I'm sure we're going to see the Saints again this season."

Notes: West El Monte has lost Fast Eddie Edwards for the season and may be without the services of Fred Ritter for the next two weeks. "What do you want me to say?" Skip Piccou said. "It's time for the next man up." The next men for the Fighting Scots are a pair of sophomores: Mike Miranda and the much discussed Billy Hudson.

We did catch one break after the El Monte game. Pasadena Marshall was our Week Ten opponent. Marshall was best known for being below average one year, losing its coach before the start of the next, and going 1-9 for two years before the cycle repeated itself. This season they started off 3-0 with a chump schedule, but were now a truly horrible 3-6.

At Monday's game planning session, Coach Jackson made it clear we were going to pound the ball with Miranda and throw high percentage hitches, bubbles, and slips to the receivers. The Eagles couldn't stop the run or the pass.

"Are you going to let me go down field?" Hudson asked. "I mean with our receivers we can put them away early and give our backups some playing time."

Hudson was such a decent soul. Always worried about the little guy, except the little guys were his sophomore friends and their highlights would be his stats. Of course, we both thought alike, but I could mask my pride.

"We're going to pound the ball, Hudson," Jackson said. "The quickest path is a short line." He pointed his red dot to the white board. "Marshall is weak up front and we've got to build Miranda's confidence. He's going to be our horse from here on out."

"If Fred's not healthy, I'm going to need more throwing reps," Hudson said.

"Show me you can master what I've given you," Jackson said, "and I'll open your packages up. Change a play on me without a green light and Omeida from the freshman team will be playing quarterback faster than you can say, 'Piccou sucks.' I'm sure you're familiar with that expression. There's not going to be one time against Marshall you're going to have to audible, not with what they have and what we've given you."

Coach Gugliotta turned the lights back on and Coach Piccou stood back in front of us.

"I'm not going to lie to you guys and blow smoke up your rears about how this team can beat you, because they can't," Piccou said. "Not even if you have the expected letdown after beating El Monte. Pasadena Marshall will not beat you, but there are two things they can do to you. First they can infect you with sloppy play, so focus on execution. Two, injuries. Those are hard to prevent, but they are easier to avoid when you respect your opposition and play fundamental football." He turned to Gugliotta and then back to the rest of the team. "If we lose somebody to a knee injury so be it, but you all better have your eyes open and your heads up. You get me?"

We nodded that we did.

"Why not just have our freshman team play them, Coach?" Pineapple said. "We'll take the week off." Some of the guys laughed.

"You need the work, Pineapple; all of you do," Piccou said. "That being said, in a contest between Marshall and Jerry's Kids, I'm taking Jerry's Kids over these guys. It's the reality of it."

I didn't know who Jerry's kids were, figured it must have been another football thing I'd learn down the road.

"Coach," Jackson said with a smile. "You better cool it or you're going to get suspended again."

He nodded. "Forget I said that guys. Let's go to work."

By the end of Wednesday's practice, it was clear to me the offensive game plan wasn't just about protecting us from Hudson's ego and getting Miranda as many touches as possible, but about getting Bustamonte's head back into the season.

Jet Sweeps, bubble-screens, slip-screens, skinnys, and every other call put the ball in his hands. Marshall was the perfect team to do it against. Even if they figured it out they had no one on their defense to stop Bustamonte. They didn't have anyone on their defense to prevent a bad snap by Basler from turning into a touchdown for us.

Maez dropped a pass when practice started. Hudson didn't dare get directly in Maez's face, but let go of a string of profanities about how he needed help and it was time for the team to step up. It was good motivation for me not to have a letdown. I hated Hudson so much I decided I'd catch everything he threw my way just to keep him from talking to or about me.

The Hudsonites were working the boards about how much sharper and crisper the West El Monte practices were looking this week:

"The team isn't going to miss a beat against Marshall thanks to the way Billy Hudson has stepped up."---MaxAtax

It was gross, not even Grip Teague was commenting on it because everyone knew where it was coming from. The theory continued to be pushed about how much better off we would have been if Hudson had been the quarterback all season and Ritter the running back.

Before practice on Thursday, Piccou had us meet at midfield with Crumsey. Another wave of fear passed over us. How many meetings had there been like this so far? Three, four? Any suspensions now would crush our season. We couldn't even afford to lose Hudson. The sun was setting, the sky was darkening; it was Halloween week. A pleasant lingering cold was beginning to settle in.

"Gentlemen," Crumsey said, getting our attention. We'd all taken a knee. Behind us, Fred was standing in civilian clothes with his arm still in a sling. "We've been down the road of respect and character before, and my presence here is to demonstrate how important it is to West El Monte Poly. With that said, Coach Piccou has something to share with you. Coach?"

The tone was far from an end of the world feel. Piccou appeared more perplexed than stressed. When he looked at Crumsey, and not at the ground, and gave him a nod I knew it wasn't too serious. He pulled a piece of paper out of his pocket.

"Earlier this week I made a thoughtless reference to Marshall and how they would lose to Jerry's Kids. This was wrong and insensitive on my part and I need to apologize to all of you. Again, I am not perfect but in my role as a coach and leader of this program I need to hold myself to a higher standard. Such derogatory remarks are never appropriate, and especially by someone in my position of leadership at West El Monte Poly. I again apologize if I offended you, or someone you know that may suffer from disabilities."

I didn't know who Jerry was, but my first thought was Hudson and his family had done it again. Who else? My second thought was to get Gelbaugh and Pineapple to hold Hudson's head inside of a loaded toilet while I flushed it. Coach Piccou would have been blamed for that too so I let it go.

"You have a question?" Crumsey said, pointing to Patterson who had his hand raised.

"I don't know who Jerry is. Are his kids on the team?"

"I was thinking the same thing," Lee said. "Who's Jerry?"

"Yeah," Gelbaugh said. "Who the f-bomb is Jerry?"

"This matter is closed," Crumsey said shaking his head and holding back a smile. "The only thing left for you to do now is to get a victory on Friday night for West El Monte Poly."

I finished my pregame power nap by waking up to the aged ceiling of the Pasadena City College locker room. From the floor, it took me a few moments to adjust, coming out of sleep I was usually disoriented. For all I knew I could have been on Mars or waking up from a carpet snooze when I was seven.

The naps took a while to get used too, but by midseason they'd taken hold. As I stretched, a final yawn came out of my relaxed body and I knew I was physically ready for the game.

Marshall didn't have a home field with lights and often played day games, but tonight was homecoming and it secured the bigger venue at PCC. West El Monte Poly had been a good homecoming match for many schools over the years so it was just bad luck they had to play us this season. Even without Fred-X we were going to blow up the party.

A very reasonable Coach Jackson sat with us in a corner of the locker room with his dry erase board. He scripted the offense's first twenty plays. The plan remained the same. Pound the ball with Miranda and restore Bustamonte's confidence with easy touches from Hudson. Jackson gave our quarterback no audibles.

"You're only a sophomore, Hudson, and you should be the quarterback next year," Jackson said. "Marshall is only going to have twenty-one in uniform. Tonight we can win this game without you, but it's important for all of us to know that we can win this game with you. This means showing us you can stick to the script, work within the offensive game plan. When we see that, then we'll trust you enough to open things up."

"You let Fred-X change the plays if he doesn't like what he sees," Hudson said.

Jackson stared at him. Maez let out a laugh, and I couldn't suppress the smile coming to my face.

"What?" Hudson said. "It's true."

"Yeah," Jackson said with a sarcastic smile. "We're done, why don't you guys get back to your business."

Hudson stuck to the script. Bustamonte turned a pair of simple bubble screens into long touchdowns. Miranda ran for two more, including a seventy-six-yarder, and Hudson scored on a thirty-yard keeper. Patterson added a forty-seven-yard punt return for a touchdown. Seventeen plays into the twenty play script and we were up 54-0 midway through the second quarter.

I wasn't targeted once and was subbed out for Charlie Califf. I watched the game standing next to Fred.

Just before half Miranda slipped after taking a handoff from Hudson but then bounced the play outside. He turned it up field before a Marshall defensive back hit him high but slid off as Miranda's legs continued to churn.

The exhausted defensive back, who played receiver on offense, took a knee before standing and peeling off his helmet. He spit and shook his head.

"You cool, Charlie Wong?" Fred called out to him.

"Yeah," he nodded back at us. Sweat was streaking down his cheek. "I'm cool." Putting his helmet back on, he trotted to the other end of the field.

"You see that?" Fred said to me.

"Was he hurt?"

"Nah man," Fred said. "I used to play Junior All-American with Charlie, he just never quits. His team is going to be 3-7, and he's selling out in the last game he's ever going to play. I know you're hot right now at Hudson for not getting you the ball, but remember you got it good. Nothing is better than winning."

I understood what he was saying because it would suck to be Charlie Wong. I had been a volleyball player. No one cared, no one came, and no one talked about anything we did, this is why I played football now. Everyone cared about what we did, everything seemed to matter.

We were at the edge of the players box when Padilla walked by. It was her second week in a row on the sideline and I thought it was to lend support, but it wasn't.

"There goes trouble," Fred said.

"What do you mean?"

"I think she's here to spy on Piccou," he said.

"Really?"

"Yep."

"What does Maez call her?" I said.

"Bruja."

The action brought Piccou and Padilla our way, They both stood within earshot of us.

"You shouldn't embarrass those boys out there like that," she said to Piccou.

"They're going to start the running clock in the second half and I'm already in the process of pulling our starters," he said without looking directly at her.

She walked away.

It was 62-0 at halftime and I didn't go back on the field to start the third quarter. My stat line was all zeroes. Irked was a bad description of how I felt. I didn't know if it was the amount of fat stats that were out there for me to grab or if it was seeing Hudson raise his hands after every score in triumph.

"Tell me what's better than winning?" Fred said, rejoining me at the end of the players box.

There were so many ways to answer the question. To have Lena, with her eyes and dimpled face, look at me the way she looked at Fred would have been better than winning.

Then shame hit me. I was in trouble between the ears and worked on roughing down my thoughts as the game went on.

To catch a few passes and score a few touchdowns, to have more moments like I did last week against El Monte would have been better than winning. My big moment last week was now forgotten. Fame, I was learning, is a beast continually needing to be fed. I sure wasn't going to feed it standing on the sidelines.

The devil inside of me thought Hudson having his knee blown out on him by a defender would have been better than winning. The same devil smiled and tried to bring in another daydream about Lena.

"Coach, you need to stop this." I turned my eyes left and saw Padilla again talking to Coach Piccou as the game was going on. "You're embarrassing that team and you're embarrassing us. You shouldn't score another touchdown."

"It's a running clock and my starters are out," Piccou said. We could all pick up the frustration in his voice.

"This is terrible," she said. "It's cruel…"

"Stripe!" Piccou called the sideline official. "Can you please explain to my vice-principal what a running clock is?"

Fate did deal a sweet blow to Hudson at the end of Week Ten, and it wasn't a knee injury. No one was there to see him play except for Benny from the school paper and on the way to the locker room Hudson didn't bother to talk to him.

The team party at Gelbaugh's was good with Fred and Lena in attendance. She spent most of her time with Gelbaugh's little sister so I didn't have an opportunity to work my way next to her. I also didn't bother to find a spot to see my highlights because I had none. Except for Patterson's punt return, none of Grip Teague's show mattered to me.

Hudson's dad had already filed and sent his son's highlights for Teague and the Bald Guy to talk about. When our game score flashed on the screen the Hudsonites had front row seats to see what they had done to Pasadena Marshall.

Grip Teague: Billy Hudson had five touchdown passes, that's something. With uncertainty about Fred-X being healthy, this is bound to give Piccou confidence going forward.

Bald Guy: Really? Honestly, no offense to the Marshall Eagles but Grip you could have thrown five touchdown passes against them. Truth is, there are just two questions for the Fighting Scots right now. The second one is which team CIF is going to send their way next Friday night, and the first one is the health and well-being of Fred Ritter's left shoulder. It was

a nice game for Billy Hudson tonight, a nice preview for next year, but playoffs are a different story. Especially when you're only a sophomore.

Hudson raised a middle finger to the flat-screen. "Just give me a f-bombing shot Bald Guy and you'll see."

"F-bomb Bald Guy!" Ponce said securing his sidekick status next to Hudson. "He doesn't respect you at all."

Grip Teague: I got a comment on our board here saying Fred-X was in street clothes tonight, but his arm wasn't in a sling. So some good news for West El Monte Poly. We have to remember the injury is to his non-throwing shoulder, but he runs a lot which is a big part of their offense.

Bald Guy: And how much more running is he going to have to do with Fast Eddie Edwards gone for the season? I think the ups and downs of the season may have caught up to the Scots. They are cruisin' for bruisin.

Grip Teague: You say that here, go say it to Piccou's face.

Bald Guy: I don't have to. He's already told me what I could do to myself...several times, none of it being physically possible, but I will say super soph Mike Miranda can ball. The dude's a keeper.

"Alright, Mikey getting love from the Bald Guy," sophomore guard Matt Grieb said.

"Bald Guy and I are tight," Miranda said. "He knows his business."

"Suck up," Ponce said.

The show continued and the team celebrated. We were 7-0 in league, 9-1 overall, but I couldn't shake the anger over not getting a chance to make a play. Last week I was the guy, this week I felt like I was a fly on the wall. I hated Hudson and even if it meant Omeida, the freshman, was going to have to play, I wanted to hurt him.

After drinking a soda and watching the rest of the show, I went into the kitchen where another conversation was going on.

"Who do you think they're going to give us?" Pineapple said. Splotches of blue paint were all over his face.

Pineapple, Fred, Bustamonte, Feliz, and now myself were standing around the kitchen table double dipping tortilla chips into the salsa and guacamole Gelbaugh's mom put out for us.

"You missed some of your makeup in the shower," Fred said to Pineapple.

"No, I didn't. I'm wearing blue everywhere all week."

"Who do you think?" Bustamonte asked. His demeanor was a whole lot better. Some people needed to pop aspirin, some needed a date, all Bustamonte needed was a couple of touchdowns and he was set back in orbit.

"Bell Gardens beat Alhambra tonight," Fred said. "So they're in. I think we're going to get BG, but if we're lucky we'll get Temple City."

"Pomona's going to get Temple City," Pineapple said.

It was quiet for a moment, I'm sure many were thinking about our one loss. We all knew it, and I understood better now the Pomona game was one we should have taken. Keeping it to myself, I didn't put much hope in a rematch. Not with Fred banged up and Edwards, Escandon, Feliz, and Bobby Lucia wrecked for the season.

"Teague said San Dimas won tonight," Gelbaugh said, coming into the kitchen. His blue paint was off. "And they lost the coin flip."

"What does that mean?" I said.

"It means they're going to go into the playoffs as the third place team from their league," Fred said.

"San Dimas is good," I said.

"No jack," Pineapple said. "Somebody's going to get screwed over in the first round."

"Us?" I said and the looks on their faces told me there wouldn't be an audible answer.

The party broke up a half hour later for most of us. For the few that lingered Gelbaugh started playing *Braveheart* and it cleared everyone else out except for Pineapple, who decided he was going to spend the night on the couch.

I agreed to let Fred and Lena drop me off at home, but it was like a double kick to the gut. She was smoking hot, smoking kind, and so smoking not in love with me. Whatever happened next year they'd both be someplace else and I'd be in uniform not catching passes from Billy Hudson.

"You're too uptight, Handsdrade," Fred said as we drove near empty streets at midnight. He took it slow, not wanting to get pulled over for having too many people in his car. Neither Fred nor Lena were eighteen yet. "You got it good."

"Why do I have it so good?" I said, from the backseat, unable to even shake the depression out of my voice. I tiredly rubbed my forehead into the palm of my hand for comfort wishing I wasn't making my pettiness so obvious.

"Because you could be Charlie Wong," he said, "or somebody else could have gone out for the pass that day at P.E. You ever think about that? Imagine what we all would have missed out on?"

For the half he knew, Fred was right. Where would I be right now if I hadn't played football? Playing X-Box with some volleyball geeks and clinging to a relationship with Desi? I shuddered.

"Besides," Lena said turning back to look at me. I could have sworn her eyes were sparkling through the running shadows between street lamps. I could see the dimples and her smile. "We never would have spent so much time together."

Was she doing this to me deliberately?

Saturday morning I jogged the track with Maez and Miranda. Physically I felt like I had taken another week off. Mentally I knew I needed to grow up and do what needed to be done for the team. If I'd been hit or clocked by Marshall, I probably would have felt better. Strange how for the briefest of moments after Gelbaugh plastered me back in August I thought I might not keep playing, and now I was going through withdrawals without contact.

"Good job last night, Hudson," I said, coming into the film room. He didn't know how much I despised him.

"Thanks, Handsman," he said surprised.

Fred, sitting behind him, gave me a thumb's up.

Pineapple and Gelbaugh came in with donut boxes in both hands and fresh blue paint covering their faces.

"Sons of Scotland? What will you do with your freedom? Will you fight?" Pineapple said to the rest of us who were sitting down.

"Go back to the Jesus fish," Bustamonte said. "It looks cooler."

"Aye," he continued with a horrible accent. "Fight and you may die, quit and you may live. But many years from now when you are in your beds and old..."

"No, no, no," Gelbaugh interrupted him. "It's supposed to be, 'many years from now when you are old and dying in your beds'... come on, if you're going to do it, you've got to do it right. This is *Braveheart*, not some *Transformer* movie..."

"Sons of Scotland...!" He started again.

The lights to the classroom were flicked off and on by Coach Jackson.

"Gelbaugh, Pineapple, sit your big butts down," Jackson said. Piccou came in behind him, followed by Gugliotta and the rest of the staff. "We've got a load we need to clean up this morning."

"We won seventy to nothing Coach," Ponce said.

I was still new to football, but the stupid sophomore should have known better. Instead, he opened the door for thirty minutes of hell. How the team didn't do this, and how the defense didn't do that. Why the offense only worked because it was playing the worst team in the division.

Excluded from the coaches swarm of tirades were Fred and me. Everyone else took a beating, especially Hudson. Piccou and Jackson alternated ripping into him about not calling out the reads at the line of scrimmage, not altering his cadence enough, and all the things he did with his vision and footwork to tip off defenders.

"I ran the offense," Hudson said.

"Big f-bombing deal," Jackson said. "You want a medal for running the offense? I think he wants a medal for that performance last night."

"I'll give you a f-bombing medal when you start playing better football," Piccou said. "You think you're going to get away with that against San Dimas? Bell Gardens?" Piccou then stepped back and addressed the rest of the team. "Do any of you? You play like this next Friday night and you'll be turning in your gear on Saturday morning. I kid you not. Big f-bombing deal so you beat Marshall, so you can play a little football, but can you play real football? Are you ready to play some playoff football? I didn't come all this way just to lose in the first round and I'm cussing because I don't give a f-bomb anymore!...I'm sick of dealing with all of it!"

I could only assume Padilla's nagging of him on the sideline was much the source of his frustration.

"You think God's going to make Ritter's shoulder all better by next week? Are Edwards or Feliz suiting up? This has to get better, if it doesn't get better we might as well end it right now."

I loved nearly all of it. It made me want to strap it up and get into some head knocking. The guys loved it. Gelbaugh and Pineapple were beating the tables. It was a great rah-rah moment taking us through the game film, but no one was talking about the one thing that had me nervous: the thing about God healing Fred's shoulder.

I'd assumed Fred would be back on Friday night. There was room for error in what coach was saying, but I weighed it with the way he cut into Hudson. Enjoyable as it was, it was almost like he was trying to prepare Hudson to start another game.

"You playing next week?" I asked Fred in the parking lot as we were leaving.

"For sure," he said.

"I was getting a bad vibe from Coach in there."

Fred shook his head. "Coach is going to worry until I get official clearance from the doctor on Monday."

"Are you going to get it?"

Fred raised his left arm and began windmilling it around in circles. "I don't know," he laughed. "Doesn't seem to be any range of motion in this shoulder."

I should have known better. Fred-X was incapable of doing anything without giving everyone a thrill. Immediately I relaxed knowing he was going to play. If everything went well I had four games left with him as my quarterback, but only one was guaranteed.

Getting home, I began watching a college game but fell into a long afternoon nap. The snooze felt almost eternal. Extremely deep. It was like I had landed in the real world and this one that I played football in was really a dream.

In the other world, I was at a college in Nebraska. I didn't know if it was Grandview or not, but there were large lawns of green grass and brown autumn leaves on the ground. It was serene and peaceful. Except for Maez, my friends on the team were there.

The dream worked in rational fashion bouncing around the campus and then, as time began to run, my friends started quitting school and leaving one by one. Pineapple, Gelbaugh, Edwards, Bustamonte, Fred, and finally Lena was leaving. I asked her why.

"Because it's my time to go," she said.

"You don't have to go," I said. "You can stay. Stay with me."

"I have to go," she said and made it worse by smiling. "It's my time." She waved goodbye.

Then I was alone on a campus somewhere in Nebraska. Alone, but an odd comfort came to me with strange faces. I kept asking myself why I wasn't missing the old ones, I wanted to miss them, but no answer came.

I spent Sunday morning fighting the urge to go to church before giving in. A few weeks before, not wanting to be around Dad was the issue, now it was facing a unique Lena disappointment. I'd get her alone and someone else would show up. Mr. Umphries would invite me to lunch, her mom would say it was time to go, she was sick, or I couldn't track her down, it was always something. Then again, I was hopeful. Trading my shorts and a tee shirt for Gap khakis and a blue button down, I left out the door. It felt good to be out walking, smelling the day, and seeing the things that went with autumn.

Besides seeing Lena, the smart thing was to go to church. It worked when I was afraid of losing my job to Ponce at the start of the season and it sure wouldn't hurt our chances for a good playoff draw. I knew it was silly, as if God cared about the first round of the CIF playoffs, but it was crunch time.

The dream was bugging me. It was a stupid dream like all dreams were stupid dreams, but this one made me think about separation and mortality. Death didn't feel like it was coming anytime soon, but the football season felt like it was in the balance. So many guys were wrecked along with Fred. I couldn't bear the thought this part of my life might end Friday night.

The feeling of pending doom was enabled all the more knowing the playoff pairings were being released in an hour. God, football, Lena, I didn't know the order they should be in. To be perfectly honest, God was only a factor as to how he could help me out with the other two.

I took my spot in the back section of pews as the worship band finished its set. People were going to the altar as Pastor David came to the microphone. He was younger than Domres, had more hair, and I believed his job was to run the day to day operations of the church. He never preached, except when he prayed and then it seemed like he could turn minutes into hours.

Standing with the rest, I closed my eyes and bowed my head. Unsure if I was supposed to be repeating what Pastor David was saying about the Holy Spirit blessing this service or if I should have been offering my own words. I held still, showed respect for the moment, and waited for it to end.

I felt the presence of someone to my left and smelled the aroma of Royal Jasmine. When the amen came I opened my eyes to see Lena had taken the seat next to me. I thanked God.

"When I know I'm not teaching," she whispered. "I oversleep sometimes." She playfully bumped her shoulder into mine. "Look at you, Mr. Regular Attendant."

We didn't talk, but every few minutes exchanged a smile during Pastor Domres message. Twenty of the fastest minutes of my life, rivaling with the best, went by. We weren't rushing somewhere, Fred wasn't around, and there wasn't a football related discussion to be had. I breathed her in. Was God doing something here? Was this really happening? Could momentum be swinging my way?

Over the last few months of attending church, I'd seen people write notes on the blue cards stuffed into holders on the backs of the pews. Could I write her a note now and tell her I loved her?

Could I just put my hand out and have her take it? What I was feeling now was bigger than anything I felt playing football, hauling in the touchdown pass against El Monte, or being in the presence of Fred-X.

All I needed was for Pastor Domres to keep preaching.

Lena reached into her purse and looked at her phone very discretely. In my peripheral, I could see a small acknowledgment come to her face and then she carefully put her hand out in front of me. Our eyes met and she motioned down to her phone. It was a text from Fred.

'**San Dimas**' was all it said.

So much for trying to score football points with God. She tilted her head and gave me a tough luck smile. No worries, I thought, everything was going to be okay as long as Domres kept preaching.

"Would you stand with me as we close in prayer…"

Up to this point in my life, it was the only time I ever felt robbed by a preacher. Like there wasn't another verse to read? Another story to tell? It's not like these guys didn't have stories, Domres was full of stories.

When the prayer ended everyone was emptying into the aisles. Because we were in the back we had an easier escape. I followed Lena through the side door and then out to the church courtyard.

"They're going to ask me to babysit for the fellowship they've got going tonight," she said. "I kind of want to get out of here. Let's go through the breezeway out to the street."

The breezeway was the narrow, covered, outdoor passage between the sanctuary and church office. I didn't have to think about it or consider another option, I followed her. We went undetected down the shorts steps to the sidewalk.

"I think you made it," I said.

"I hope so," she smiled. "I usually don't mind helping, but I'm backed up on homework. The AP classes are killing me."

"Are your parents here?"

"Not today, they're visiting some friends," she said. She looked over my shoulder to make sure she was clear. "You go the same way don't you?" I nodded. "Walk with me."

The day went from good to very good. It was autumn, it was cool, there were clouds, and the air tasted like God had just created it. Then again, it might have just been the Royal Jasmine. She was wearing a light brown dress that hugged her torso and flowed outward as it reached her waist. It covered the edges of her shoulders and exposed an area of skin beneath her neck. A cross hung in the center.

I became lost searching for the words I'd rehearsed whenever I dreamed of a moment like this. It took everything I had to remember the basics of breathing, exhaling, and stepping to the outside of her as we went down the sidewalk.

"So what do you think about San Dimas?" She said.

Who the heck cared about San Dimas right now? Delfman, Bazooka Joe? Forget those guys and forget the Fighting Scots of

West El Monte Poly because the trifecta of Lena, the day, and the Royal Jasmine were doing their thing.

"I don't think the guys are going to be happy," I said.

"You want to know the truth?" She said as we continued to walk. Her black hair, down to the shoulders, hung around the sides of her face. Bangs covered her forehead.

"I don't know if I want to know the truth. Sometimes the truth is scary."

"So you don't ever want to know the truth, Handsman?" She smiled.

"Like I said, the truth is scary." It felt like she was setting me up for something. Something great I prayed.

"Don't get mad," she said. We were a block away from where she turned off to her home. It was only two houses down and unless she was ready to proclaim her love for me it would be awkward to walk her the whole way.

"I won't get mad."

"I don't want it to happen, but I think you guys are going to lose to San Dimas."

"You really think so? Fred's coming back."

"Fred's hurt," she said. "He's going to get cleared but his shoulder is getting worse and he knows he shouldn't play."

"I saw him yesterday and I saw him move the shoulder."

"Remember the night at The Boat when I told you Fred wasn't leaving?"

"Yes," I said. We reached her corner.

"We never got to finish, but he's not leaving because he's got no offers. Not one, nothing except for the Division-three schools but those are just offers to put together financial packages for him. He's only playing because he's convinced winning will get him a scholarship."

I didn't know what to say to her. This was my moment with her and we were still talking about Fred.

"I'm only telling you because I need to tell somebody," she said. "He's dying on the inside and I'm the only one who really knows, but he's drifting from me. Everyone thinks he's a god and when this scholarship thing doesn't happen he's going to need a friend. He's going to need someone like you."

"I'll be there for him, but one thing about Fred I've noticed is he always surprises me," I said feeling the flood of depression coming in.

"I hope he surprises us all," she said. "I really do." Then she side hugged me before going her way. I waited and watched until she got to her house and went up to the porch. From there she gave a short wave similar, in style and hurt, to the one she gave me in Nebraska.

We were getting San Dimas and Sunday night the subject caught fire on the message boards. Chat boxes, tweets, and statuses were rolling. Not wanting to jump into any of them, I got away from my computer and thought about downloading *Braveheart*. It had some encouraging scenes about how to beat the odds. At least for a while it did.

The season couldn't end. It couldn't, but if it did what would happen? There were still seven months of school. We'd see each other. We'd still workout together. There was the winter formal, the awards banquet, and signing day.

There had to be a real moment coming for Lena and I.

For me, Grandview sounded nice even if it was in a dream place like Nebraska. I'd be away from everything I didn't like, everyone I didn't want to be around, and playing football. Still, my thoughts remained anchored at West El Monte Poly. These were the guys that brought me in. These were the guys that made me "Handsdrade." It seemed inappropriate for the season to end so suddenly. I didn't want to dwell on the future and Nebraska, I wanted to think about this place and winning on Friday night.

Fred and Pineapple were sure to sign and Gelbaugh was bound to get some interest. Even in my selfishness, I wanted something good to happen for Bustamonte because he was going to be devastated if he didn't play next year.

He's not leaving because he's got no offers.

Where was Fred going? After all he'd accomplished I was certain he had options we didn't know about. A miracle was never out of the question when it came to Fred-X.

Getting back online I went to the prep page for scouting and followed the ridiculously long route to find the right region, then state, then position. I clicked on a link for the Top Fifty Quarterbacks in California.

There I found the big names I'd learned about over the summer, and heard about during the season. At the top of the stack was Meisner from Capo Valley, then Parker from Servite, a guy from De La Salle named Douglass was third, and fourth was Jammon from Dominguez. Fred told me first-hand stories about Jammon and the things he could do.

I scrolled through the rest of the top ten, went through the top twenty, then twenty-five and scrolled through the first forty...forty-one: D.K. Germany, El Rancho...forty-two...forty-three...forty-four...forty-five...forty-six: Shane Delfman, San Dimas...forty-seven...forty-eight...forty-nine...fifty.

I'd missed something. Going to the search box, I typed in Fred Ritter. Nothing came up. I typed in Frederick Ritter knowing sometimes search engines could be anal about how a name was entered.

Nothing.

I'd seen the stack of letters at Fred's house so I knew this wasn't right. I keyed in another recruiting site, entered in all the information: nothing.

In the search box, I typed in: Carl Bartholomew

Bartholomew, Carl: G/T Rk: 97th
Offer: Humboldt State.

I put Fred's name in again, then tried it a different way, nothing came up. I typed in his name on Google and all that came to the screen was a string of game stories he'd been mentioned in, our team page on MaxPreps, his highlights on Hudl, and the West El Monte Poly website.

There had to be a mistake.

WEEK ELEVEN
(PLAYOFFS)

Read The Blitz
By Grip Teague

CIF didn't do West El Monte any favors here. San Dimas is not a third place team and everyone knows it. Skip Piccou knows it and he's losing hair trying to game plan this thing out...Regular season is over so the coach replacement season has begun. First on the list? Tom Crawl, La Serna has announced he will not be back as the team's HC. The job's been posted and a teaching position comes with it. Crawl could not be reached for comment...No truth, so far, to the rumor that Jefferson Pham will be coming back to California next fall. One rumor popping up in our comments box had Pham returning next season to play at Burbank. I like Arroyo, I just don't like them traveling to Lancaster to play Paraclete. That's a lot of gas wasted for a quick turnaround just to see Calvin Greene. Keep an eye on Mayfair, I've said it before. No one is talking about the Monsoons but if they get by Downey their bracket sets up for a long run...Cathedral will beat Burroughs...El

Monte gets Northview...The Lions looked hungover this weekend in their win against South El Monte. They better snap out of it if they intend on competing with the Vikings.

"Hope you all got familiar with San Dimas online," Piccou said in Monday's meeting. "Back in the day they used to run the Delaware Wing and did all sorts of variations off of it. What you saw shows them running something that looks like an old Wishbone attack, but functions like a spread. It's different, it's unique, and it's a pain."

The San Dimas offense was playing on the wall behind Piccou. The dark room was serious. There wasn't any joking. If Temple City or even Bell Gardens had been put in front of us there might have been room for a little screwing around. As it was, facing San Dimas felt like an insult. We were 9-1, they were 7-3 but hadn't lost on the field and were being treated like a third place team. To the suits structuring the playoffs, going 7-0 in the Mission Valley League earned us nothing. There was no place to appeal, no time to vent. Complaining to Trudy Shields or Grip Teague would have made us look like whiners.

"Coach, I saw everything on them," Gelbaugh said with a raised hand. "They didn't run an option down the line once."

"Good to know you can watch something besides *Braveheart*," Piccou said. "No, they haven't. They pound, they hit the corners, and constantly use play action. You can see for yourself." He gestured to the video. "They haven't run one option all season or used one straight drop back. You see Delfman here..." He used the laser pointer to highlight the Saints' quarterback. "He'll fake the dive to the fullback, go down the line but not once all season has he pitched it. He's passed, he's run, but he's never pitched it out to Eric Johnson. Look at your notes, they've thrown 257 passes this year, not one was without play action. They ran 400 hundred times and passed over half that many times out of a wishbone formation."

"I hate Delfman already," Dinh Lee said, which brought a smile to everyone's face to hear our very mild mannered free safety chime in.

Shane Delfman, at six-two, 210 pounds, was ranked number forty-six on the list for the top quarterbacks in the state. It was hard to believe he was only a freshman.

"You should," Gugliotta said. "He's trouble and he doesn't play like a freshman. The sooner we stop him, the sooner he can transfer out of our division to a private Orange County school."

"They're not any bigger than us," Fred said.

"It's real simple, they have great technique and they hit. Those skinny little receivers of theirs hit. Those backs, they hit," Piccou said, "but we've got a game plan. Coach Jackson?"

Coach Jackson stood in front of us. "We think they can be exposed up the middle, which, with Edwards out, they think we're going to ignore."

"You going to pound it with me?" Miranda said with joy.

"We're going to pound it with you, but we're going to feature you in the running game." Jackson pointed at Bustamonte.

"I've been running the Jet Sweep all year, I don't think that'll be a surprise," Boosty said.

"You're going to be running out of the backfield. Physically you're the strongest skill player we have, Coach Piccou and I talked about it yesterday after the brackets came out. We want you to carry the ball between the tackles this week. You down with that?"

Bustamonte's face lit up. "I'm down!"

"That's not a shot at you Miranda, Boosty's just stronger right now," Jackson said. "We're also going to work Patterson into more of the game plan."

Jackson broke down the plays and packages we were going to run and the adjustments we were making to the existing plays. He increased the pre-snap use of motion, which was something that totally baffled me at the start of the season but could now grasp after ten weeks and a torso turned plum with bruises.

"Fair warning," Jackson said. "Because I'd want to know if someone was out there looking for me. Receivers keep your eyes open for Bazooka Joe, dude is a wrecking ball."

"Who's tougher, Bazooka Joe or Gilliam Gilliam?" Fred said and then grinned at me.

"I'd rate them the same," Jackson said, "but Handsdrade will probably be able to give you a better assessment after."

"If he can still talk," Maez said.

"I'll try not to lead you too much on the slant," Fred said.

"Not taking a shot at our defense, but we want to help them," Jackson went on. "So we're going to change our pacing, use motion to create uncertainty, and extend the snap counts. Ritter you're going to have to milk the play clock, take us right to the brink. Everyone is always working hard to limit our touches but this Friday we're going to need to limit theirs."

After we broke, Fred left for the doctor's office.

Later, when we were on the field going through a soft work-out, Coach Piccou's phone dinged with a text message saying our quarterback had the green light to play on Friday night. Part of the honor of knowing Fred was the feeling of all things being possible. I loved Lena, but she was wrong. He could and would accomplish it all. The news he was going to suit up against San Dimas in the first round of the playoffs had a Christmas morning effect on us.

Except for Hudson. The sophomore didn't sulk, kept throwing, kept up appearances, but I could see he was disappointed. I didn't know for sure, but it was never about the team with him.

Hudson? How about you? My own voices convicted.

Practice continued.

The ball was snapped and I took off on a skinny-route. I was healthy, which was nothing to sneeze at given all I'd experienced and seen around me this season. There were bruises, an especially deep one in my thigh from the South El Monte game, but I was running. The ball glided towards me and I hauled it in, effortlessly, before sprinting to the other end of the field.

When I turned in the end zone, I saw the empty stadium. In the distance, I could hear the coaching staff applauding my effort. The next play was being run and Hudson hit Ponce with a perfect pass on a corner-route.

"Handsdrade! You coming back?" Piccou yelled. "Are you waiting for the band to start playing?"

A breeze hit against my back. Even in my health and good fortune, I felt like a dead man. In another month, if not sooner (San Dimas was a great dream killer), Alonson Stadium would look like this. The marching band wouldn't have to compete for time and all of us would be setting sail in different directions. Nothing could prevent it.

Chanos was out to interview Fred on Tuesday, and while Fred was polite he cut the interview short with an apology. "I missed a week, I got to get caught up, but thank's for coming out. I'll see you on Friday."

A jock sniffer deluxe, Chanos didn't get upset but said he wanted the first interview after Friday's win over San Dimas and Fred told him he'd get it.

Chanos was positive, but Grip Teague wasn't. He took San Dimas, 35-30, on his Tuesday show. Bald Guy was still advancing his theory that we were cruisin' for a bruisin and said the Saints were going to take us out.

On Wednesday Kiel Basler's heavily taped right wrist finally gave out. The injury he'd been coaxing along since early in the season finally snapped when he rolled the ball to Fred while in formation. He cursed when it happened, and then cursed much more when Sondra took a look at it.

The results of the x-rays were texted to us. They showed a fracture and torn tendons. Basler's season was wrecked. Sophomore Hector Cardenas would take his place.

On Thursday at lunch Pineapple removed Trudy Shields from his 'To Do List' after she published her previews and predictions for this weekend's games. Shields had us losing 35-21, writing that we'd be worn down by the fourth quarter.

We were sitting on the stone benches, near the flag pole, outside the lunch area. The guys pulled out their phones and tablets and began sharing the story.

Game Night Column
By Trudy Shields

"The game will be close for a while, but the San Dimas offense will break West El Monte's back in the fourth quarter. The Fred-X Show closes down forever."

The comments box underneath began to fill.

"The secret weapon for the Fighting Scots this season has been Dale 'Handsdrade' Andrade. Bustamonte makes big plays, but he's inconsistent, Handsdrade has been bailing Fred-X and the offense out all year."---War Eagle

"It's a mistake to undersell the Fighting Scots. They have a great quarterback and great receivers. They also have the area's next great running back in Mike Miranda."---Wolfman

"San Dimas is going to kill them at the line of scrimmage. It might get my butt kicked on Flair Drive, but the Saints have a better quarterback in Delfman than the Scots do in either Ritter or Hudson."---Sunshine

"@Sunshine that is the stupidest thing I've ever heard. Fred-X makes miracles happen."---Bad News

"@Bad News well its going to take a miracle for them to beat San Dimas with Billy Hudson on the bench."---Cool Jets

"Ritter's banged up, Edwards is out, Basler is out, Feliz is out, Escandon is out, Lucia is out, and even when everyone was playing West El Monte was having trouble stopping the run. Do you really think they are going to be able to do anything against that mutant-bone offense SD runs? Thanks for playing we have some lovely parting gifts for you..."---Trotsky Lives

"The West offense will score, but they won't be able to stop the Saints."---Kansas

"The key to this game is Fred-X. If he is standing and throwing West El Monte is going to win."---Big Tony

"Hudson will rally this team. Wait and see."---MaxAtax

"@Cool Jets what has Hudson done to make you believe he's something special? All I've seen is a lot of whining out of his family this year. I can tell you Ayala didn't cry any tears when he left."---Wolfman

"Uh, try five touchdown passes last week."---Cool Jets

"Uh, that was against Marshall."---Jorge Grande

"With Basler (starting center) out it means three sophomores starting on the offensive line. It's going to be a case of the spirit is willing, but the flesh is weak against San Dimas. Fred-X and friends just aren't going to have enough…"---Trotsky Lives

"Prediction: Delfman throws for two hundred yards and three touchdowns, Ritter is knocked out in the second quarter, and Hudson throws five interceptions in the second half. Saints win."---Kansas

"---DELETED--- you Kansas!"---Cool Jets

We were told to stay away from the message boards, but we never did. In previous weeks, at worst, there seemed to be a split among fans and writers about how we would do against a certain opponent. This week everybody was picking against us.

It should have motivated us, but instead Thursday's practice felt depressed. No one said anything, no one complained, but I noticed it. We took our steps, but we weren't planting them. We ran through our plays, but we weren't feeling the same buzz we felt from them before.

Sitting on the sideline watching us were Feliz, wrist in a cast, Basler, arm in a sling, and Escandon on crutches. It might have been better if they hadn't shown up. For all practical purposes they were dead men, wrecked, they weren't coming back. Instead, they were reminders, I thought anyway, of what we might become in another day. I didn't like seeing them.

Even Fred was less electric. In normal interactions, he was always Fred, but on the field or when the football was in his hands he was Fred-X. He was probably getting focused, but all he seemed to be doing was making his reads and his throws. No hand clapping, no joking, no back slapping, no whatever it was he had that made every moment of the last eight months special to be around him.

Was it a playoff attitude I couldn't understand? I doubted it. No one had been in the playoffs before.

Coach Piccou didn't get in our faces because on the surface, there was nothing to get in our faces about. We'd played ten games, won nine, worked through the summer, started in the spring and most of the team had been lifting weights since the previous December to get to this moment. Yet, something was missing...or something had arrived.

We were playing a team that should have been ranked number one in our division and so many of our guys were wrecked or banged up. What arrived was doom. I was becoming an expert in recognizing the onset of doom. I was in love with a girl I had no chance with and every hour of every day raised hopelessness and brought her graduation in June closer.

We weren't talking about it, but every moment ticking Friday closer felt like the end of all things was closing in on us.

After practice, several of us hit the different fast food joints on Flair Drive and came back to the stadium. In the bleachers, we ate our dinner and watched folks walk and run around the track in the early shade of the evening. Stretches of time would pass without any of us speaking.

We'd seen all the film we could see to this point. We were as healthy and as in shape as we were going to be. We knew the game plan, the packages, the audibles. There was nothing left to do but sit and wait for the remainder of Thursday to expire.

"What are you thinking about Fred?" I said.

"I'm not thinking," he said suddenly looking very old. Like a grandfather looking back over his life knowing there were no adjustments he could make to alter what happened way back when. "I'm just remembering."

"What happens if we lose?" Pineapple asked no one in particular.

"You can't think like that," Gelbaugh said. On another day, in another week of the season, Gelbaugh would have exploded if he heard that comment.

"What I meant was, if we do lose, it means all of this is over." Pineapple looked back at Fred and then at the rest of us. "It means this part of our life is finished. No more practices and no more being together like this."

"Carl Bartholomew getting all philosophical on us," Fred said. His arms were back against a bench, his legs stretched out across another. The varsity jacket on his frame was stitched with countless kudos, plaudits, and honors.

"Are you saying we've already lost this game Pineapple?" Bustamonte said.

"No," he said, but it was easy to see he was thinking about it. We all were.

The pressures of the week, the momentum of the message boards, and what our own dark fears had built because we'd seen the film and knew what we were taking into battle were wearing us down. We were league champs, but they were a better team right now. Instead of thinking about winning we were scared of losing and too scared to admit it.

"Don't even think about it," Gelbaugh said. "It's just fear trying to get at us."

It was a nice effort by our middle linebacker, but fear was already inside the walls.

"What happens if we lose?" Fred pondered back to us. "Besides hugging and crying, and turning in our gear? Everything gets dark. For days, we won't want to think about anything and when we do we'll cry while we're alone. So we won't watch any football and we won't want to be around each other because we won't want to be reminded we're dead. Then a big old hole opens up inside of us and nothing we do, for the rest of our lives, will ever fill it. Except football, except if we can find a way to keep playing football. We'll go to the junior colleges and when we're done we'll try to play semipro and then we'll even reduce ourselves to seven on seven sports bar leagues. We'll try coaching, but it won't be the same and then we'll come back to stand on the sidelines at home games like Horse and those poor guys who played before us do with their twice shrunk varsity jackets...How does that sound?"

I don't know how everyone else felt, but I was stunned. I'd never heard him speak like that before.

"Don't be so f-bombing positive Fred," Bustamonte said.

"Anyone disagree?" He said, not moving from his spot. He stared at the empty field with the stadium lights shining down on it. "I think I'm more afraid of that happening than losing. I know what we're all thinking, I know what we're feeling, but we still have four quarters to play and change it." Finally, a spark of energy came out of our quarterback's eyes. "Why don't we make San Dimas sorry they lost the coin flip and had to face us in the first round? Let's admit we're the underdog and do everything we can to wreck their season."

On Friday, the skill players sat in the film room and watched highlights of the San Dimas defense. Fred, myself, Bustamonte, Maez, Miranda, Patterson, Ponce, Califf, and even Hudson.

Bazooka Joe didn't look any tougher than Gilliam Gilliam to me.

The message boards were alive with threads about Hudson's pending transfer once the season was over. I read and believed them, but Fred didn't treat him like any less a citizen of the team. Fred told Hudson, with complete honesty, if he got knocked out he had to be ready to go.

Being home provided some hope. No bus to get ready for and meet with all of our gear. No foreign locker room, stalls, or showers. Being home was an advantage and it added to our preparation. The stretching was easier and the pregame nap fuller.

Guys got taped and eased into their routine. They hit their familiar stalls and let loose their growlers. Some contemplated throwing up, but no one did. It was comforting to see Bustamonte working on his hair. The defense was all painted up and the seniors on offense added blue crosses to their foreheads.

Edwards came into the locker room on crutches after we were dressed. His best face was there for us to see, but it was clear he was doing it to feel connected to the team. I couldn't blame him, but then again didn't every ghost want to be in fellowship with the living?

We hugged him, shook his hand, and helped him hop over to the bench in front of his locker.

"I wasn't going to let you guys go out there without me," he said. "Win tonight and maybe I'll be back in time for the finals."

"Put this in your locker, and you can take it home after the game," Fred said spinning a football, now covered in ink with our signatures and thoughts, to Edwards. "Lose it and the Moanin' Samoan will put you on his 'To do List.'"

Fast Eddie's eyes stared at the ball. There was a tremble in his shoulders letting us know the gift touched him. Lee and Maez put their hands on his back. It was a tough moment, but I didn't think it was the one we needed.

I loved Edwards, but his presence didn't inspire me to play harder. It didn't make me think I had to win this game for him. My feelings were I had to win this game to stay alive. I wouldn't let anyone else know my thoughts, but I felt nothing for him because he was already dead. The fellow solider who didn't make it off the beach, you couldn't mourn for him because there was still a battle to be fought. If you did you'd end up in the same place he was: the bleachers, which was just another name for a cemetery.

Coach Piccou delivered his speech. He was calm, measured, and told us flatly everything was in our power to make happen. Nothing had changed since Week One. Everything we wanted was there for the taking.

"Right now, in your way, take a moment to thank your maker, your creator, for the opportunity to play this great game of football." This was a first. We had fifteen-seconds of silent team prayer. No atheists in foxholes? I wasn't sure, but Coach didn't seem like he was too concerned about what the administration or others might think.

We honored his words, but I didn't know if the other guys prayed. I offered up a "please let us win" but it was with half a heart. I didn't know how to pray any other way except in desperation and I felt guilty for it. I didn't really even know how to say thank you, and if we lost what would there be to be thankful for? The game would be lost, the girl I wanted would be lost, and, maybe, I would lose the connection to all of my new friends.

"Amen," Coach Piccou said.

Our helmets came on and we lined in pairs. Jesse Maez was my marching partner. There was no alba gu bràth moment. The tension of the locker room was intensified by the growing heat from our breathing. We waited for the double doors to open. The sound of the stands, muffled, was buzzing.

The doors opened, and the night air hit us. We marched across the cement, our cleats clacking, and through the gates the noise level of the fans picked up. The band started playing the same ancient rock and roll song it always played, but it didn't sound like dance music. It sounded like the music anyone would want to hear when everything they dreamed of or wished for was being put on the line.

Every tangent dream we had about our lives and this season was connected to this playoff moment. Dreams of the girl, of college, of legacy, and eternity, lit our minds like a furnace forging memories as real, as tangible, as any sod or dirt we walked on. How could you get to USC without winning this game? How could you achieve in life if you didn't win this game?

Was I a selfish young man? Yes, I was. Was I someone who dreamed dreams for myself and not others? Yes, I was, but we all were. We all had desires and ambitions of what we wanted. I was all of it as I marched with Maez to the music and approval of the fans. If this was to be my only moment, then I was proud this was it.

A feeling of gratitude struck me as I looked at my marching partner and tugged his hand. "Thank you," I said.

Maez looked at me and nodded. He understood. "Handsdrade," he said with a small smile.

We came together under our goal post. At the fifty Fred, Bustamonte, and Gelbaugh went out met with the San Dimas team captains. They were in their white uniforms with their blue Michigan helmets with maize stripes. The banner we were supposed to run through blocked most of my view, but when I heard the crowd cheer I knew we had won the toss.

The captains jogged our way, but no rah-rah was rising out of us. We had amped ourselves up so much over the course of the regular season we were emotionally drained. Pomona, Arroyo, and

El Monte were exhausting games, and tonight there was the cloud of doom fogging our thoughts.

When we ran through the banner, the sophomores led the way. The fans loved it, but two and a half months in for me...whatever. What I needed most was to get hit, and quick, to get my mind right. I was ready to run right into f-bombing Bazooka Joe. Let him light me up and then I'd light up his defense on a corner-route to the end zone.

Meeting again on our sideline before sending the kickoff team out, Gelbaugh took off his helmet. On cue, wind flapped the back of his hair up. His face was painted half blue on the right side, three finger length stripes were horizontal underneath his left I. It was a good look for him.

"Sons of Scotland! What will you do with your freedom? Will you fight?"

"Yes!"

"Will you?"

"Yes!"

"Alba...!"

"...Gu bràth!"

The team came to life and, finally, it felt like we were ready to play.

We no longer had the weapons we began the season with. We were still no huddle, we were still spread, but now, when forced into punting situations deep in our own end, we punted.

It didn't feel as much like a step back as it did a smart adjustment. The punting did give our defense help, but the offense hated not being on the field for fourth down. We saw what it did to defenses when no punt team came from the sideline. No matter, it was about getting the win, about staying alive. Our vice had been the thrill of going for it on fourth down, now with the season well aged it was time to live responsibly.

Gelbaugh, Lee, and the rest played the opening of the game like folks did when others believed in them. They were sold out. The first two possessions for both teams ended with punts. Which meant twice we faced the Saints' wishbone-spread and twice we got them off the field. Towards the end of the opening quarter, I caught my first pass on a dig-route and Bazooka Joe Natalia lit me up.

I was decleated, it hurt, and something tightened just below my right shoulder, but it felt horribly good. I held onto the ball for a seventeen-yard gain. Popping up I gave it to the official ready to do it again.

On our third possession, Bustamonte broke off a thirteen-yard run before the quarter ended. Mike Patterson, running a skinny, knifed right through the San Dimas defense. Fred-X's pass was on target and we set up first and ten at the twelve. One play later Maez ran the jet sweep to the left with Pineapple making a double block and we were up 6-0.

The stadium cheered the way it always did. The band juiced more emotion out of us and there was only a brief hiccup in the applause when the two-point conversion failed. Jackson's most recent numbers showed us being successful over fifty-six percent of the time. No one ever panicked when we didn't convert a deuce except for the Hudsonites, but right now I couldn't hear them.

Following the kickoff, San Dimas's offense came onto the field at their own twenty-seven.

"It's going to be open all night," Jackson said, pointing at his laminated game plan and talking to Fred. I was standing behind them. "Patterson's too fast, they're running a cheap looking Cover Two, but Bazooka Joe can't get back fast enough to clog up the middle. So they're going to start cheating."

"Then we got Handsdrade and Maez up the sidelines," Fred said. His eyes were atomic.

"You don't even have to read the safeties. If Bazooka Joe starts stepping back audible out, and pound Bustamonte and Miranda."

As our offensive game plan began to take hold our defense began to show its first cracks. The Saints running game pushed the ball to our nine. On first down Shane Delfman, faked the dive to the fullback and ran to his right before pitching it out to halfback, Eric Johnson.

"Option!" Gugliotta yelled.

Johnson took the ball into the end zone untouched and, after the extra-point, San Dimas led 7-6.

The defense congregated around the bench and, as I prepared to go back on the field, I could hear Gugliotta shouting at them. "Did you think we were going to be the only ones to add wrinkles tonight? Clearly they were saving this, so adapt and react! We've given you answers, execute them!"

It wasn't my problem.

Taking over at our twenty-two, we put the ball into Bustamonte's hands on consecutive plays and picked up a first down. If I enjoyed getting hit in a game, Bustamonte thrived on it. The average was two, and on occasion three, defenders were required to bring him down.

I caught an out-route to the right to keep the defense honest and got blasted out of bounds with a shot to the center of my back. I felt nothing. We were marching and using everything in the playbook except for Fred running the ball. As long as we had Bustamonte to run Power, we didn't need Fred to expose his shoulder.

On first down at the fifty, Fred faked a handoff to Miranda and hit Ponce on a slant. The sophomore carried the ball to the San Dimas thirty-nine. The next play I escaped the line of scrimmage without getting jammed and turned to Fred on my corner-route in time to see him get slammed from behind.

The Saints had sent a cornerback blitz from the blindside.

Fred jumped to his feet, got us at the line of scrimmage, and went to Bustamonte on the next play. Three yards later we were facing a third and seven at the San Dimas thirty-six. The second quarter clock showed 4:20 to play.

The signals were barked. It was going to be Patterson on another skinny-route, my route was an out and up. The same one I burned Billy Camacho on in Week Nine. I was told it was once called a

'Staircase' pattern, another description described it as a 'Fork' or a 'Chair.' I liked it because if the defense bit, and they should, I was going to score.

They bit, but not Bazooka Joe. He blitzed, first time all night, up the middle and flattened Fred as he released the ball. The pass fell incomplete and we were looking at fourth and seven.

Fred hopped to his feet again, but a pensive expression was on his face. It was as if he was trying to hold something down. He waved us to the line of scrimmage and then the signal came from Piccou for a timeout.

"Boosty," Fat John said. "You've got to pick up that blitz!"

"I was swinging," Bustamonte said. "What do you want me to do?"

"You guys have got to protect Fred-X or we ain't getting out of here," Pineapple said to the interior linemen: Matt Grieb, Hector Cardenas, and Ben Montoya. "F-bombing sophomores start playing like men!"

The girls with water bottles came out and Fred walked to the sideline. Behind the bench, in front of where the cheerleaders stood on their boxes, a football was being thrown.

Billy Hudson, who should have been standing alongside Coach Jackson with a clipboard, was gone. We didn't have to hear the words, we could see it in the body language Piccou was asking Fred how he felt.

"No matter what," Maez said. "We've got to protect our herma-no. Give up your body if you have to, Fred needs to stay in this game." We all nodded

Fred came back and we huddled.

"You okay?" Pineapple asked. His face was drenched with sweat, the blue war paint was smeared everywhere.

"Just give me time," Fred said, ignoring the question.

He gave us the play and we went to the line of scrimmage. I was going to run a dig-route and sit down just past the first down marker in the soft part of the Saints zone. Expecting the blitz, Bustamonte stayed in to protect.

The ball snapped. I shoved aside the light linebacker trying to jam me, made my cut inside the hashmark. The perfect pass would have been low, where I catch it and just get tapped down. The next best one would have been chest high, I catch it and get tackled. The worst...the one I got...was the pass went high.

A high pass, in the middle field, even against Pasadena Marshall, at any time, was like begging to go to a local ICU. It felt like I had a second to make my decision to climb the ladder and thirty-one days to consider the ferociousness waiting for me on the other side.

Middle of the field, high pass; best hope was it would land incomplete, the worst was an interception. Football did make you consider things you never would have before. Like going on a roller coaster without being strapped in. Never in your right mind would you do it, not even for a thrill.

You wouldn't do it for football alone, but you would do it for your teammates, and I knew I would do it for the most special of all my teammates. I'd do it for Fred-X.

I leaped high and my right-hand cupped the nose of the ball. As I tucked it into my shoulder, I felt the pressure of a defender pushing up underneath me, and the crushing wave of Bazooka Joe knocking me into a near death experience.

From the left corner of my eye, I saw the ancient looking official signal first down, but it was all I saw. There was a slow spin going on around the outside of my eyes and in front of them I saw sporadic flashings of stars.

I was in trouble, but if anyone knew I was in trouble I'd be done for the night. So I went into fake mode. I held the ball up from the ground, smiled at Maez and Ponce as they pulled me off the turf. Picking my feet up off the ground was pushing it as I trotted to our side of the line of scrimmage. Clapping my hands, I got my answers ready. They would be asking me numbers and the name of the school and where we were at. My mind was still working through the fireworks show, but all my numbers were in a row.

Jackson subbed Patterson in for me. I was still seeing stars and things were flashing, but I put my hands out going to the sideline to give the impression I was okay. It was a good sell.

"Handsdrade, you alright?" Jackson said.

"I'm cool!" I lied. "Get me back in the game! I want back in!"

"Check him out!" Piccou ordered the trainer. I was escorted to the bench and forced to sit.

"I'm fine!" I said with a little more attitude. Sitting out a couple of plays to get the spinning and flashing to stop would be a good thing, but if I admitted to anything my night would be wrecked.

"This is crazy! I held onto the f-bombing ball! I would have dropped it if I had a concussion!" I said to our trainer. She was blonde, middle-aged, sort of attractive, and a complete stranger to me at the moment.

My brain searched for her name while it worked overtime to uncover who we were playing. I knew they wore blue and yellow, but I forgot who they were. Fortunately, those weren't the questions.

"What school do you play for?" She asked.

"West El Monte Poly, right here on Flair Drive."

"What is the name of your head coach?"

"Skip Piccou and he got suspended this year for using racial slurs against Pineapple."

"What's Pineapple's name?"

"Bartholomew." I didn't have his first name ready, but she didn't ask.

"What's your phone number?"

I gave it.

"How many fingers?"

"Three, two and a thumb."

She put a penlight into my eyes. "Stop moving...Stop moving!"

"I'm good!"

"Squeeze my hands," she said. I squeezed her hands. "Wait here until halftime."

A minute later, Fred and the rest of the offense came off the field. I learned we turned the ball over on downs and the other team had it at their own twelve with less than two minutes to go in the quarter.

"You gonna live?" Maez said.

"They're making me sit until halftime, I'm good though."

Ordered to sit, I couldn't see the plays, but I heard the screaming from the stands and the cussing on our sideline. The other team had reached midfield. Four plays later they scored as the whistle sounded to end the half. Adding the point after, we now trailed 14-6.

Heading for the locker room, I jogged next to Bustamonte and tugged at his elbow.

"What?" He said.

I looked around. "Don't tell anybody."

"Tell anybody what?"

I looked around again, and let the rest of the team pass. "Who are we playing?"

"Are you f-bombing with me?"

I shook my head.

"San Dimas."

"Boosty, don't tell anybody."

"F-bombing Handsman," he said as we ran into the into the locker room. I didn't know what he was going to do or if he'd say anything. By the time I sat down on the locker room bench, the flashing and spinning were gone. A headache was building, but I had aspirin in my locker. Best yet, I knew now we were playing San Dimas. *San Dimas, San Dimas, San Dimas,* I repeated silently in case it slipped out the backdoor of my brain.

There was no pep talk. Piccou and the coaching staff broke down the excellent job our defense was doing to this point, and if we could be a little more efficient with the ball on offense in the second half we'd win.

"We've got thirty minutes to live guys," he said, clapping his hands together. "You've been doing it all season, you're going to do it now. Sons of Scotland?"

"Alba gu bràth!"

We began to line up, but I drifted back to Gelbaugh, who was by his locker. I motioned to the makeup jar behind him.

"What?" He growled.

I reached around him and cupped my fingers into the blue cake and smeared it on my forehead and cheeks. "Alba gu bràth," I said.

"Mother-f-bomber!" He said back to me and slapped a fist into my shoulder pads. "Handsman has arrived!" I hammered his pads in like fashion.

"Let's do all them f-bombers!" I said.

"F-bombing A!"

We marched out of the locker room and busted through our banner to our sideline. Bustamonte went to the goal line to receive the kickoff. I took short ten-yard sprints to make sure my legs were loose.

"We're not sure about you," Piccou said. "You sound fine, but we're not sure about your eyes. How do you feel?"

"I feel like a Son of Scotland," I said. "I'm ready to go, Coach."

"Not dizzy? Nausea?"

"No."

"You lying to me?"

"No way Coach. You want my phone number, my Social Security number, Fred-X's number? I got them all, which one do you want?"

"Okay, let's play some football."

Bustamonte nearly cracked the return but got tripped at our thirty-nine.

First play Fred faked the Jet Sweep to Maez and connected with me in the flat. Catching the ball, I turned up field and went fourteen-yards before Bazooka Joe racked me out of bounds. The throbbing in my head was down a bit and the punishment to my body felt great. Every pass could be over thrown tonight, and I was going to go up for it. I didn't care.

The next play I took a slant from Fred and collided with Bazooka Joe. He fell back and I pinballed the other way. I stayed on my feet long enough to gain another twelve-yards.

"F-bomb you Joe!" I said. "F-bomb you!"

The next play signaled out to us was Twenty-four Slam. Maez moved to my spot in the slot and I dropped into the backfield to an H-Back role a yard behind Fat John. The ball was hiked and quickly given to Bustamonte. I led him through the B-gap, between the right guard and tackle.

The Saints strong safety came up and I fearlessly launched into him. Before Bazooka Joe could slide over, Bustamonte was running free and was dragged down only after crossing the goal line.

Someone else made the call, Bustamonte made the play, and no one was cheering for me, but it felt like I'd scored the winning touchdown in the Super Bowl. We were back in the game. The constant war between my heart and head battling glory versus shame went away. It amazed me how being a part of something, instead of *the* part, could make me feel so good.

For the deuce, we ran my favorite Smash play and I caught the corner-route over the five-seven cornerback lost between Maez and me. The score was tied: 14-14.

"Hey, Joe!" I yelled. "You want the f-bombing ball! F-bombing take it!"

The San Dimas middle linebacker started to come after me and some weird gear switched on and moved me towards him. Our teammates and officials kept us separated.

"You want to get thrown out of this game?" The official yelled at me. "Do you want to get thrown out of this game?"

"No," I said as Maez pulled me away.

"Then shut up!"

When I got to the sidelines I tore off my helmet and screamed to my teammates. "We're gonna do this! Nobody quits! Nobody quits! I'll f-bombing kill anybody that quits! F-bombing Gelbaugh! Make a play out there!"

My motor wasn't throttling back. If I didn't know for sure it was aspirin I took at halftime, I would have thought I took some kind of speed, meth, or coke. All I knew was nothing mattered in terms of well-being. It felt like every pore in my skin was finely tuned to absorb the universe of this football game and solely the universe of this football game. Nothing mattered, nothing but staying alive. Nothing but winning. I wasn't going to end up watching from the grandstands, I wasn't going to end up in the f-bombing cemetery.

I'd become the madman I saw Gelbaugh as.

San Dimas had given up its passing game and was now punishing our front seven with dives and testing their patience and nerve with its option attack. The bodies weren't thudding together, but cracking. Facemasks were being broken, each play someone was going out with something wrong with bone, muscle, or equipment failure.

Lee broke his shoulder pad. The Saints' Delfman left for a play after getting the wind knocked out of him. Gelbaugh was the definition of possessed as he shed blockers and blew up runners. On a third down and half a yard at our forty-two, he paid no attention to the option Delfman was running, but exploded into the quarterback. Running through him, Gelbaugh stumbled to the ground five yards behind the line of scrimmage. San Dimas, after helping Delfman off the field again, punted.

From our sixteen, Fred was able to get a flair pass out to Bustamonte for six-yards but we went nowhere after that. Another blitz caught Fred for a sack, and on third and a dozen his scramble for the first down ended a yard short. He landed out of bounds with Saints defenders piled on him.

He got up, slowly, and walked to our side of the field. Five weeks before he would have picked up the first down with a leap, but was too banged up now.

"Hudson, warm up!" Piccou said.

Fred pulled at his chin strap and smiled at Piccou and Jackson.

"What are you laughing at?" Jackson said. "We're punting the f-bombing ball, you shouldn't be laughing."

"I got kicked in the money-spot," Fred said. "If I don't smile, I'm gonna cry. It hurts."

"Can you play?" Piccou said.

"F-bomb yeah, I can play!"

Bustamonte, now handling all the kicking duties, punted away. Ten-seconds later, we wished he hadn't. I didn't know who Brad Beasley was before, probably a backup receiver, but he broke through a cluster of our special team players and went fifty-seven-yards for a touchdown.

The bad news was they were up 20-14. The good news, besides them missing the extra-point, was they scored quick and didn't beat our defense up doing it. Gelbaugh and friends didn't have to wear this touchdown or let it linger in the back of their minds. We were all equally shafted over by our punt coverage.

"We'll get it back!" I said. "I swear we're going to f-bombing get it back!"

"Handsdrade, take it easy," Fred said, coming alongside of me.

"We're going to get it back!" My voice raised for the first time to the guy who was everything I wanted to be. "I'm f-bombing serious!"

"I'm f-bombing serious too, so how about a little Gun-Power?"

"Oh yeah!" I said and we put our helmets on and retook the field at our twenty-four.

Jackson wanted us to run a Jet Sweep on first down. At the line of scrimmage, Fred changed colors, which meant he was changing the play. For the first time in three weeks, he ran Gun-Power with himself and San Dimas was flat footed. Then he ran it again.

On our third play, he faked the Jet Sweep to Maez and a delayed hand off to Bustamonte, who picked up the blitzing Bazooka Joe. Running a double move, out and up, he hit me in a near repeat of the touchdown I scored against El Monte. I was driven out at the Saints nineteen and our crowd let me experience the ultimate effect only a wall of audible praise can bring.

"When someone wants you, Dale, appreciate it."

We lined up, there was 2:44 to play in the third quarter, and gave the ball to Bustamonte who was hit for a three-yard loss. Before second down, Pineapple's leg quivered and he was called for a false start. When we ran the next play, Bustamonte picked up the blitz, but Fred was forced to throw the ball away. On third down I was double teamed on a corner-route and Fred was sacked for a nine-yard loss.

It was fourth down and twenty-seven from the San Dimas thirty-six. Piccou burned a timeout and the offense came to the numbers. The girls were working the water bottles around. Pineapple was groaning, hurting, I'd ask after but not now. I didn't want to know now, all I wanted was to win this game. Unless blood was geysering out of our bodies, it didn't matter. Maybe not even then. We were all tired, we all hurt, to talk about it was meaningless.

"What do you want to do, Skip?" Jackson said. "We got a whole fourth quarter and we're only down a score."

"We're going to do what we do," Piccou said and everyone on the offense nodded in agreement. "We punted when we never punt and that's why we're down. We're gonna do what we do. Live with it, die with it, I need a Fred-X touchdown delivery."

"I got you, Coach," Fred-X said, his eyes lit like lightening. We all came closer and bunched in tight around him. I felt my teammates breath, sweat coming off their skin mingled with mine, and I knew this was why people played football.

"Then let's Scram those mothers," Jackson said. "They ain't going to blitz with us empty and spread. If they do, you make the read, Ritter, and make'm pay for it."

'Scram' called for us all to run deep verticals. The whistle blew and our offense coming back onto the field was no surprise, but I saw the look in Bazooka Joe's eyes when Bustamonte motioned out of the backfield to his traditional wide spot. I covered the right tackle, and Maez was between Boosty and me. Miranda and Ponce split to the left.

As they adjusted their coverage, Fred called for the ball. Exploding off the line, I sold the corner-route with a look and slight dip of my shoulder. It wasn't much, but it gave me enough to get inside the safety.

When I hit the ten I turned to look for the ball. Fred-X was coming to me. The safety on the other side was a fraction late and I was now between both deep men. The pass hit my outstretched hands in stride and before I could think about it I was crashing into the end zone turf.

In Sunday School as a kid, I'd heard the stories of Moses parting the Red Sea and Elijah calling fire out of the sky, but who would ever believe the stories about Fred-X? He wasn't just good, he was perfect. Off the field I knew he cut and bled, but on the field he was immortal.

Teammates surrounded me, but thirty yards away I saw Fred going to Jackson for the next play. The easiest part of life was knowing exactly what Fred wanted and what he didn't. He wanted a scholarship and only a championship would get him the attention he needed playing at West El Monte Poly. What he didn't care about was another round of glorious suffocation in celebration of a touchdown.

I loved it because it felt like it brought me closer to being like him. Hearing my name over the speakers and the band blasting away with the ancient rock song, I mattered now, and I would always matter. In twenty years when they talked about this season, they'd mention me. Even if only briefly, I'd be mentioned in the same breath with Fred Ritter.

Jackson gave the play and Fred-X wasted no time getting us re-set. Calling the signals, his voice began to crack and then the ball came. Bustamonte took the handoff and made the first guy miss, but Bazooka Joe tied him up around the ankles.

The score was tied, 20-20.

Things would have felt better on the sideline if we had converted the deuce, but they were far from glum. Watching the kickoff team stretch across the field, I could hear Gugliotta empowering his defense.

"We got to make about three get off the field plays in the next twelve minutes! Finish them off!" The defensive coordinator said as the unit squeezed in around him and Gelbaugh at the far end of the bench.

Sitting, I turned to my left and saw Pineapple, at the other end of the bench, trying to rock away whatever pain he was feeling. Lying back on the trainer's table was Lee, his jersey and pads on the dirt track. Our trainer, whose name I still couldn't remember, was wrapping a large bag of ice around his left knee. He was wrecked.

Fear seized me. I ran my numbers again in my head and was able to remember we were playing San Dimas.

"What do you think?" I said to Fred.

The Saints got the ball at their eighteen with 1:02 to play in the third.

"I..." Fred paused to grimace. His jet black hair hanging like a drenched towel, he pushed out a smile.

"What?"

"I think I cracked a rib the last time I was sacked." Then he looked at me. "If you say anything I'll kill you."

I laughed.

"Why are you laughing?"

"My head was spinning so much at halftime I had to ask Bustamonte who we were playing. I still don't know our trainer's name. I know Pineapple has her on his list, but I can't remember her name."

We smiled together in our physical misery. The pain he was in was sharper and more crippling than the building throb that was returning between my temples.

"Her name's Sondra," he said.

"Thanks," I answered.

"What's your woman's name?"

"Lena," I said without hesitation.

"Cool," he said while gritting out another laugh. "Love you, Handsdrade."

Delfman, using play action, dropped back and went down the middle of the field. Gelbaugh got a hand up and tipped the ball to himself. Our sideline began to jump up and down, I raised my helmet, Fred did nothing as Gelbaugh returned it to the Saints 26.

"Let's do this right now!" Piccou said.

"Ritter, Trips Right Ritchie," Jackson said.

Fred nodded and took us to the line of scrimmage. His voice growing raspier by the word seemed on the verge of being overtaken by the cheering of our fans. He gave us the signals and snapped the ball. First looking downfield, Fred swung a pass to Bustamonte before a defensive end crashed into his blindside.

The ball landed uncatchable as Fred was driven into the ground by the weight of the lineman. When he started to move, I looked towards Jackson to get an idea of the next play. The offensive coordinator's eyes were on Fred. In the background, I heard Piccou's voice call for Hudson and then I shifted my eyes back to see Fred hunched over on his knees, fists pushing into the grass to pacify the pain.

"Come on, Fred, you ain't soft!" I said. "Get up! You ain't soft!"

"What the f-bomb were you doing, Pineapple?" Bustamonte screamed. Our left tackle, exhausted, was holding himself by an arm and down on a knee. He gave no defense or response. Tired, hurting, it didn't matter, he missed his assignment and our quarterback got mangled.

I thought Fred would get up because he always got up. He didn't. I thought when our trainer came out he'd get up and be out for a play or two. That wasn't happening. Piccou and, I believe, Sondra rolled him over and he let out a sick groan only someone dying could make. The throbbing in my head got louder.

They got him off the field to cheers, but we felt finished. When Maez told Bustamonte to calm down, Boosty answered back. Miranda joined in, Pineapple was eating pain just to stay in the game and our quarterback wasn't there to shut it all down.

Hudson came in to run the next three plays, and three incomplete passes later we turned the ball over on downs at the San Dimas twenty-six. The third quarter ended and the teams began the long walk to other side of the field.

As the chains were moved, I caught a glimpse of Fred being laid out on the trainer's table. Lee had been relocated to the bench, his face sullen, knee wrapped, streaks of blue stained his Under Armor shirt.

"Hudson, you did good," Jackson said. "You did good. Nobody was open and you threw the ball away, nothing you can do when you got nothing. Son, remember this game is tied. We're not trailing, so you didn't need to take that chance. You're going to get another shot. Good job."

I patted him on the butt. "I got you, Hudson, we all got you," I said. It was forced. I was lost in the twilight of crying for Fred, crying for my headache, and at least making the arrogant sophomore believe I believed in him. "We're with you."

We slapped hands because there was no other option.

The whistle blew for the start of the fourth quarter. Shane Delfman dropped straight back, there was no play action, and Preece, who was playing Lee's spot, got caught creeping forward in anticipation. Patterson, at cornerback, gave the San Dimas receiver, Kris Barkley, the inside lane thinking he was going to have help. There was none. Barkley ran by Preece, the pass hit him in stride, and seventy-four-yards later he was in the end zone. They added the point after and we were down: 27-20.

"We got time," Piccou said. "There's more than eleven minutes for us to do what we've been doing all year."

Except the guy who had been doing it all year was flat on his back and in terrible pain. Except now we were going to have to do it with a sophomore whose only numbers came courtesy of Pasadena Marshall. Except now, the three guys blocking for him in the interior of the line were all sophomores and the left tackle was hurting.

To help Pineapple in the deep drops, Jackson had us back in a short passing scheme. I caught an out-route, Maez an in-route, and Miranda took a swing for nine-yards. A Jet Sweep to Maez running left caught San Dimas off guard. That was followed by a Jet Sweep the other way to Ponce, which left them shaking their heads. When I caught a slant and carried it to their twenty-two, the Saints called a timeout.

Bazooka Joe was screaming at the top of his lungs. I screamed back at him. We stared at each other, but surprisingly we had the good sense to go to our respective sides of the field.

Jackson was out of body calling the plays. Everything looked the same, but nothing ever was. The Jet Sweep with Ponce was the first time he'd run the play this season. All of it was building the confidence of the already, overly, confident Hudson.

Jerk or not, Hudson was one thing Fred wasn't: healthy. His jersey was clean, his body wasn't aching, and his reflexes were quicker. It was unlikely they would blitz him because he was mobile.

Thinking the defense would adjust for the short pass, Jackson called for Patterson to run the skinny from the left and if it was there, great. If not, I was running the out and up from the left slot.

The ball was hiked. They weren't coming, and my bruised mind rejoiced. We were going to beat them deep. The safety wasn't buying Patterson but eyed me. It was perfect. When I made my second move up, Patterson was wide open but the ball never got there.

I didn't see it until much later, but Hudson came my way with the pass as if I was running an out-route. The ball was behind me. I heard the reaction of the crowd as the interception was made and returned to the San Dimas forty-three.

Coming to the sideline, Hudson reverted to form and gestured to me but Jackson pointed a loud finger at him. If he hadn't implied I ran the wrong route, Hudson would have been shown the scheme on a dry erase board and carefully had things explained to him. Instead, he went looking for a goat and Jackson pointed the index finger openly, and directly, at him five yards onto the playing field.

The coaches hated a rat who wouldn't man up.

The defense retook the field and before they could settle in, Delfman snapped the ball on the first sound. Using play action this time he went back and Barkley was streaking through our secondary. Gelbaugh, over reacting to what happened before, went back deep, Patterson was all over him, and Preece was there this time.

Barkley burned us again. He reached for the pass and caught it over his shoulder, with outstretched arms, in front of our three defenders. They tackled him, but it was too late. San Dimas had a first down at our eighteen. Their side of the stadium exploded, their players celebrated, and something convulsed inside my stomach.

My headache was worsening, and I knew I was about to throw up. Two dive plays took it to the twelve, and an option pitch to Johnson set up first and goal at our four with the clock continuing to run. There were less than five minutes to play.

On first and goal from the four, Delfman faked the handoff and bootlegged around left end. Gelbaugh recovered enough to shove him down but not before the ball touched the pylon and the side judge signaled touchdown. The Saints side erupted again and I heaved. I heaved repeatedly until things began to get blurry around me.

"Handsdrade?" Maez asked. "You cool?"

We were down by two scores, Gelbaugh was thrown out for firing his helmet, Fred-X was out, I was puking, and there were now less than four minutes to go. I had a f-bombing concussion.

"I'm cool."

When the extra-point missed wide, part of me still believed we had a chance.

Piccou called the team together before the kickoff, but I couldn't understand what he was saying. Slurping water, I couldn't feel any emotions. It was as if everything had been siphoned off. We were like a boxer out on his feet. Bustamonte picked up the rah-rah part and told us not to give up, but he had tears because he knew it was over.

I ran my routes. Hudson's first two passes were incomplete. Pineapple hobbled off the field, bouncing on his right leg, before third down. On third down Hudson's pass to Bustamonte over the middle was incomplete and before he could get back to our side of the line of scrimmage, Boosty was thrown out of the game for taking a swing at Bazooka Joe. We were set back fifteen more yards.

On fourth and thirty-five, I looked around me and noticed Fred, Bustamonte, Pineapple, Edwards, Feliz, Basler, Lee, Escandon, Lucia, and Gelbaugh were all gone. I ran my route through the headache, but my legs could hardly carry me. Hudson completed a seventeen-yard pass to Maez and we gave the ball back to San Dimas on downs.

If death hadn't arrived, it was at least ringing the doorbell. I felt rooted to the spot where my route ended, just beyond our forty. My hands were on my hips and I felt like I couldn't leave. The Saints offense came in around me. Our defense came on the field, and for a second I figured I was dead. San Dimas was going to run a play, what was left of our defense was going to try to stop it, and I didn't matter at all. They'd run right through me.

"Son," a hand touched my back, "you're going to have to get off the field."

I looked at the official, he looked back at me.

"You okay? Do you need some help?"

No words formed and no answer came.

He blew his whistle and waved for the trainer to come get me. "Just hold still. You're going to be okay."

I assumed it was Sondra who came jogging across the field. Fred had given me her name, but now I wasn't so sure. Piccou was with her. "Handsdrade! Let's go!"

"Coach," the official said. "This kid's bats. I think he's got a concussion."

I was escorted to the bench to wait out the end of the game. All around me guys were crying. Pineapple was now on the trainer's table. Bustamonte, at the end of the players box, was down on one knee, his forehead in the palm of a hand. Hudson's arms were folded.

My emotions were short-circuited as I sat sipping water.

When time expired, I didn't do the post-game handshake or hear the post-game speech. Instead, I was taken to the hospital where my concussion was officially diagnosed. It never left me that we lost, but I didn't get worked up about it until Saturday afternoon when things unblurred.

PART III

1

Wind and rain bought up the time on Saturday. With foggy eyes, I saw the storm falling sideways and small rivers, with strong currents, out of my bedroom window. It drove trashcans down the alley to some unknown place. Staying in bed, the bad from the night before remained unclear, and I drifted back to sleep.

When things cleared enough, I got up. Padding to the door in boxer briefs, I cracked it open to make sure Mom was gone, and Dad was doing something else.

I did remember seeing Mom at the hospital and having her come home with us. She was very motherly and made sure I had everything I needed. Then she pelted Dad with jabs about letting me play football.

"If you didn't want me to play you never should have split," I was sure I said to her. I couldn't remember when, but I did remember the look of horror she gave me. At some point during the weekend, I'd regret it, but then, and even now, I was in too much pain to care.

The living room was empty. My ears caught the sound of Dad snoring through his bedroom door. The clock on the oven said 9:45. If there had been a team meeting I'd already missed it.

On the dining table, there was a discharge paper from the hospital that said 'mild concussion' next to my name. It didn't feel mild, but whatever they saw after running me through the machines didn't require an overnight stay.

Chasing cobwebs with a cold glass of water, I felt my body and emotions return. Everything hurt: my thighs, my shoulders, the old Downey ache across my chest, and something attaching neck to upper back was stiff as well.

I sat on a barstool and began to cry when the results from the night before became clear. Wiping my eyes and mouth, I searched for places in my head to store the pain. There was no place to take my thoughts, I was marooned in the present.

After taking a shower, I got back into bed for the rest of Saturday. Dad checked on me several times, brought me something to eat in the afternoon, and it wasn't until late in the evening I felt I could tolerate being awake.

I went online and clicked the recording of Grip Teague's show.

Bald Guy: Trudy Shields called it, Grip. She said they would be even until the fourth quarter, and then San Dimas would pull away.

Grip Teague: How easy was it to pull away with Fred-X and everyone else out?

Bald Guy: That's the point, Teague. She called it.

Below were 154 comments confirming, praising, or attacking all being said by the duo. Somewhere in the thread, word emerged I played the second half with a concussion. A whole new discussion began about player safety.

Piccou was labeled the devil, again. He was the author and finisher of our disappointing season, again. Everyone said we were a good team, again. Our destiny was to be great, to win the whole thing, we had the talent to do it, and, again, Piccou failed us.

My body was still sore and I was grateful. The last eight months felt like they hardly took place at all. The bruises, the stiffness were like poor man's Purple Hearts confirming I'd done my job: Proof I really lived through these experiences.

"Hey, you made it." Mr. Umphries greeted me as I came in through the church's glass doors on Sunday. "I heard you had to go to the hospital after the game Friday night."

"You knew?"

"When I heard about it, I prayed for you," he said. "Glad you're feeling better."

"Thank you, I am."

"Go on in, your dad's sitting in the middle to the right. I think they're getting ready to start." The sound of the worship band came out of the sanctuary. "Oh, I guess they just did." He smiled.

We nodded at each other, and I went in and sat three rows behind Dad.

"...And they will gather to themselves teachers who will tickle their ears and will turn aside the truth for mythology. In fact the Greek word is 'mythology,'" said Pastor Domres.

He came across as angry this morning. Angry enough for me to take better notice, but like every Sunday morning I was looking for Lena. I wanted to see her, I wanted to see if there would be anything different with the season being over.

"...More and more these days, people that look like me, people that sound like me, they stand behind these pulpits and are more concerned about giving you what you want to hear instead of what you need to hear, and what you need to hear is the truth of God."

He pushed past noon, and when he stopped talking, the altars filled. More music played, and people started praying loudly. They prayed more this Sunday than any Sunday I could remember before or since coming back to church.

I stayed in my seat until the point of embarrassment. Lena didn't exit with the children. If she was at the altar I didn't know because everyone, including my dad, was there. The singing continued, and I bailed.

2

Read The Blitz
By Grip Teague

Arroyo's upset of Paraclete, on the road, has to be the shocker of the season. Matt Burns's three touchdowns, two on punt returns, and Connor Stone's game management have put the Knights into the second round...Coaching casualty: Nick Chalmers has resigned at Alhambra. This means La Serna, Alhambra, and Burroughs need HC's...Don't take your eye off of West El Monte Poly. A lot of changes expected...

On Monday morning, the follow up with the doctor produced a clean bill for me to be sent back to school. In the end, it didn't make any difference. If we'd won, I would have been ruled out this coming week. Instead, we were all like Fast Eddie, coming into the locker room on crutches. We were ghosts.

Going through the halls, I saw nearly everyone. Fred was walking with Pineapple. Gelbaugh was making a feeble attempt at talking to a girl. Bustamonte was going into English class when we traded nods of acknowledgment. Everything was flat between us as teammates and the atmosphere, the urgency, was gone.

There was a team meeting after school to give the break down of everything we would be doing to close out the season. We filed into the film room and took our seats. The staff came in, distributing copies of equipment checklists we'd signed back in August.

"First of all, you guys didn't let anybody down," Piccou started with us. "We were marked from the get-go, and everybody we played gave us their best. That's an honor because every one of those teams looked at us like they were playing the CIF champs. Be proud. We didn't lose. Like the old line goes, we were just a little behind when the clock ran out."

Gugliotta said to have all of our gear turned in and signed off by the next day. Then told us over the course of the next two weeks we'd all have exit interviews. For the seniors, it would be about sharing anything they needed regarding game film or letters of recommendation. Because of the holiday schedule for the school and staff, the team banquet would be in January.

As they spoke, I rubbed hands over my face and held my emotions in quiet transit between tears and no expression. It was over. The best year of my life was over. Now all the cool guys were leaving the party.

The meeting ended with a pathetic team break and tired voicing of alba gu bràth.

The kidding around was light. There were no big laughs. No one seemed to want to go for them. Pineapple didn't do anything naked. Gelbaugh had put *Braveheart* on the back burner. The blue face paint was gone, and no one was talking about being a son of Scotland anymore. Sadness strangled everything.

"How many fingers am I holding up, Handsdrade?" Pineapple said, raising a thumb. "You were *Looney Tunes* Friday night."

"I don't remember," I said. Some things were coming back to me, but I didn't feel like getting into a conversation about it. There was also a lingering thought I might have done something else, something stupid, but I couldn't recall it. "So, what are they going to tell me?"

"They're going to get you and everybody else, back in the weight room right after Christmas," Bustamonte said.

"That sucks," I said as we all headed out.

"Aren't you going to be one of Hudson's boys?" Pineapple said.

Feeling the crispness of a true autumn day, I shook my head.

"Jackson's going to give you a diet to follow, workouts to do. He's going to tell you not to do anything stupid like skateboarding or surfing. Just before spring workouts he'll give you an updated playbook," Bustamonte said. "My advice is listen to him."

"You're giving me advice?" We'd come so far from my first day in the spring when Boosty wouldn't even speak to me.

"Take it from the best. You played hard man, but if you had been in the weight room with us in January, you might have held up better," Bustamonte said. "Look at you. Right now you're a wreck and I'm still going."

"What are you guys going to be doing?" I said.

"We're seniors," Pineapple said. "We're going to enjoy ourselves."

We spoke nothing about San Dimas or Pomona, or even Arroyo who was still alive in the playoffs. I stayed away from Grip Teague's blog because I couldn't bear to read about us in the past tense.

For months, I'd heard 'Handsdrade! You need a ride?' but no offer came today. Fred didn't say a word to me and very little to everyone else. He walked silently through the rest of us. Thoughts came that I didn't have to talk to or see him again. We didn't share any classes, there were no more workouts, and there would be no more time spent together at The Habit. The days of breaking down plays on napkins over burgers and fries were finished.

He opened the door to his truck, then looked at me from over the hood as I started to walk away.

His smile came. "I guess there have been worse seasons in history."

"For sure," I said, elated with the interaction.

"You were great, Handsman."

"Thanks."

He nodded, looked towards the stadium, then got inside of his Frontier and drove off.

We all left school in different directions, feeling strange and detached. It was an odd, round moment, attempting to fit into a square situation. Like being in some alternate universe, how could this team not be playing anymore?

Monday night I was back online. A thread was started by Trudy Shields on her site about Billy Hudson withdrawing from West El Monte and going to Upland. Her story was based on a tip about Hudson's father being displeased with the offensive philosophy and feeling like his son was being singled out for the team's first round loss to San Dimas.

The anonymous comments immediately began to fry Piccou and Jackson in cyberspace. Fred was attacked for being too short and being in the game too long when it was clear he wasn't healthy. Gugliotta's defense was trashed. Using fake names, I easily recognized, our guys argued in support of the staff.

On the bright side, I was being universally praised as the team's best overall receiver for having talent and toughness. They also said Hudson and me, if he stayed, would make a great pitch and catch tandem next year.

3

Now that the on-the-field portion of the season is over, I can admit where I was wrong and wrong again. Everyone has a tough stretch as many of the coaches we cover would agree. Yes, I took Mayfair over Dominguez in the finals and I was wrong. Alec Jammon is just so freaking good. I know I took West Covina over Bonita. I thought the WC had enough offense and I underestimated the Bearcats, who finally got payback for what happened way back in 2010. But, do I get credit for Arroyo's upset over Pomona in the semis? I know I didn't exactly say it would happen, but I did say the Knights could pull something and they did. At least until they got to the finals and were hammered by San Dimas. Still, with post season victories over Paraclete and the Red Devils, it was a great run for Arroyo...

Notes: The University of Idaho has offered San Dimas Saints linebacker, Bazooka Joe Natalia, a full scholarship...Former Diamond Ranch HC, Kent Miller, has been hired by Alhambra...Tab Figueroa has resigned at Arcadia...Former La Serna HC, Tom Crawl, will serve as El Rancho's defensive coordinator next year...Senior cornerback, Mike Patterson, has withdrawn from West El Monte Poly...And my pre-pre-preseason pick for next year is...(drum roll please)...Monrovia!

By the middle of December, we were surprised Hudson was still enrolled at West El Monte, but Patterson's departure didn't shock us at all. He was cordial, we were cordial, but he always felt like a guy who was just doing his football time. We didn't know where he was going, but figured, most likely, it was back to Pasadena to graduate.

The 'All Mission Valley League' teams came out. Fred told me, in the spring, he would make me an all league receiver. In the minds of everyone, except the coaches in the league, he had. With anticipation, I read the list and felt the disappointment when my name didn't appear until I got down to the honorable mention section. Even that was ruined when I saw it was next to Ponce's name.

It wasn't all bad, Grip Teague and Bald Guy became my biggest advocates. They shared on their show, and in columns, how I was robbed by being named honorable mention.

"Handsdrade, you got jobbed and I'm going to tell you why," Coach Jackson said. He called me in during lunch break for an exit interview. We sat down by my locker. "I know you're probably upset, but I want to explain this to you."

My problem right now wasn't being 'All Mission Valley,' it was being out of orbit from the team. The seniors had moved on, and I felt increasingly lost as the days passed without hearing from them.

Online I saw a picture of Fred and the guys at the Santa Anita Mall's food court. A few months before I would have been given a call to hang with them. I couldn't remember the last time my phone rang or my message box lit up. It hurt, and the hurt made me feel soft.

"Coach and I think you're the best receiver in the league. We think you're better than Bustamonte, but we'll never admit to it in court. It's just that he's a senior and there was no way to get both of you onto the first team. And if you're not first team then you're not up for All-CIF consideration."

"I didn't know they were connected," I said.

"Never mind any of it. You're tall, you have decent speed, some hops, and great hands. What's your GPA?"

"Three-point-nine," I said.

"If Bustamonte is going to have a chance at staying in school and getting a degree, it's going to be because he's playing football. There's no interest in him right now, but being first team MVL and making CIF might raise his profile a little bit."

I nodded.

"Just so you understand, these teams are meaningless except sometimes they might enhance a resume or college application a little bit. You're not the only one getting jobbed either. Lee made second team, but Feliz has to live with honorable mention as well."

Fred, of course, won everything except 'Coach of The Year,' and he probably should have picked up some votes for that.

Pineapple was 'Lineman of The Year' for the coaches and the media. He was a lock to be All CIF. Gelbaugh would get a spot on CIF. He was already being named to multiple media teams at linebacker.

When the CIF choices did come out, Bustamonte, Pineapple, and Gelbaugh all joined Fred on the first team. Paraclete's Calvin Greene won 'Player of The Year' and everyone, not living in the desert, wondered why. The message boards blew up over this slight to Fred-X, but I didn't know what Fred thought because he hadn't said a word to me in weeks.

After Christmas vacation, I half heartedly returned to the weight room. No mood existed inside me to play next fall, but for nine months the weight room had become home. Sweating resurfaced good memories about the recent season. I did make some great catches.

Two days later I got a message from Lena.

Lena Durkin:
Hey Handsman, how have you been? I miss talking to you. Haven't seen you in church for a while.

Lena reaching out to me washed away a lot of loneliness. We hadn't spoken for a month. Partly because it had been three weeks since I last went to church, but mostly because without football our paths didn't cross anymore.

Dale Andrade:
Just busy, started getting back into the weight room.

I didn't hear back from her until the following night.

Lena Durkin:
Have you talked to Fred?

Dale Andrade:
About what?

Lena Durkin:
No reason.

Dale Andrade:
I think he's just trying to decide what he's going to do, I wouldn't worry about him. Probably got a lot on his mind.

I assumed Fred had distanced himself from her in much the way he did from me. He had heavy thinking to work through about the future and where he was going to play.

Lena Durkin:
No offers came.

Dale Andrade:
I saw the letters.

Lena Durkin:
Letters, not offers. I thought he might have talked to you about it, he really likes you.

My mind replayed the wave off she gave me through the sliding glass door at her place.

Dale Andrade:
Fred hasn't spoken to me in weeks.

Lena Durkin:
I'm sorry, I didn't know that.

The conversation ended.

I went back to the scouting websites and, again, Fred's name did not appear. I looked at the top prospects, the passers we'd been talking about all season, and they had multiple offers. Even quarterbacks Fred outplayed over the summer were getting offers with stats nowhere close to his.

Fred-X was off the radar.

4

Read The Blitz
By Grip Teague

West Covina linebacker, Courtney Graye and Downey linebacker, Gilliam Gilliam, have both verbaled they will attend APU in the fall...Whittier HC, Matt Sisson has stepped down saying he wants to spend more time with his family...Could a certain Mission Valley League coach on the outs with his administration be Sisson's replacement? I won't say a word, but the coach in question is a Whittier alum...Pomona defensive back, Stephon Stukes, has decided not to play football next fall. Cal Lutheran was recruiting him, but the talented corner has decided to enlist in the United States Marine Corps. "It's something I've always wanted to do, and I know I won't be able to play football forever."

For the banquet, we wore our home jerseys with button down shirts underneath and ties. Some argued it should have been more formal. I agreed with the crowd that said it was a football banquet and not the f-bombing prom. My side won. Jerseys and button downs it was.

"You all did a terrific job this year," said Principal Mathers. "Not only was it record breaking, but you represented the finest of the West El Monte Poly spirit. In these cases, wins and losses never matter, but did we show spirit? The answer to that question is, yes you did. I've never been so proud of a football team as I've been of this one. For the seniors, may this past season be a spring board to future success, and for those of you coming back next year...Go get'em Scots!"

"Didn't he say last year he'd never been so proud of us?" Fast Eddie said. His leg was still in a very serious looking brace, but he was moving around on his own. I was impressed with his positive attitude. With the heavy metal hinges surrounding his leg, he kept talking and joking even as the topic of Arizona State vanished like a lost childhood toy. He was set to major in business at Northridge and happy with life.

They played the team highlights. It was over thirteen minutes long, and while I thought Fred looked good, I fell in love with myself. The catches were great, the hits I survived were better, but the best of it was being part of the team again. All of my regular contact with them had dried up since the San Dimas game so just sitting with them was special.

"Who has to give a speech?" I said, seeing a table on wheels roll into the banquet room stacked with trophies. "Does everyone?"

"Coach will give one, so will Jackson and Gugliotta," Maez said. "Then Fred will give his speech after winning all the awards. Then we get dessert." He checked the time on his phone. I didn't have to ask why. Maez was going to start taking night classes in February so he could work during the day.

Technically, Fred hadn't been named our MVP, yet, but everyone knew it was going to be him. I think even if the players blew the vote, the coaches would have made sure he got the honor.

Rumors still had Billy Hudson transferring out, but another turn of the message boards was causing more angst. Grip Teague blogged that Whittier High School, Coach Piccou's alma mater, had asked him to interview for its job opening. It was just a rumor, but it made things uneasy.

As the night progressed, the expected winners won the awards everyone expected them to get. I got 'Rookie of The Year,' which, if it didn't surprise me, did move me. I took the trophy, shook the coaches' hands, and kept my head down to keep my prideful smile hidden.

The trophy was plastic, not brass, the name plate was glued on, and very little distinguished it from the others handed out. Except this trophy was mine. My name was on it, it was going home with me, and it would always be someplace important. I had proof beyond a picture in a yearbook or internet archives I not only belonged but achieved. Only Lena would have felt better in my hands.

When Fred went to the podium, multiple trophies, including the MVP award, were placed around him.

"Wherever I go, wherever I play," Fred said, well rehearsed and less electric. "I will always be a son of Scotland." We applauded him. "Mr. Mathers," he looked to the side where our Principal and the rest of the key administration people were seated. "I don't want to take this MVP trophy home. I want it to stay here in the school's trophy case with a different name plate. I want it to read the MVP for this season was all the Fighting Scots."

More cheers came. Of course, I knew, only Fred-X could do something like that. He had his trophies, he had his awards, he had his recognition, but what he didn't have was an offer in writing to play football on a full athletic scholarship.

Fred and I hadn't spoken since the day in the parking lot, but I knew this was still the case regarding his status next year. Now would have been the time to announce it. My quarterback, the guy with the bravado to try anything, the guy who could make you believe in anything, looked like he was living off of fumes. Maybe nobody else saw it, but I did. He wasn't the same.

As Piccou began his speech, I waited for him to say he wasn't coming back. Why would he want to come back? Most of the skill players were moving on, he was constantly hassled by the parents and the administration, who needed any of it? It was only going to get worse because Padilla was expected to replace the retiring Mathers.

"I'll never forget how this team stood together when things got tough. When things got tough for me, heck, when things got tough for all of us." His voice labored as he choked back tears. "You've read the rumors about Whittier asking me to interview..." It was coming, I knew it was coming. My breath shortened. "It's true. They did ask me to interview...and what Grip Teague didn't write was I turned them down."

Hands hit the tables in applause. The team stood and everyone else followed.

"I'll be back next year."

Pineapple and Gelbaugh carried a plaque to the podium and gave it to Coach Piccou.

Taking a peek across the room, I searched for Hudson's response, but couldn't find him.

"Coach, you are a true son of Scotland," Gelbaugh said. "So we're giving you this plaque that the team chipped in for. It says, 'Scotland Forever!' but it should also say, you'll be our coach forever."

Everyone clapped before Pineapple stepped forward and raised his hands for quiet. He put a finger to his lips and made a downward motion for us to sit.

"We've got one more gift for Coach Piccou," he said. "Come on out!"

Jackson and Gugliotta came from back stage wearing plaid kilts and presented one to Piccou. As the hall erupted in laughter, I thought about all the times I hated each of them. I couldn't stand them for the way they looked down on me when I first came out. I would have agreed with anybody wanting to slash the tires on their cars, but not now.

Fred talked me into football, made me believe in what football could do, but Piccou, Jackson, and Gugliotta were the ones who operated on me. They cut out the soft parts, sewed in the fundamentals, and did the things necessary to make sure the skills I had been blessed with at birth became useful. They made the volleyball guy into a football player. I applauded harder than anyone else because I understood what they had done for me.

We sat back down as cake was being served.

"Western Oregon is getting ready to offer me," Fred said from across the table. He threw it out not in response to a question, not as part of a conversation, but it came like a sudden sneeze or cough. We were all caught off guard.

"Awesome," I said. Finally, he said something that felt directed enough at me to allow a response. His voice and tone were still lacking the confidence of Fred-X. Last June he was talking about USC and PAC 12 schools. Now he was optimistic about Division-two Western Oregon. Nervously optimistic.

"Sweet," Maez said. "It was just a matter of time." He bumped fists with our quarterback.

"Yeah," Fred said. "It's cool."

"What about you and Lena?" I asked.

"We broke up. If I'm going to Western Oregon, there's no way it's going to work out." There had never been anything fake about Fred until now. I felt bad for asking about anything. Giving answers looked like torture for him. "Don't worry I put a good word in for you."

"With who?"

"Lena," he said, and, with perfect clarity, the stupid thing I had said at the end of the San Dimas game came to me.

"I had a concussion. I wasn't trying to steal your girlfriend."

He smiled a hollow smile. "Don't worry about it. We're good. It's time to get on with the rest our lives, Handsman."

Coach Piccou tapped the microphone. He tapped it again. "Excuse me, can I please get everyone's attention. You can go back to your desserts and ignore me in a moment, but I've got something in this envelope. It's a surprise for one of our best and an honor to share with all of you. Earlier this season, you heard Carl Bartholomew was offered by Humboldt State...Pineapple, come up here."

Pineapple came back up with his jersey, shirt, tie, khakis, and hair all looking like they had spent the last ten minutes inside of a tornado. For a guy who reveled and marched in untempered nudity, he suddenly appeared shy. I didn't think shy was possible for him.

"It's my honor to present you this offer for a full athletic scholarship to UC Davis!"

Pineapple's mouth fell. Screams of joy exploded and everyone jumped up to applaud. His family came out of their seats to hug him. He began to cry, and his parents and siblings squeezed around him all the more. Then he broke away from them and went to Coach Piccou. They bear hugged each other.

I knew Fred was standing and applauding, but I didn't look his way. I didn't need to see him to know how much this was carving at his heart.

5

Read The Blitz
By Grip Teague

Talk had Skip Piccou leaving West El Monte Poly, but now the talk is Billy Hudson is as good as gone. Bald Guy says over the weekend he got a tip that Hudson would be transferring down the 605 to La Serna. La Serna has been without an HC since mid-November... Cathedral guard, Josiah Chavez, has verbaled Western Oregon...Word leaking out to us about Charter Oak quarterback, Del Chance, is not good. His grades are not in order and will most likely go the junior college route next fall...Bob Aberdeen has resigned at Heritage Christian...Kelvin Smith has withdrawn from Duarte. Smith rushed for 1,003 yards and nine touchdowns this past season. No word yet on where he'll land, but I'll give you odds if you want to guess.

When signing day came, we met in the football room. Gelbaugh, Feliz, Fast Eddie, Basler, Lee, Bustamonte and I were there to stand behind Pineapple as he inked his deal with UC Davis.

Then Coach Piccou and Coach Jackson stood behind him for another picture. Pineapple's family came up, and they all looked the same, hair flopping everywhere with thick skin, tired eyes and much love for everybody.

Grip Teague and a photographer were doing business. Chanos had an intern filming, and Benny represented the school paper. Principal Mathers and Athletic Director, Crumsey, were there.

Everyone who needed to be there was there, except Fred. It was Pineapple's day and while Fred had been around at every other important moment, he was missing from this one. It was easy to see it hurt the big lineman to not have his quarterback present, but he pressed on.

Out of uniform and out of season, I was back to being a junior and out of the loop. What everyone else knew, but I didn't until later, was Fred had not been in school for a week.

Lena, with a friend, stood by the door. She gave me a smile and a wave. I hadn't had much interaction with her other than a few 'hellos' and 'goodbyes' when I drifted into church. She was a senior, and time was going by at the speed of light.

Grip Teague brought up Fred's name, but Piccou deflected it by talking about what a great story Pineapple was. While Fred not being in school was a mystery to me, I did know no offers came. I looked at the Western Oregon website and they didn't make an offer. His best options now were academic packages to schools in the midwest or junior college.

"I want to thank my teammates and the Coaches..." Pineapple gave his speech. Public Speaking would not be his major at UC Davis, but it didn't matter. He was the kind of guy we all rooted for. "This was hard but worth it..." Crying, again, the Moanin' Samoan went to hug his mom.

"Have you talked to Fred?" Lena said, arriving on my left. I shook my head and motioned for her to back away from the front of the room with me. We kept our eyes on Pineapple and started to talk.

"I haven't spoken to Fred since the night of the banquet," I said. "I think he's..."

"He's embarrassed because Pineapple got a scholarship and he didn't," she said. "He's a mess right now. You know we broke up?"

"Yeah," I said. "You two going to get back together now that he's not leaving?"

She didn't smile her smile of creased dimples and green lit eyes. Instead, she gave me a pained look. "Do you know how awful that sounds?"

"What?"

"That since he's not going anywhere that means we're getting back together?"

"I didn't mean it like that," I said. "It's just, if it wasn't for Fred I'd still be playing volleyball and going through the motions. I love Fred, almost as much as I love you."

...And that had to have been concussion hangover.

Did I really just say that?

"What did you say?" She turned to looked straight at me.

Was it rude? I didn't know. Had I insulted her? I didn't know that either. I surely surprised her, almost as much as I surprised myself.

"Say what?" I attempted to bluff.

"You know what you said."

How many daydreams had chewed away minutes and hours of my life longing for a chance to say what I just said to her? I dreamed about it at night. I said the words in the shower. I turned scenarios over in my head when walking to school. Instead, when it happened, I vomited it out. All I wanted to do was run.

"Come on," she said. "Own it."

I surrendered. Maybe this was my moment.

"I didn't think I'd ever have the courage to say it," I said, feeling a weight come off my shoulders. This place was already turning miserable; the team was going to be miserable; I was going to miserable for the next year, playing football without my friends. In the end, though, when all the misery was totaled and columned, the one thing I wouldn't be miserable about was that I had finally told Lena Durkin I loved her. "Yeah, I love you." I gave the smile to her I'd been waiting months to give.

"Is that you talking or is it the concussion?" She gave me some of the look I'd fallen deeply for, but not all of it.

"No, I'm saying it. I hardly see you anymore and my day is great now if I just see you walking across the campus. So I told myself before graduation day comes, I was going to tell you how I feel about you. I wasn't going to say anything as long as you were with Fred, but now you're not with him. Lena, I can't think of a future without thinking about you. I get sick thinking about you graduating and all the days after." A fleeting whisper suggested caution, but caution would have kept me from playing after Gelbaugh decked me or Gilliam Gilliam assaulted me. The best things in my life since last spring came when I ignored caution. I ignored it now. "I've been in love with you since that day you said, 'hi' to me at graduation last summer. It's like you've latched yourself to me, and I can't shake you."

Who knew what girls thought? I didn't know what she was thinking, but I could tell she wasn't mad or insulted.

"I don't want another boyfriend right now," she said. Her look gave a different impression than her words. Her tone didn't even make her words sound effective. She was taken back.

"I didn't ask you to be my girlfriend," I said. "I didn't ask you to go steady or to wear my varsity jacket, but..." I touched her elbow and moved both of us further into the corner to keep our conversation private. "...This party is over, and I don't want to be stuck here with the people that are staying behind. I know you're graduating. I know you are leaving West El Monte..."

"...I'm leaving Dale," she said. "I'm going to Trevecca University in Tennessee. I'm leaving all of this. Fred didn't break up with me. I broke up with Fred because he can't think about anything but that scholarship he's never going to get."

"Forget Fred. What if I came to Trevecca after next year?"

"Why would you come to Tennessee?"

"Do you know..." I said, taking my voice lower to not be over-heard. "Do you know what it's like to hear you call me 'Handsman' or just seeing you work with those little kids at church? I love you. I..."

"I'm sorry." She put a soft hand to my shoulder. "I'm so sorry, but I can't." She bent at her hips and gave me a hug. "We have different paths to follow. I can't stay here and you can't follow me. After a while, you'll see, it will be okay."

"No," I said. "It won't. Stay here and give me a chance."

"Dale," she carefully smiled. "It's my time to go." She walked away and my body went numb.

I kidded myself with the thought that at least she knew how I felt about her...at least she knew. The good feeling it gave began to subside and rejection, with pain, crept in. Another concussion, another body slam by Gilliam Gilliam, were the only things that could blunt what I was feeling.

6

Read The Blitz: Breaking News!
By Grip Teague

"Piccou Steps Down at West El Monte Poly"
Sources have confirmed, West El Monte football coach
Skip Piccou resigned Friday afternoon to become the HC
at Huntington Beach High School...

G rip Teague published his story at 6:30 on Friday night and it achieved the desired effect. Everyone was clicking and commenting: the deniers, the affirmers, the shocked, the hurt and the angered.

"Piccou lied to his team at the banquet when he said he was staying..."---Cool Jets

"Now I know why Hudson wanted to transfer! What a piece of garbage!"---Kansas

"He's got another job lined up somewhere and I don't blame him. Come on would you want to work for that administration?"---Bad News

"Can't complain about lack of loyalty when you don't show it yourself."---Sunshine

"Huntington Beach versus West El Monte Poly? Mmm? Let me think...Yeah, Piccou made the right choice."---Wolfman

"Teague you're a piece of ***DELETED***! You didn't even give him a chance to tell his team."--- Big Tony

"I told you."---Jorge Grande

A message came through our phones that Coach Piccou wanted to meet with the football team at lunch on Monday afternoon. I held little hope the story was going to change. Confirmations of Teague's story were already bleeding through. Coach had informed the administration but wanted to wait until Monday to break the news.

The seniors didn't care because they were half way out the door. Piccou shared with us in the film room his intention was to stay at West El Monte, and he had indeed turned down an interview from Whittier High School.

"Huntington Beach is closer to my home, it's a level higher, and its district is going to honor all of my years teaching. I had to make the switch," Piccou said. "I wanted to let everyone know right away but was convinced to wait until Monday. Someone leaked it to Teague, and I'm sorry. Teague and Bald Guy have ears everywhere."

This was a kick in the gut and a good reason not to play next year. The idea of transferring flirted with me, but where was I going to go? Private school? My folks didn't have Maranatha money or the option to get me a better address. Glendora? I wasn't about to move in with Mom.

It was going to be an entirely new staff. Jackson and Gugliotta were leaving with Piccou. Gugliotta got a teaching job, and Jackson was going because he had the financial flexibility to work as a walk-on. Crumsey said a new coach would be in place in a month, and Coach Von Huson would manage the workouts in the meantime.

When it was over, the seniors led the way to the front of the room. They gathered around Piccou and the staff. Hugs, handshakes, pictures were all getting done. Fred made it to the meeting. He was back in school, still respected, but looking like a diminished star. He came nowhere near me and left quickly. I tried to think of something I'd done but knew it was really nothing more than football being over and them being seniors.

I waited a little while then started to take off. There would be a chance to say goodbye to Coach later on. He wouldn't be leaving until the end of the school year. I exited out of the film room and into the locker area when Coach Jackson came through the double doors calling my name.

"Handsdrade! Where you going?" He was wearing his black muscle shirt, red shorts, and sandals, his bald head hauling in the glare of the lights. "I ain't done with you!"

"Sounds like you are," I said, turning back to him. "Tell me at least Hudson is going to transfer?"

"Nope," he said. "I don't think he is."

"F-bomb me," I said.

"So should I give you this or not?" He held up an envelope.

"What is it?"

"Have you been to the doctor's lately Handsdrade? Have you had yourself measured?"

"No, why?"

Jackson closed in on me, close enough for me to see we were at eye level. "I think you've slipped in another inch, inch and a half on me since last August. I think you're pushing six-two." Then he handed me an envelope. It read, 'UC Davis Aggies Football.'

"You're kidding me," I said.

"When they saw Pineapple on film, they saw you," Jackson said. "It's not an offer, but that's a Division-one double-a school. You're officially on the radar, Handsman. Now, are you still going to quit?"

"I..."

"Don't lie," he said. "I know you're thinking about it with all the changes."

"Well..."

"My guess is when they put together your current size, with last season's film, and your grades, you'll be getting offers by this summer. Probably invites to some camps. Double-A schools, D-two schools, maybe even a legitimate D-one opportunity because your butt is growing you into a scholarship. The question you have to ask yourself is, are you ready to take advantage of it?"

"You guys are leaving. I don't know what the next coach is going to do. Should I transfer?"

"Listen," Jackson said, making us sit down on the bench in front of my locker. "I'm not your coach anymore, but the best thing for you to do is to stay right here. Get in the best shape of your life, and you're going to have to do that on your own, the only thing Von Huson is going to do is unlock the weight room. There's not going to be any more leadership on this team, no one to hold your hand, or walk you through things."

This was big boy stuff. Did I love football, or did I just love Fred-X and the guys? This was the letter Fred, Boosty and Gelbaugh never got.

"The next guy, if I'm correct, is going to be a West Coast offense guy. After running what we ran this past year, it will be a piece of cake for you. You'll be split out wide. I'll tell you right now the team's going to struggle. You probably won't make the playoffs..."

"...But won't that kill any scholarship offer?"

"No," he said. "You've got the body they're looking for, and they have your film from this year. What they'll want to see next year is a hard working guy who got in shape and played through distractions. You're not going to get an offer from USC, but who knows? Southern Utah? Maybe an outside chance at New Mexico? I don't know, but if you do what I tell you, you'll get an offer. Hudson has a way better arm than Fred. He's more athletic, he's taller and he's going to keep growing, but he's not a decision maker. He thinks too much, and when he f-bombs up he blames someone else. You got a great aptitude for route running, so learn your playbook. If Hudson disrespects you on the field, take it. Kick his butt in the locker room, but be a pro on the field. Don't show up any of your teammates in public, even if you hate their guts."

It felt good to have Coach Jackson talk to me about football and all the things that have to happen before a touchdown is scored or a game is won. It was like being in a Monday meeting and game planning for Friday night.

"Is Fred going to go anywhere?" I said.

Coach Jackson pressed his lips together before he spoke. "Coach Piccou and I have talked to him until we are blue in face about taking advantage of one of these D-three offers, but he's not having any of it. He still thinks he's got a shot..." Jackson stopped and shook his head in sorrow. "...He's not going anywhere."

7

Read The Blitz
By Grip Teague

Former Heritage Christian HC, Bob Aberdeen, is now the top guy at West El Monte Poly. The second thing to go on Flair drive will be the high voltage, no huddle, live on the edge of the volcano, offense. The first thing to go already has, sophomore running back Mike Miranda has withdrawn from school and enrolled at Crescenta Valley... Former Duarte running back Kelvin Smith is now at Los Altos...(Not where I thought he'd go.)...El Rancho quarterback D.K. Germany has officially signed his letter of intent to play football at Fresno State. He's expected to redshirt next fall and be converted to cornerback because of his size...

Two weeks before the end of the school year, Grandview scout, James Splitorff, took a job in Michigan, and that's when I got an official offer from Division-two Grand Valley State. The letter said they'd love to have me play for the Lakers.

It was great to get an offer, but it didn't change things the way I once thought football validation would. Old teammates didn't put me on their shoulders, and present ones just went about their business. Grip Teague didn't mention it, probably didn't even know about it.

Lena didn't hate me after I confessed my feelings to her, but she didn't suddenly want me either. She gave me a letter I kept in my backpack but didn't bother to open. We exchanged smiles in the hallways at school and passing each other in the foyer after church. I was tired of dreaming dreams with happy, but impossible, endings. Her letter was going to be something about us always being friends and that it was great to get to know each other. Being Lena, she would also encourage me to keep going to church and get closer to God.

Virtuous, but not what I wanted to hear.

Sometimes I'd run a finger over a map to see how far Grand Valley was from Trevecca and then get a rush as a dream would attempt to develop a game plan. Like an alcoholic only needed one drink to reignite the fire, I only needed one daydream about Lena to start believing in the impossible again.

New head coach, Bob Aberdeen, didn't seem impressed with my Grand Valley offer or too enthused about anyone else. I didn't hate Aberdeen. He was just this skinny, bald guy who acted like he was perpetually sitting on a tack. There was nothing engaging or fun about him.

Plugged in as a starter, I worked hard, but it was different. When Jackson, Gugliotta, and Coach Piccou were cursing at me this time a year ago, I hated them. Now, I appreciated them even more.

Aberdeen didn't care about how we executed as much as he did about making sure we did everything his way. We had to make sure our shirts were tucked in his way. We had to make sure our shoes were tied his way. We had to do our stretching his way or hit the road.

All of it was okay, except he didn't get on us about passes being dropped or routes being rounded off. No one on his staff spoke to Hudson about his footwork or reads. Talking to each other was forbidden while doing drills. Mentioning that something sucked bought you a lap around the track. If a position squad was caught chatting, then the entire team had to run.

He also ordered the team to call me Andrade, not Handsdrade or Handsman.

When graduation day came, I ditched a beach chair behind the hedge plants before practice then made it a point to be the last one to leave. It was Hudson and Ponce's locker room. When they joked, it came across as mean, when they were encouraging, it came across as fake. So I practiced, I dressed, and I kept to myself. When word got out about my offer, any attempts to trash talk me by the new leaders evaporated. They had to give me grudging respect.

I texted Dad and told him we'd meet at Jack's in a couple of hours. He texted back that he had a date and would see me later tonight. He was doing well, and it was easy to figure being back in church had brought him out of his funk. I was happy for him but would always be leery of another bad stretch cropping up.

Everything on my side of the campus faded down to just me and the breaths I was taking. The stadium was filling and conversations could be heard sifting through the air. I sat outside the double doors in the same place I had a year ago with Fred. That night I was dreaming about the season, about playing football, and fitting in. He was dreaming about championships, scholarships and life far away from West El Monte.

The last time I saw him was in May. The chiseled appearance he had during the season was losing its edge. The aura around him was gone as he leaned against his truck and watched a baseball game while I went to the football field. I played football because of him. I caught passes, and I made plays because of him. I had the time of my life because of him, but once the season was over, when all the plays had been run, he rendered me obsolete.

The music began as the graduates entered. Sealed off from them, I was officially alone. I let a dream play of them calling me over to see the ceremony. Not to graduate with my friends but just to be with them again, talking football and dreaming dreams.

The speeches started. The same speeches I heard the year before.

The dream turned into Fred popping up from around the corner and saying, "I was hoping I'd find you here." A big smile on his face, the Fred-X smile.

Fred Ritter didn't turn the corner and say he was happy to see me.

I sat in the beach chair and listened. The sound out of the speakers was still lousy but distinguishable. The swelling noise of the crowd would rise and fall.

"Carl Bartholomew." Cheers rose. Bustamonte's name was called and cheers came.

Another dream ran across the back of my eyes of Lena turning the corner, looking like she did last June, coming to tell me she shared my feelings. I jumped out of the chair to greet her, and we shared a magnificent kiss.

Lena Durkin didn't turn the corner and say she was in love with me.

I reached into my backpack and pulled out the letter she wrote me. Sliding a finger between the envelope and the adhesive, it split open.

Dear Dale,

I wish this letter could say what you want it to say, but it can't. I think the world of you, but it will be impossible for us to stay close. I'm in one place in life, and you're in another. I'm beginning the journey to where God wants to take me, and you're still discovering it.

When you discover where God wants to take you, you're going to find out real fast your feelings for me weren't all that important--just part of the pain and learning we all go through in life.

I want you to be happy. I want you to pray for Fred. I want you to be kind to him, but don't be him. His life is trapped, and yours doesn't have to be. I know you have a great future in front of you. Be happy and open yourself up to the Lord.

I wish I could say we'll always be friends, but maybe the best for now is we will always have good memories and thoughts of each other.

Lena

"Lena Durkin." The applause was significant enough to melt away her image and words and remind me I was sitting in a beach chair. She was several hundred yards away, picking up a diploma and officially stamping herself out of my life forever.

The names kept being read, and the urge came to go, but the feeling was countered by the question: where would I go? Who would I call on this night? Old volleyball friends? Anything or anyone I had something in common with was graduating tonight. How was it someone could be in physical proximity to a thousand or more people and still feel so completely alone?

Names continued to be read: some I knew, some I didn't and never would. Dad was hours down the timeline, but I heard his voice.

"When someone wants you, Dale, appreciate it. Because they're not always going to want you."

"Fred Ritter." Pam Padilla said into the microphone, and Alonson Stadium erupted one last time for Fred-X.

I'd spent a year wanting to be respected like Fred-X: treated like him, admired like him, even wanted the kind of girl Fred-X dated. In that moment, as I was all alone on the other side of the campus, as they were calling out his name for the final time, it came to me.

I was Fred, he was me, and as wonderful as the ride had been, time was tossing us both to the curb. Neither one of us were wanted anymore because our time was up, our story line was finished.

"So what separates us from the love of God?" Pastor Domres preached. "Would you like me to read you the whole passage again? I can. I will. It's a marvelous read out of Romans eight..."

The Sunday after graduation I was in church with Dad. The place felt different. I never thought of it as hostile, but it never felt comfortable. This Sunday it felt comfortable, and I didn't know why.

"The truth is, that no matter what you think, feel, or are told, you are never ever alone. The world is a bitter place. It's a harsh place. It is a place made much worse when fools behind a pulpit try to convince you that there are ceremonies, rituals, and hoops you have to jump through to get to Christ..."

Everything I dreaded came to pass. The football season ended, Lena never became my girlfriend, Piccou quit, Fred disowned me, and my football family was scattered. I was still breathing and the sun was still coming up, but I couldn't shake the loneliness. I knew I'd go on, albeit with dried tears and a few inner scars.

"He loves you and he knows the plans he has for you. The plans to bless you and prosper you..."

For the first time since I'd come back to church, I was in a service not hoping to keep my starting job, hoping for a win, or looking for a girl. I was free. Pastor Domres kept preaching and, for the first time, I leaned a little bit forward in my seat to hear what he had to say.

8

Read The Blitz
By Grip Teague

There is an excellent article at 605-Football about first year La Serna HC, Tab Figueroa, and his family's health issues. We wish him the best...If you are ready to hear it, I am ready to share it, so here it goes: by some alchemy unknown to common man, Jefferson Pham will be eligible Zero Week for the Burbank Bulldogs. You can't make this stuff up...Former Arroyo bookend defensive ends Chao Estrada and Miguel Ruiz have landed at Citrus College...With summer over and the season ready to start, my number one passer in our coverage zone is former El Monte quarterback, and current Temple City starter, Anthony Ledesma. I love his arm and the way he makes plays out of nothing...Note to the Hudsonites at West El Monte: This is not a personal attack on Billy Hudson. I just think, right now, Ledesma's better.

W hen kickoff time came in the fall, I was six-two, and everything Coach Jackson told me would happen, happened. We were terrible, there was no leadership, and Billy Hudson was no Fred Ritter. He knew how to blame somebody, knew how to bad mouth somebody, knew how to talk trash, and talk about how good he was. He just didn't know what to do with the football besides throwing it real hard.

By Week Three, he and Ponce were enemies, and I quietly became his most trusted target. We weren't friends, and I never became a Hudsonite, but I encouraged him through the difficult team parties and didn't join Ponce's brigade of complainers.

I played the game, I ran my routes, I took pleasure in my blocking, and said, 'Yes, sir' and 'No, sir,' to the coaches. I was such a good soldier, I didn't have to defend myself when Hudson or the coaching staff was looking for somebody to blame.

I had nothing to say, but my actions, like Coach Jackson said, won me respect. I was the guy who played on the winning team. Not just a winning team, but the best team in school history. I didn't have to give speeches, I stopped worrying about my touches, and stayed positive. If I knew more about the game, I would have taken someone under my wing like Fred had done for me.

As our record worsened, the message boards heated up about what a flop Coach Aberdeen and his staff were. It got tough, and I wanted to rip into the team for not working hard enough. I didn't because it would have been another loud noise in the locker room, a locker room already too loud and a lot less fun. Never thought I'd miss seeing Pineapple walk around naked or the smell of 'Crushed Pineapple,' but I did.

At the end of September, we were 1-3. We lost to Pasadena Marshall in the league opener the week before, and now we were playing South El Monte. The sports sites, and the schools tried to build excitement because South was improved this year.

It was a big game, a big game we weren't going to win with the disfunction we had. The third quarter ended with South leading 42-7 (Thanks to La Mirada transfer, tailback, Kennedy Jaynes), and the coaching staff ordered us to raise four fingers.

"Get your fours up!" Aberdeen hollered, going down the sideline. "I want to see them! The fourth quarter is our quarter!"

Dad, who had not missed a game, smiled at me when I turned to him in the stands with my four fingers raised. He gave me four fingers back and so did his girlfriend, Julie. Being on the same team with Hudson and Ponce was easier than raising four fingers. I felt as stupid as the guys we mocked a year ago for doing it.

I didn't play in the fourth quarter. Against Marshall, I tweaked my ankle, so when things got out of hand, Aberdeen pulled me saying he wanted me healthy for next week. I said, "Yes, sir."

Standing at the end of the team box, holding my helmet by the facemask, I looked at the sparse crowd in the stadium and then down at the end of the field. On our sideline was Horse, and standing next to him was Fred Ritter.

I had not seen him since the spring. There had been a few interactions on the internet with comments on the same thread but no connections or time together. He looked shorter and out of shape. I couldn't tell for sure if he was over dressed or if it was a bit of a gut sticking out from the center of his varsity jacket. Unable to leave the box, I wanted him to look my way, but his attention was on the field.

Boosty was at East Los Angeles College and getting playing time. Gelbaugh was on the roster at Mt. Sac, but not seeing many minutes. There had been talk of APU, but Gelbaugh didn't have the wheels to play for the Cougars. Dan Feliz, Dinh Lee, and Edgar Escandon decided not to play. Jessie Maez was married, working, and raising his family. Fast Eddie was at Cal Sate Northridge and having a great time based on his Facebook postings.

Lena was happy at Trevecca. Every now and then, by way of a tag or suggestion, I saw her. I tucked the picture of her and me away inside of my yearbook with the letter she gave me. She was so boxed away in my emotions that by September, I'd stopped looking at anything connected with her altogether. I didn't need to see the pictures of her new life and new friends. They hurt more than they helped, so I preferred not to dwell on Lena. It was a rabbit hole too easy to get lost in when I did.

The Eagles scored another touchdown, and I shifted my eyes to the far end of the field. Fred, still there, watching the game without expression, never turned my direction. Rumor had him going to D-three Cal Lutheran, but because of his timing and the school's success recruiting other players, like Del Chance out of Charter Oak, the financial package was gone. He could go, but there wouldn't be any guarantees. The other D-three offers withered.

I heard he was going to Pasadena City College. Another report had him playing at Citrus and then Landestoy Luke, with 605-Football, published a small item about Fred withdrawing from school. Word was circulating he didn't have the speed or the arm strength to play at the next level. Everyone knew he didn't have the size. A year ago I would have laughed at any assumption about him lacking arm strength, but, after going to several camps over the summer and catching fastballs from Hudson, I knew it was true.

For me, there were five offers on the table. If I took the Davis offer I'd be reunited with Pineapple, who was redshirting this season after wrecking his knee in August. Southern Utah State, Grand Valley, and APU all offered. Eastern Washington officially offered me on Monday of this week.

"Did they pull you?" Grip Teague said, coming next to me on the right.

"Yeah, Coach wants to protect my ankle for next week."

Not wanting it to appear we were uninterested in the uninteresting game, we stood shoulder to shoulder, looking towards the field with false interest.

"Excited about the latest offer? Eastern Washington, gotta be awesome." I'd worked from hating Teague to just disliking him. He was a vulture, all the reporters seemed like vultures now. If I told him I was considering Grand Valley instead of Eastern Washington, and to keep it under his hat, it would have been on his blog soon as he found bandwidth.

"It's great," I said. "Did you see who's down at the other end?"

"Who?"

"Fred-X is down there." I gestured for him to look.

"Cool," he said, glancing briefly. "When do you think you're going to make a decision?"

"Dude," I said. "That's Fred-X. He threw a thousand touchdown passes last year."

"Where's he playing this year?"

"Really?" I said, finding Teague's indifference unbelievable.

Teague smiled, then used his stylist to record statistical information on his tablet.

"Is that weird?" I said. "You and Bald Guy were all over him last year. You loved him."

"He had a great year, but you see that guy over there?" Teague pointed to the other side of the field, directly across from where Fred was standing. A heavy looking guy with a shaved head was wearing an El Monte varsity jacket. "Do you know who that guy is?"

I shook my head.

"Justin Ta'amu. Does it ring a bell now?" I shook my head again. "Nine years ago he ran for two thousand yards, was All CIF, and was our MVP. He got a D-two scholarship to Humboldt State. D-two for a running back from this area is a pretty big deal. In the middle of his first season, he got homesick and came back. For the next three years we kept getting items he was going to play at ELAC or PCC, but he never did. Now he's just some fat guy, like me, who used to play football, watching his little brother play for South El Monte, and no one cares."

My eyes went from Ta'amu back to Fred and then back to Ta'amu. Teague took a step closer and dropped his voice a notch.

"I know what people think of me and, for the most part, they're right, Handsman. I always want a great story, and I don't say this to be mean, but there will always be another you, another Ta'amu, there will always be another Fred-X."

"Fred was special," I said, feeling odd for trying to defend my former quarterback, who now wouldn't even look my way. "There's not going to be another..."

Teague tapped his stylist to tablet again. "There's not going to be another what? Delfman? Anthony Ledesma? Kennedy Jaynes? Mike Miranda is going to finish this season with a thousand yards and twenty touchdowns for CV. There will always be another Fred-X."

Hudson was picked off, and South El Monte got the ball back inside our fifty. I didn't know what to say to Teague because I didn't know how to dispute it. Isn't there always a part of us that hates it when somebody tells us the truth?

"I think you get it," he said. "Football opens a small window for you to go through and experience what may be on the other side. Enjoy it, have a blast, but when the ride is over go find another one. There are a lot of great rides out there. Too many are waiting for this football window to open bigger but for ninety-eight percent of them, it never does. Why dream about what used to be when you can dream about what will be? You know what I mean? You're one of the fortunate ones, Handsman, but that window is going to close for you too."

Fred stood next to Horse. I saw him glance at his phone, put it in his pocket and walk back through the gate into the cemetery.

"The seasons come and go, Handsman," Teague said. "You go, Ritter goes, Ledesma will go, Coach Aberdeen will go...Only the fat guys get to stick around."

ABOUT THE AUTHOR

Joe Torosian, raised in the San Gabriel Valley, has been a minister for 26 years, married for 24 years, and writing prep sports for 20 years. His next novel, *The Dead Bug Tales*, will be released in the spring of 2016.

Made in the USA
San Bernardino, CA
18 February 2016